UBUNTU AND PERSONHOOD

Ubuntu and Personhood, Professor James Ogude's edited collection of essays, achieves three critical objectives among others. Firstly, the work defines Ubuntu from an exceptionally wide and diverse array of angles, using debate and inventive analysis to squeeze every drop of meaning out of the concept. Secondly, the collection demonstrates Ubuntu's relevance and applicability to various academic disciplines, including philosophy; religion; literature; orature-inspired compositions; history; political science and nursing. Thirdly and most importantly, by discussing Ubuntu on its own terms—as an African-rooted example of indigenous knowledges, yet one that has universal impact—the book affirms the African continent as a site of knowledge, a fact ignored by colonizing and dominating cultures even up to this day. Through this bold effort, mainly by a younger generation of African scholars, Ogude and his contributors have succeeded in creatively transgressing colonial and neo-colonial imposed academic borders. I have often argued that if we as African scholars are to be taken seriously, we need to bring home-bred theories to international conference tables instead of regurgitating what we learnt from colonial and neo-colonial classrooms. This work certainly belongs to a much-needed tradition of resistant and original, self-defining scholarship.

—*Mīcere Gīthae Mūgo, Ph.D.*
Emeritus Professor of Teaching Excellence
Department of African American Studies
Syracuse University

Ubuntu and Personhood brings together some of the most incisive thinkers on the question of African being. It will be an essential primer for readers interested in debates on the status of the person in Africa and the role of metaphysics and morals in the imagination of selfhood, communitarian identity, moral leadership, and the ethics of care.

—*Simon Gikandi,*
Robert Schirmer Professor of English,
Princeton University

UBUNTU AND PERSONHOOD

EDITED BY
JAMES OGUDE

AFRICA WORLD PRESS
TRENTON | LONDON | CAPE TOWN | NAIROBI | ADDIS ABABA | ASMARA | IBADAN | NEW DELHI

AFRICA WORLD PRESS
541 West Ingham Avenue | Suite B
Trenton, New Jersey 08638

Copyright © 2018

Cover art: from https://www.dreamstime.com/ with
          permission
Book and cover design: Lemlem Tadesse

Cataloging-in-Publication Data may be obtained from the
Library of Congress.

ISBNs: 9781569025819 (HB)
       9781569025826 (PB)

CONTENTS

≠≠≠≠≠≠≠≠≠≠≠ ✳ ≠≠≠≠≠≠≠≠≠≠≠

ACKNOWLEDGEMENTS

We owe great gratitude to the Templeton World Charity Foundation for making this study possible, especially in providing the funding to undertake research and a series of colloquia that brought us together to explore the value of this vexed concept in advancing our development and inter-dependence as the human community. The Templeton World Charity Foundation gave this funding in honour of Archbishop Emeritus Desmond Tutu for his life-long work in advancing those spiritual principles that encourage our mutual dependence and obligation to others. The aim of the funding was to deepen and enrich not just our knowledge of the concept, but also to generate positive awareness of Ubuntu that was so central in galvanising the post-apartheid South African community, especially during the Truth and Reconciliation Commission (TRC) hearings, that the Archbishop chaired. I hope the publication of this book is, in part, a major fulfilment of what our funders wished for. And to our Vice-Chancellor, Cheryl de le Ray, who showed confidence in me when she insisted that I lead a team of equally outstanding researchers (Professors Julian Muller, Christof Heyns and Maxi Schoeman), on the project—thank you. I hope this book will be a positive tribute to your visionary leadership.

The bulk of the material used in this book came out of papers presented at colloquium on "Ubuntu and Personhood", held at the Centre for the Advancement of Scholarship, University of Pretoria, in April 28 – 29, 2015. The contributors to this volume were themselves instrumental in providing insightful reviews of the papers, and in the process generating rich dialogue around Ubuntu and personhood within the group and I thank them for the layered and complex engagement with the idea of personhood, especially relational form of personhood that Ubuntu entails.

Finally, to my research assistant, Uni Dyer, for her sense of commitment and dedication to the project. Her clinical archival work was central in surfacing a range of hidden issues that only became apparent as we delved into the meaning and value of Ubuntu in contemporary times. Uni also organised the colloquia and seminars at which a number of difficult issues on Ubuntu were debated, not to mention her relentless communication with the contributors to the volume to deliver on time. You proved to be a great interlocutor in your own right and with a passionate defence of the place of repressed indigenous knowledge systems within the academy. Thanks too to the Project Assistant at our Centre, Kirsty Agnew, who took over the support network that Uni left behind as she moved on to undertake her PhD. Lastly, immense gratitude to our Administrative Assistant, Cecelia Samson, who made the travel and accommodation arrangements for the Ubuntu Fellows and delegates during our series of colloquia.

Introduction: Ubuntu and Personhood

==========*:*==========

James Ogude

> As the German Immanuel Kant suggested, the notion of the person, the ultimate question of anthropology, underlies and is assumed by all other questions, suggesting also thereby that the ubiquity of the idea of the person in cultural expressive forms is hardly an African peculiarity.
>
> —D. A. Masolo (2010, 135)

If there is anything that defines Ubuntu and distinguishes it from other value systems, it is the fact that it is premised on a very specific understanding of personhood and that is that the full development of personhood comes with a shared identity and the idea that an individual's humanity is fostered in a network of relationships—*I am because you are; we are because you are.* In other words, to talk meaningfully about Ubuntu we have to grapple with the notion of personhood, specifically the relational idea of personhood, which Ubuntu entails. This, though, is not something new because over the years a number of African philosophers and political thinkers have argued that the African idea of self or the person is not only more attractive, but also stands in sharp contrast to the view of the individual found in European thought (Wiredu 1980; Masolo 2010; Nyerere 1966; Nkrumah 1964 and Senghor 1964). It is for this reason that D. A. Masolo has argued that: "By articulating the pre-metaphysical social genesis of the individual and his or her dependence on others for self-actualization, African philosophers have contributed significantly to the establishment of an alternative normative standpoint for viewing the world from a communalist rather than the individualist perspective...." (2010, 139 – 140). This understanding of personhood contradicts the understanding of the individual dominant in European thought that sees the individual as a free and intentional agent and therefore social relations between people and society stems from the fact that individuals are autonomous and rational, and the principle of individual freedom is the source of all rights and responsibility in contemporary society. African philosophers insist that even at the most basic level, human beings are always in communication and it is this act of interactive engagement that transforms them from human beings to persons. Wiredu argues that: "Without communication there is not even a human person" (1996, 13). Alternatively, as D. A. Masolo observes:

> This process of depending on others for the tools that enable us to associate with them on a growing scale of competence is the process that makes us into persons. In other words, we become persons through acquiring and participating in the socially generated knowledge of norms and actions that we learn to live by in order to impose humaneness upon our humanness (2010, 155).

And yet, the argument I am making here should not be confused with the strand of scholarship, largely championed by some of the foundational scholars cited above (Senghor, Nkrumah, Nyerere), that sought sometimes to posit African identities in racial terms and in so doing grounding the distinctiveness of 'the African person' in an essentialized racial category while pointing to how different it is from the Western person. If in their reaction to the schism created by colonial modernity these foundational thinkers found it prudent to respond to a generalised African person in essentialized terms, it is important to draw a distinction here, and that is that a conception of personhood, gleaned from a range of cultural practices in Africa, cannot be reduced to a racial category very much in the same way that Western individualism and discourses on individual agency, rationality and autonomy are not, even when they work to support certain racial stereotypes. We cannot reduce the European idea of a person to a racial concept because it is a marker of the ascendance of a certain dominant philosophical thought in European history, namely, the enlightenment period and the age of reason. It is also fair to argue that Africa's foundational thinkers were responding to a specifically coded colonial discourse, which sought to deny the colonised people any form of rationality, often reducing them to the traditional category and a thoughtless herd. The dominant assumption was that agency only resides in individualistic, self-determining and autonomous bodies. Any attempt to forge a communitarian self-determination and collective expression of agency or relational forms of personhood is generally seen as undermining human independence and individual personhood, often detached from the whole—the community. Michael Lambek (2008, 102) has made a compelling argument against this understanding of individualistic agency, which he thinks is both naïve and romantic because they posit agency as "a capacity of fully autonomous individuals rather than relationally constituted social persons: and... that action occurs without respect to convention and commitment, that is, as if agents were not specifically located social persons operating within moral universes, with respect to prior and binding commitments both to specific liturgical orders [...] and to specific other persons". Lambek concludes, "That the existential emphasis on the freedom of the individual self is very different from the moral questions facing the relationally embedded person. There is a difference between exercising one's judgement and claiming absolute freedom of choice" (2008, 102).

The argument I am advancing here, and one which most of the chapters in the volume take up, is that personhood is attained through complex processes of exchange and engagement as people interact and communicate with those around them and with the totality of their environment. It is for this reason that I argue here that Ubuntu as a specific strand of Africa's expression of personhood is a moral obligation and aspirational. Christian Gade (2012, 499) is therefore wrong when, in a highly controversial and very questionable study in terms of its research methods and approach, argues that "exclusive ideas about the nature of Ubuntu underpin group segregation; more specifically, segregation between those who are part of the 'community of *persons*' and those who are not. This distinction devaluates those who are not part of the 'community of *persons*' since they are not considered to be possible subjects of the positive moral quality of *Ubuntu*". The first point to make is that all moral values have a gradation system and ethical standards that allows their practitioners to make value judgement. Nevertheless, they are hardly used, even at the best of time, as instruments of discrimination, or, prejudice, but instead as providing the ideal moral conduct toward which we must all aspire. True, these may be abused or distorted as with all human values, but the ideal expression of Utu or Ubuntu must entail "the recognition of the moral equality of all people" (Masolo 2010, 27). In other words, Ubuntu is not an ideology that works to impose a programmatic set of rules of insiders and outsiders, even when it talks of our moral obligation toward those around us. In addition, when it talks to our moral obligation toward other people judgement comes into it. There must be ways in which we can measure our responsibility toward others within a community of people. It is not surprising that even within Western societies, largely driven by the principle of individualism, the principle of basic or minimum human rights, as a standard for how everyone ought to be treated is highly cherished and privileged. The West too accepts that judgement will come into what counts as minimum principles of human rights and proper conduct within a community of people. What the values of Ubuntu do is to provide us, contrary to what Gade argues, with grounds for a moral critique of social and other forms of exclusion, and it does not matter whether the basis of these forms of exclusion or discrimination is gender, race or class. It is about what Masolo, after Wiredu, calls the principle of "sympathetic impartiality" (2006, 27) in this volume. Group solidarity in the form of herd mentality or pedestrian groupism is not the defining principle of Ubuntu as Gade argues in his paper, but rather an awareness that our wholeness—the realisation of our full humanness—is achieved through our interdependence and consensus building. That is why, as I have argued elsewhere, Ubuntu is used as a vehicle for the reconstitution of community, often during moments of crisis, but only through consensus building as opposed to group tyranny. And because Ubuntu is a process of becoming and aspirational, one cannot talk of it being "bound together by the *exclusive* possession of the positive moral quality of *ubuntu*" as Gade suggests (2012, 499). Besides, the danger of pushing values such as Ubuntu to some absolute category is not something unique to Africa, but is also found in certain strands of unbridled individualism that privileges self-interest at the expense of social or communitarian values as we have seen with neo-liberalism in the era of globalisation.

As some of the chapters in the volume demonstrate, Ubuntu is earned but it can also be lost. Therefore, the idea of Ubuntu suggests that personhood is experienced and performed in the practical exercise of living and coming into being. In this respect, the gulf between the compulsion of the 'I' and that of the 'self' concerned with public moral value, or immersed in the practice of public reason, becomes the seat of our self-assessment and the assessment of us by society. The management of our own practical identity is then what drives who we come to be perceived to be by society or in society.

My interest in this book is not to revisit the tension between European and the African conceptions of the person. After all, so much scholarship has been devoted to this tension and there is now a consensus that there may be a measure of complementarity that exists between European and African ideas of personhood (see Masolo's chapter). This is what Gykye refers to as "moderate communitarianism", which calls for a dialectical view of individualism and communitarianism. This volume therefore seeks to move beyond these debates and to examine the multiple ways through which a dynamic understanding of Ubuntu, reflected in the majority of the essays in this volume, extend and deepen our understanding of personhood. What does it mean to be a person? Does Ubuntu share any similarities with other intellectual and philosophical streams from the African continent? If the idea of personhood suggested by the term Ubuntu comes with moral obligation and ethical demands, as they should, how are we to understand our material obligations to those who are less privileged in society and how does material lack affect the realisation of full personhood?

One of the first themes that this volume grapples with in various ways is how personhood is achieved, hence the broad consensus that Ubuntu like personhood is acquired and not given. What this means is that relationality as Wiredu would aver, is the primary condition of human existence. According to Masolo, Wiredu's philosophical anthropology "recognizes the biological constitution of humans as a necessary but not sufficient basis for personhood, because human beings require gradual socio-genic development to become persons. This relational condition circumstantiates not only the physical existence of things and our development of persons but also our cognitive and moral experience of the world" (2010, 156). Herein lies the convergence between communitarian understanding of personhood and Ubuntu's idea of personhood as an inter-dependence not simply between human beings, but also with the broader world, physical and spiritual—the entire universe (Ramose 2005). Looked at this way, personhood cannot be a complete state but a process of being and becoming. A number of chapters in this volume underscore the sociality of personhood and its relational quality as the basis for understanding the idea of Ubuntu. It is what the South African writer and essayist Antjie Krog calls "interconnectedness-towards-wholeness", as Jacomien van Niekerk's chapter demonstrates.

However, the chapters in this volume also insist that in order to talk about Ubuntu as a concept underpinned by interdependence of human beings we need to go beyond ontological, normative and epistemological perspectives and include material dimensions. Indeed the re-emergence/emergence of Ubuntu in recent intellectual discourse, especially in South Africa, has been characterised by a singular focus on its capacity to bring about harmony in the community and to generate the kind of dialogue that would allow for restorative justice. In framing, Ubuntu as an ethical tool for peace and harmony, the material conditions for creating a stable and harmonious community and for attaining full personhood, is often ignored. Some of the chapters argue quite sharply after the Kenyan philosopher, Henry Odera Oruka (1989), that full personhood must come with the provision of basic economic needs or what Oruka calls the human minimum aimed at taking care of bodily and physical needs of people; that conditions of deprivation dehumanize and could easily lead to stifled growth of full personhood. Although Ubuntu as a concept calls for empathy and sharing of resources as a moral and ethical principle, unless this translates into the practical level of distribution of resources among members of society, Ubuntu would remain a mere ideal and a pipe dream. One of the lingering criticisms against the South African Truth and Reconciliation Commission (TRC) was its inability to rise above the rhetoric of forgiveness and reconciliation, because the emphasis was on restorative justice without economic redress. That is why, allowing Oruka's philosophical approach to enter into dialogue with the basic tenets of Ubuntu, as some chapters do in this volume, can only enrich our understanding of the concept.

Ubuntu in this sense is required to become a disruptive and subversive philosophy in contexts where inhumane practices have become the norm. It becomes both insurrectionist and a vehicle for self-determination. Although in this volume, Augustine Shutte confines self-determination to individual agency and therefore to European thought, I wish to add that self-determination is also about the collective desire to repudiate conditions of servitude. It is therefore very much a function of a communitarian drive and collective agency seen here as the broader communal desire for freedom and independence. Besides, individually driven desire for freedom and autonomy need not always be inward looking, but also an outward attempt to connect those with similar desires and goals, and in the realization that inter-dependence is also a source of strength and creative imagination to move forward and bring about change for all. Thus, for Ubuntu ethic to have relevance it has to move from the realm of theory to the practical, and it has to become the instrument for mediating relationships between people; between different races; between different classes and between professional workers and those that they serve.

But recasting Ubuntu in these terms also means that we must be prepared to change what are often presented as immutable values for all time, while insisting on epistemic justice that takes due cognizance of repressed knowledges among postcolonial subjects—by having a conversation between European modernity and local knowledges— thus challenging social inequality and existential inequality as Aloo Mojola argues forcefully in this volume. It is for these reasons that this volume is, in certain ways, an exploration of how productive Ubuntu can be creatively understood without reducing it to the category of the traditional. Seen this way, Ubuntu is likely to offer alternative and radical ways of approaching debates around communitarian forms of personhood, especially when evacuated of its racial or ethnic baggage as the Arch-Bishop Desmond Tutu tried to do in South Africa. By appropriating Ubuntu to mediate the racially charged processes of the Truth and Reconciliation Commission in South Africa, Tutu was rescuing Ubuntu from the prison house of tradition and ethnicity and elevating it to a universal ethical and moral category. He was transforming the concept into an implement for clearing and thus destabilizing Apartheid racial hierarchies. He was also questioning the racial prism as the only matrix through which we could glean South Africa's ugly past. He was also pointing to the re-discovery of a relational value system among the marginalised and the possibilities that it offered for the re-imagining of a new South Africa. It was about how local idioms continue to offer the potential for generating or articulating insight and revising dominant Western views of autonomous selfhood and agency. Some of the chapters in this volume echo some of the values that Ubuntu espouses. These include the capacity for communal forgiveness and reconciliation in contexts of conflict, or, in societies that have undergone traumatic experiences of violence. In such societies, modern conventional forms of justice may not offer redress, and only a recuperation of indigenous forms of redress can open a chance for justice and restoration (see Dominic Dipio's chapter). Other chapters point to the challenge of policing and safeguarding the exacting demand of the Ubuntu morality, especially in a postcolonial context where neo-liberal values are cloaked in the grammar of human rights, self-interest and personal responsibility, often in total disregard for social forces. Henry A. Giroux refers to these as engagements in "promoting the virtues of unbridled individualism [that is] almost pathological in its disdain for community, social responsibility, public values, and the public good" (2014, 2). We ask in the same vain whether the form of morality embedded in these neo-liberal values and grammar engender an ethical value system in our public institutions and those who service them to embrace social responsibility, especially for the most vulnerable in our societies. Put differently, can the re-discovery of the ordinary values wilfully relegated to the category of the traditional, be mobilised in the transformation of service delivery with a human face in our public institutions such as schools, churches and hospitals? We are aware that there may be no easy answer to these vexed questions, but as some of the essays suggest, Utu/Ubuntu-inspired frameworks may well offer new ways of thinking about the possibilities for the future.

Finally, whichever way one looks at Ubuntu/Utu, what is evident from this volume is that it has been the subject of scrutiny in many areas and genres of social discourse, not least among them, works of fiction and essays, also examined in this volume to put a sharper nuance on our understanding of what is a vexed subject; a concept that continues to be mediated by Africa's past and recent histories.

BIBLIOGRAPHY

Gade, Christian B.N. 2012. "What Isubuntu? Different Interpretations among South Africans of African Descent". *South African Journal of Philosophy*. 31 (3): 484-503.

Giroux, Henry A. 2014. *Neoliberalism's War on Higher Education*. Chicago: Haymarket Books.

Gyekye, Kwame. 1995. *An Essay on African Philosophical Thought*. Philadelphia: Temple University Press.

Lambek, Michael. 2008. "Rheumatic Irony: Questions of Agency and Self Deception as Refracted through the Art of Living with Spirits". In *Readings in Modernity in Africa*, edtied by Birgit Meyer, 98 – 106. Bloomington: Indiana University Press.

Masolo, D. A. 2010. *Self and Community in a Changing World*. Bloomington: Indiana University Press.

Nkrumah, Kwame. 1964. *Conciencism: Philosophy and Ideology for Decolonisation and Development with Particular Reference to African Revolution*. London: Heinemann.

Nyembezi, C. L. Sibusiso. 1983. *Izibongo Zamakkozi*. Pietermaritburg: Shuter and Shuter.

Nyerere, Julius K. 1966. *The Basis of African Socialism*. Dar es Salaam: Oxford University Press.

Oruka, Henry Odera. 1989. 'The Philosophy of Foreign Aid: A Question of the Right to a Human Minimum." *Praxis International* 8 (4): 465-75.

Oruka, Henry Odera. 1997. *Practical Philosophy: In Search of an Ethical Minimum*. Nairobi: East African Educational Publishers.

Ramose, Mogobe B. 2005. *African Philosophy through Ubuntu*. 2nd. Ed. Harare: Mond Books.

Shutte, Augustine. 2001. *Ubuntu: An Ethic for a New South Africa*. Pietermaritzburg: Cluster Publications.

Senghor, Leopold Sedar. 1964. *On African Socialism*. New York and London: Frederick A. Prager.

Tempels, Placide. 1965. *Bantu Philosophy*. Paris: Presence Africaine.

Wiredu, Kwasi. 2006. *Cultural Universals and Particulars: An African Perspective*. Bloomington: Indiana University Press.

CHAPTER 1. SELF-CONSTITUTION AND AGENCY

≈≈≈≈≈≈≈≈≈≈≈ ❖ ≈≈≈≈≈≈≈≈≈≈≈

D. A. MASOLO

PREAMBLE

Who am I? What is a person? Is "person" the same thing as "self", and does it add anything to the concept of "human being"? In what senses are the three English terms—"person", "self", and "human being"—identical or different in their meanings? And in what ways would the English terms, on the one hand, be identical with, or different from, say, the Kiswahili term *Mtu*, or *Umtu*, and *Umuntu* in other central or southern African Bantu variants? While "human being" refers to the biological species, "person" is subject to much debate and is defined with differences across disciplines. And because the same words are used for both in some languages—for example the Luo of Kenya use the word *"dhano"* for both, just like the Kiswahili and Bantu terms indicated above do—the term "person" has required analysis and delineation from use for "species." Some people think that one does not need to be a human being to be a "person" while others, called animalists, believe that one has to be at least an animal to be a "person." What, then, is implied when the term "person" is used for human beings? And would the term "person" used for "human beings" bear the same meaning when it is used for, say, the clever, sophisticatedly computerized machine standing before me and which is ready to give me cash when I ask it to? I have in mind that fact that some philosophers have defined "persons" as "thinking substances," and our clever computer was doing some thinking when communicating with me. So while I have no doubt that you are a person, I can only say that you are probably a human being too, because you could be of the same "species" as my compute here. But that view gives the impression of the "thinking thing" that Descartes talked about. We shall mention that later. The famous British philosopher John Locke defined "person" as "a thinking intelligent being that has reason and reflection, and can consider itself as itself, the same thinking thing, in different times and places; which it does by that consciousness which is inseparable from thinking..." (Locke 1956, 127). There too, there are discordant views about who qualifies to be a "person", and to be regarded and treated as such, based on how the term has been used in some socio-political systems where it has been denied, as shown in practice, that all human beings are "persons."The fundamental question, then, is what is in a "person"? Or what is personhood? Does the English abstract "personhood" adequately correctly translate the Kiswahili abstract from "*Utu*"? or its Bantu and Nguni variants "*Umuntu*" and "*Ubuntu*"? I should have asked this question in the reverse, namely whether the Kiswahili and Bantu and Nguni forms adequately correctly translate the English term "personhood," but the focus of this book is not the English language formulations of these concepts. Rather, it is the vernacular formulation, which is what has been evoked, as is to be found in Bishop Desmond Tutu's now famous aphoristic saying, "*Umuntu ngumuntu ngabantu*, (One is/becomes a person only through other persons)" as a reference to address the collective need to reevaluate values as part of the post-apartheid societal readjustment in South Africa and other places of socio-political schisms and conflict. The point is, then, not to compare the conceptual contents of "*Utu/Umuntu/Ubuntu*" on the one hand, and of "personhood" on the other, but to understand and conceptually unpack "*Ubuntu*" while writing in the English language rather than in any one of the African vernaculars where the terms find their meanings. Hence the comparison is accidental rather than the focus either of this particular chapter or of the book as a whole. Also, as we embark on this task, the human "person" is the only use we shall consider out of the English language use as it is the one comparable to the referents of the African vernacular uses of *Mtu/Umtu/Umuntu/Dhano*.

The concept of a "person" is central to a metaphysical understanding of the kind of reality that humans are, and it has been an object of philosophical speculation since antiquity. Grand theories about history, about morality, or about the ideal political order assume some understanding of what humans are meant to be. Everyday relations and how people treat each other, or government policies in healthcare across the globe assume no less significant understanding of the nature of humans than what great thinkers have proposed. In all these analyses and suggestions are controversies that reveal the elusiveness of the idea of "a person." Resulting from them are two separate but related emphases in the discussions and debates about the nature of persons. Differences in the emphases are influenced by a variety of inherited historical-cultural concerns and problems. Traditions with emphasis on the constitution of reality take a predominantly metaphysical path to understanding the nature of persons with a focus on identity. They are predominantly Western. Traditions with emphasis on relations in nature, on the other hand, take a moral trajectory in their discussions or informal assumptions about the character of persons. These are predominantly non-Western, and specifically African in this separation. The cultural emphases are however not mutually exclusive and thinkers on either side of the divide either discuss or implicitly suggest the implications their positions may have for the other perspective. Discussions on the morality of abortion hinge on the onset of the conventional constitutive elements in the metaphysical identity of persons, just as (Wiredu's) critique of the correspondence theory of truth addresses the non-metaphysical nature of mind.

The two approaches to the idea of persons make the debate particularly interesting in the South African context. Evoked by Africans as a critique of the social-political system erected exclusively by and for the interests of whites as the descendants and cultural heirs of European settlers or later immigrants and as an attempt to put in place a new, post-apartheid moral and political order, the term *Ubuntu* seeks to bring into dialogue the two approaches to the idea that were traditionally not known to have much to do with each other either theoretically or in the historical reality of South Africa itself. This chapter seeks to chart an understanding of the moral content of the term Ubuntu and its linguistic and conceptual cognates as it appears in the related Bantu languages, and to show how its meaning therein informs the moral visions of a post-apartheid social and political space.

PERSONHOOD AS PRIVATE AND PUBLIC

As each one of us sits or stands here, or any other human being out there in the world, we are made of bodies, with all kinds of materiality that constitutes each one of us, and also with all kinds of psycho-somatic processes going on inside of us at any given time that enable us to move, think, talk, see, hear, be able to taste, etc. But how often do we consciously make reference, or even assume these physical make-ups of other people or the physical events happening inside them when we talk with or about people? How many times do we identify others with the textures of their skin, or with their blood type, or even their IQ so as to identify for sure who it is we are talking with or about? We don't, unless we were peculiarly detail-obsessed with the texture of nature in general. But hardly any of us cares to be that nitty-gritty. If we were, whether introspectively about ourselves, or about others, there would be no difference between looking at me and looking at a worm slithering across the surface before me. Our eyes would see and our ears would hear, or our bodies would feel, our consciousness would make us aware of our experiences, including our memories—if all our sensory organs and our brains were healthy and functional. As living organisms, perhaps we would merely respond to different instinctive urges to satisfy natural inclinations, and that would be it. This would correspond to the domain of "things." The occurrences and experiences therein are completely private as constitutive of our subjectivity. But humans do not just gravitate toward these pre-defined ends. Rather, because we are endowed with language as a primary human tool, our languages name or describe the world as statements of complex relations. While "things" are simply there in the privacy of their metaphysical or pre-given constitution, with language we impose signification, definitions, and meanings upon them. To make a statement such as "This is..." is to claim that "things are, or this object is in a certain way", thus imposing a specific conception or understanding of them or it. So when I say "This is Onyango," or merely call out the name "Onyango," there definitely is the unspoken assumption that who I mean is made up of such things as skin texture, blood type, DNA, mind, etc., as the details of his unreplicable identity, but these are hardly what I refer to when I say "This is Onyango," or when I call him out by his name. And those who hear me make the statement or call out the name do not turn their attention to his skin or want to know his blood type, DNA, or how many teeth he has in his mouth. Their attention is drawn instead to the individual in the context of his social identity, namely the one who answers to the name. They think of "Onyango" as a person. When he jumps up to answer to the call, it is all the particular "things" he is made of that bear upon his identity—"what the person called Onyango is made of"—yet many of them will be irrelevant to how "Onyango" answers the call. He will need to hear and remember his own name. If there is more than one individual with the same name, we will need to distinguish who exactly is the target of the call, and we will hardly make this distinction by carrying out a physical examination beyond what our perceptions—such as seeing that one "Onyango" is taller or lighter-skinned than the other, etc.—give us. Rather, we are likely to resort to social references, including height or skin color, which gives us a (social) separation of one from another. In today's world of travels and immigration, we may also distinguish ourselves by our nationalities or other social indicators. All these descriptions and practices suggest that we are as much private in our persons as we are social or public. Put differently, personhood is as much the concept we descriptively form in our minds when we think of some elements in the metaphysical make up of humans as it is the idea that emerges out of our consideration of all the physical elements of the metaphysical make-up together with their functional roles as enabled by the social circumstance of human nature. In other words, persons are not just the kind of beings made in a particular way, but that their species- defining mark or make-up, only a potentiality at birth, is made real by and in service of the marker itself, namely their social and moral agency and roles.

Perhaps better informed by anthropological and psychological analyses of the experience of self, there is ground to believe that we are normally born into a world that those who preceded us have already definitionally structured—one in which we separate ourselves daily from others more often by our names than by the differences in our skin textures, blood type, or DNA, heart rates, and so on. This is the world in which we play by the roles we are given. In other words, we are born into existing familial relations, as someone's child, grandchild, sister, brother, etc. Like I have said before[1], being asked to travel on errands across a vast clan territory, or sometimes even longer distances to deliver messages or goods to distant relatives was not always a single-objective event. Not only did the youth on these errands learn how to traverse strange neighborhoods in their best manners that earned them security or praise, they also learned along the way their family or clan boundaries as they acquainted themselves with different homes and their residents. When they were finally sat down for these important lessons, they would be able to learn how physical and social contours of spatial geographies unevenly intertwined, and that they would gradually learn how to navigate them based on this important knowledge.

The picture that emerges from the overlap of social and physical in both spatial and personal identities is one that, as outlined in the work of some recent anthropologists and philosophers (Mauss 1939, Lienhardt 1985 and Rorty 1989), identifies and pits two layers or realms of social experience: one whose "focus is on the idiosyncratic, inner, elusive experiences of the self," on the one hand, and "the outer or mask which a person presents to the world" on the other." Mauss referred to the first as the realm of the *moi*, the awareness of the private one-self, and the second one as that of *la personne morale* or the ideological definition of personhood in terms of rules, roles and representations that has encounters with the external world of other selves. Visiting relatives in the vicinity or in distant locations enables one to develop a sense of the integration of both the objectified and the subjectively apprehended aspects of social life as equal components of how life is experienced. Humans live lives in which the private *moi* and the public moral person are layered and constantly alternate as identity mechanisms. They are constituents of a "thought-world" that lies at the base of most of our conscious actions and decisions.

The naturalist approach to the understanding of personhood as proposed by the Ghanaian philosopher Kwasi Wiredu views human experience as involving both the *moi* and the *personne morale*. While it is grounded in empiricist beginnings, he explains, human experience involves concept formation on which communication depends, and

---

1   See "Critical Rationalism and Cultural Traditions in African Philosophy", in *Explorations in African Political Thought* ed. Teodros Kiros, (New York and London: Routledge, 2001) 81-95.

also from which it emerges. The only alternation that grounds this experience occurs between what Mauss calls the *moi* and the *personne morale*. This alternation is similar to what we said earlier, namely that sometimes we experience ourselves in the depth of our individuality, and sometimes in our sociality as connected and responsive to rules and roles. According to him,

> No human society or community is possible without communication, for a community is not just an aggregation of individuals existing as windowless monads but of individuals as interacting persons, and an interaction of persons can only be on the basis of shared meanings. Indeed, without communication there is not even a human person. A human being deprived of the socializing influence of communication will remain human biologically, but mentally is bound to be subhuman (Wiredu 1996, 13).

It is this order (from *moi* to *personne morale* or person as the socialized human being) which, according to Wiredu[2], regulates the formation of perceptual knowledge on the one hand, and normative knowledge on the other—one, the *moi*, which is based on or addresses individual sensory experiences, desires and motivations, while the *personne morale* regulates the threads of the social world made of general moral laws and political goals. In this respect, Wiredu appears to concur with Mauss's conceptual distinctions between the *moi* and *personne morale*. But because in one sense "*moi*" is not an object of perception or direct private experience but rather an idea that emerges from the self's distinction from other selves, it is not synonymous with Wiredu's unsocialized biological human being. On the other hand, Mauss may have used the "*moi*" in Wiredu's sense of "human being" who, despite not being able to think of self as "I" or "me," is nonetheless capable of emotions such as feeling pain and being aware of it, or is capable of remembering past perceptions.

---

2 Both Wiredu's *Philosophy and an African Culture* (London: Cambridge University Press, 1980), and *Cultural Universals and Particulars* give clear expositions of his idea of the sociality of personhood and its defining characteristics. The discussion of "Truth as Opinion" in the first book is built on the idea of knowledge as a social enterprise that brings into dialogue perceptions of reality from different points of view which are subjective or private.

Thus the concept of a person takes two dimensions, one metaphysical, and the other social. In the first instance, metaphysics asks questions of the constitution and identity of a person, drawing up the contours of personhood. The concerns of this approach are the distinguishing attributes of the species—such as the role of reason or specifically human intelligence. Its basic question is: *What* is a person? In the Western tradition of philosophy, this orientation finds its culmination in the metaphysics of Immanuel Kant, although it is best associated with, and remembered from the philosophy of René Descartes. For a long time, many philosophers there thought of persons as immaterial souls or Egos who were only contingently attached to the material body, laying the ground for what is known in metaphysics as the mind-body problem. Descartes himself inherited his own view, called substance dualism, from a long-standing history that went back as far as Plato in classical Greece who taught that reality was made of a combination of imperishable essences and their accidental worldly material appearances. Plato became influential to Christian metaphysics generally, and to human metaphysics in particular. Aristotle who influenced St. Thomas Aquinas expressed this dualism in the vocabulary of form and matter which he thought to be inseparable except in thought. Although few philosophers now accept the core position of this dualist view of persons due to a number of theoretical issues it raises—such as interactionism and the possibility of the knowledge of other souls—much of Western philosophy continues to think of a person as a sort of entity that possesses a mind and, in that virtue, possesses a range of sophisticated mental states like we have said above, including, like we said, self-reflective mental states, those by which a person becomes self-aware as being themselves with a distinctive identity, as the *moi* of Mauss. But thinking of persons in these manners brings out a lot many other questions of identity—such as whether persons are necessarily material or immaterial entities, or whether they are necessarily of animal type, or whether, if they are not necessarily of some sort of animal type, then artifacts with artificial intelligence like sophisticated computers can also be persons, and so on. Even as this debate goes on in the ranks of Western metaphysics, it is no longer necessarily true, or true *a priori*, that all persons are animals. In other words, while it is true that all human beings are persons in this tradition, not all persons are human beings. Human metaphysics of persons, or the philosophy of personhood as expounded by Kant and others, is about human beings, regardless of who or what else may be considered to be persons.

Kant believed that there was human nature, or a set of characteristics shared by all *normal* members of the species in different times and places. Yet, in his anthropology from a pragmatic point of view, he thought of this character as something that man creates of himself based on his freedom as a free acting agent. Hence, in this respect, he talks of this character mainly in terms of habits and inclinations. In his philosophy taken as a whole, Immanuel Kant presents the picture of humans as rational beings. The combination of reason and freedom, in Kant's view, makes human beings to have a natural purpose, one which becomes clearer only teleologically. In this particular regard, Kant paradoxically shared with Jean-Paul Sartre, the French existentialist philosopher, the view that humans only make themselves over time (Sartre believed that there was no human nature). Kant believed that human beings are driven by reason which is viewed as a tool that enables the humanly possible encounter with the external world in all the three domains of experience and sense-making: the world by means of perception; the world by means of moral norms; and the world by means of aesthetic judgements. Except in morals, Kant thought that reason appears as a formalistic tool through which the world takes a specific form or appears in a certain way. In morals, however, reason appears as the location of innate absolute laws upon which we guide our conduct. Human beings are, for him, subjects or agents through whom the world takes its experienced shape or form.

Kant resembles Wiredu in some crucial instances. For instance, Kant's idea that society does not give the individual his/her morality but rather provides the contexts in which the capacity is honed supports the idea of the role of education in the promotion of human rational capacity. In his view, humans grow into becoming rational in the sense that in society they learn to make choices, including moral choices, for their own preservation and governance. In teleological terms, humans improve their rational capacity only over time. He thought that this practice is to be found only in human beings among the many inhabitants of the earth. Informed by the variety of human relations to nature, Kant thought that only humans deliberately adapt themselves to the different natural conditions by deliberate choices (*Anthropology from a Pragmatic Point of View*). Only they are capable of culture in the serious sense of the idea as involving deliberate variations and modifications at any time in view of changeable or revisable goals. The difference between him and Wiredu is subtle. According to Wiredu, humans become rational only by means of communication with others in society. Thus, although both espouse the idea of radical indeterminacy in human nature, Kant thinks of such indeterminacy only in teleological terms. Wiredu, on the other hand, thinks of human rationality, his/her very nature as such, as indeterminate at birth, as merely a potential, and thus takes root only with communication from other human beings who have already been rationalized through socialization, that is, already in the business of general and specific workings of reason. In this sense, Wiredu's position is in agreement with the Nguni saying now popularized by Bishop Tutu, *Umuntu ngumuntu ngabantu* (a person becomes a person only through other persons)."

The prevalent Western belief in the nature of personhood was thrust into an interesting debate in the 1980s and 1990s with the emergence in the circles of psychology, of the idea of split personality, also called the fission of persons. This was the view that different personalities could inhabit the same human body, resulting in practices that could be attributed to either one of the several personalities or persons professed or claimed to exist within or to inhabit the same human being. In a curiously Cartesian manner, the body appeared to be viewed as a purely physical instrument that could be put to use by the person or personality acting within in a dominant way at any given time, hence person was viewed as that immaterial agent that determines or makes choices and commands actions—in other words, instrumentalizes the body. As the view of split personalities made its way into the discussion of accusations and attribution of responsibility for a variety of acts, it was believed that while punishment could be assessed to one, it could not to a different one who probably had nothing to do with the punishable act. Also, it was viewed that a reformed criminal may deserve less or no punishment for the crimes of their alter personalities who committed the offence(s) at a different time. These and other matters raise important questions about what it is to be a person, and what it is for a person at one time to be considered to be the same person at a later time. These are important questions, and Western philosophy takes them seriously and discusses them in a very interesting way[3]. As you can see, the concerns are basically metaphysical, and address the constitution of a person, or more generally, matters of personal identity. But African thought is not exempted completely from such metaphysical concerns or considerations nor have African scholars completely avoided metaphysical considerations of personhood, even if by way of some Western influence. Dogon thought indulges in issues of the identity of Lebe, the first ancestor of humans, by explaining—as done by the famed sage Ogotemmêli—that when *Nommo*, the seventh ancestor, consumed Lebe and gave him a life force, he gave him a spiritual principle to complement his flesh (Griaule 1965, 58-59). We can assume that the spiritual principle or substance was the basis of intelligence, mind, or reason and all the mental states that depend on it. According to the Dogon through Ogotommêli's rendition, the involvement of *Nommo* was the basis of human acquisition of the capacities to do all those things that are recognized as human activities such as, first, to design, make, and use tools, and then to use such tools to make cloth, build granaries and houses, and to cultivate crops.

In his massive metaphysical *opus* influenced by Tempels (1959), and dependent on comparisons with Aristotle, Alexis Kagame places the category of *Umuntu* at the top of all natural things due to its possession of the attribute of intelligence or reason (Kagame 1956, 104-122). According to Kagame, besides possessing the principles of life (*Ubuzima* and *Ubugingo*) as a sensitive being, *Umuntu* also possesses *igic_c_* or shadow, which is a special principle that is possessed by *Umuntu* on account of being an animal and is responsible for knowledge, love, desire, etc. This is what separates from the body at death. Ultimately *Umuntu* possesses an unnamed principle with intelligence which gives him/her the capacities of reason proper to man, such as the power to reflect, compare, and invent. These functions are contained under the principle of *Amagara*, which is responsible for a human-specific type of "life."

---

3 See, for example, Descartes, René, *Meditations on First Philosophy* (English transl. Donald A. Cress), Indianapolis, Hackett Publishing Company, 1979 (1641), Hume, David, *A Treatise of Human Nature*, ed. L. A. Selby-Bigge, Oxford: Clarendon Press 1978 (1739), and Rorty, Amelie O., ed., *The Identities of Persons*, Berkeley and Los Angeles, University of California Press, 1976.

According to Kwasi Wiredu, Akan folk thought also points to similarly multi-substance constitution of the person, all of which deal with his/her physical becoming or make-up. According to him, the Akan think of the person as constituted of the body and a combination of four "entities conceived as spiritual substances: *okra*..., *sunsum*..., *ntoro*..., and, finally, *mogya*..." (Wiredu 1980, 47). Similarly, for the Yoruba, write Hallen and Sodipo, "the essential elements of the person (*èníyàn*) when in the world are the body (*ara*), the vital spirit of that body, or soul (*èmí*), and the destiny (*orí*) that will determine every significant event during that particular lifetime" (Hallen and Sodipo 1997, 105). But human industrious capacities are hardly what lies at the heart of the idea of *Ubuntu* in the context of its recent discussions in southern African discourse.

Also, Luo traditional belief and cultural practice recognizes what is called "fission of persons" in Western discourse and philosophical debate. The belief that individuals can be possessed by the spirits—*juogi*—of the dead who can cause them to act in ways other than of their own free will suggests that an individual can be inhabited by several persons at the same time, often causing them to be conflicted in the manifestation of the capacities of their own person. The possessing spirits can either cause their individual human receptacle to "see" things otherwise hidden from other people, or to be violent if their demands conflict or get into competition with those of the victim herself or himself. In any one of those circumstances, the possessed individual manifests different personalities and can act in irrational manners as the possessing spirits "fight" with the will and intentions of their victim. At the height of the conflict, the victim may fall into a trance marked with babbling out incomprehensible locutions. In those circumstances they are said to be overwhelmed by the foreign spirits, and that they are not their own persons but mediums of other persons altogether. This inhabitation by foreign personalities or "spirits" makes the possessed person babble as a sign that they have lost control of their own ability to speak in sensible manners. They become senseless; they are said to be "sick with *juogi*." While this belief presents interesting threads for thinking about concepts of personhood in the context of identity, it also speaks to the ideals of personhood in the sense of expected exhibition of normalcy as regards the display of personhood. The possessed person loses the powers to properly use their mind in a logically and morally responsible manner. As evoked in the discourse on *Ubuntu*, the possessed person has lost the rational and moral dimensions or attributes of their *utu* or *ubuntu*. The Luo say of such a person, *"En ng'ato ma tuo* (He/she is sick)" which implies in a strong way that such a person has lost his/her social dimension. This loss is temporary until the sick person goes through treatment to exorcize the *juogi* out of them and they become "normal" or their own person again.

UBUNTU AND THE MORAL SELF

Besides some similarities and overlaps between Western and some African beliefs about the composition of personhood as indicated, there are differences as well. Western beliefs about personhood are deeply dualistic, and the dualism spans both popular and specifically philosophical renditions. By contrast, Kwasi Wiredu's philosophy on this matter is decidedly monistic. His quasi-physicalism is in contrast also to the multi-substance folk beliefs of the Akan, and suggests that there is only the human body which, by its specific endowments, is capable of activities whose products are not exactly or necessarily physical. Wiredu believes that humans' sociality is not an accidental matter. Rather, humans attain their showing and exhibit the capacities that define them in their specific difference from other animals by virtue of what their sociality enables them to develop as a result of what the body bears as its specific endowment or capacity. According to him, the mind, which is the distinguishing mark of the human species, is only a complex of aspects of brain states (Wiredu 1996, 16-17). He argues that Akan people do not list the mind as one of the constitutive elements that make up a person. Rather, the Akan usage of the term *adwene* for both thought and mind suggests that mind is the function of thought and not an entity (Wiredu 1996, 16-17). As the function of thought, mind is brought about by communication (Wiredu 1996, 21-22). The latter, for Wiredu, is the vital necessity that sparks the development of humans into *persons*.

Through communication humans not only develop and gradually refine their mind, they also grow to become self-aware and aware of others. Communication exposes the Maussian split between the *moi* and the *personne morale*, two elements that enjoy a kind of Siamese relationship, suggesting that Wiredu uses the term "person" in a sense that is more than just the Western metaphysical sense. While the Western tradition–in both its popular and specifically philosophical appearances–uses the term in its constitutive sense that is akin to what one experiences as *moi*, Wiredu uses it in a sense closer to Mauss's *personne morale*, one that emerges out of a practical relationship with others through communication. Similarly, differences emerge in the use of the term "self." As used in the English language, the term "self" appears as apposition to a noun, or pronoun, to indicate the particularity of a person or persons—me "myself", her "herself", it "itself", they "themselves", etc., meaning the same person, persons, or thing; sameness of doer and subject, such as "oneself" in "self-blame", "self-praise", and so on. Philosophers have used the term to refer to the essence or core as distinguishable from the empirical aspect of humans, the soul or the true, inner aspect of them. But because he is a monist, Wiredu probably does not draw a sharp distinction between "person" and "self," in which case his idea of both is one which is engendered through the communicative interchanges between persons who grow into it as they sharpen their potential to form and exchange thought with others. The self or person is she or he who, by virtue of her or his rationality, bears expectations from other persons with whom she or he shares both primary and extended community. She is both an epistemic and moral agent and bears responsibilities toward other persons and toward community at large, and hence is susceptible to judgement. The fundamental question in relation to this person is not about her or his constitution but about how she or he should be expected to conduct herself or himself toward other persons. According to Wiredu, "[we can] assume that every human being has a concern for his or her own interests in whatever way the concept of interest might be defined. The problem of morals arises from the fact that not everybody has a natural inclination to be concerned about the interests of others at all times in their conduct. In consideration of this, the following imperative naturally suggests itself. 'Let your conduct at all times manifest a due concern for the interests of others'" (Wiredu 1996, 29). In other words, being rational, the person can be taught, and can learn to see the grounds for or value of conducting herself or himself in manifestation of due concern for the interests of others. While the dynamics of relating to one another in society is likely to raise moral conflicts from which the person can learn about the value of the imperative, it will, as a way of countering or subverting the natural egoistic inclination in childhood or in feeble moral and social thinking in later years, usually be taught to her or him by the wise few whose consideration of the abstract principles of ethical life is aimed at "the harmonization of human interests in society" (Wiredu 1996, 29). Useful for this end is "the principle of sympathetic impartiality", which Wiredu explains in the following manner: "A person may be said to manifest due concern for the interests of others if in contemplating the impact of his actions on their interests, she puts herself [sic] imaginatively in their position, and having done so, is able to welcome that impact" (Wiredu 1996, 29). Thus when asked, for example, "why one should abstain from [their] neighbour's wife, [any ordinary Akan] would almost certainly reply 'Would you like the same if it were done to you?'" (Wiredu 1983, 7).[4] The idea, according to Wiredu, is that morality is accepted by rational reflection, a practical capability that is acquired and honed gradually with maturity in inter-personal relations and social embeddedness. The assumption behind both Akan and Luo responses is that morality in turn assumes similarity between all persons, regardless of whether or not they themselves are capable of making the right moral choices. As a minimum, people are expected to recognize this basic similarity and to conduct themselves toward them as the principle requires. If pain hurts, it hurts anybody, everybody. If injustice hurts, it hurts anybody, everybody. And if that person or those persons inflicting pain or injustice would not like it done to them, then they should not do it to anybody.

But what, exactly, do the principle of sympathetic impartiality and the golden rule teach? And what, in the context of South Africa's contemporary social, moral, and political discourse, do they require of people in their conduct? It is obvious from their general framing that these principles are merely general guides that do not teach how one ought to act in particular instances or cases. They leave the determination of conduct in particular instances to evaluation according to their guidance. They teach us above all that our judgement of the conduct of others presupposes a norm, one that we already know or take for granted, namely that there are expectations of how people ought to be treated, because we would demand them of ourselves. Negatively, we presuppose that there are some ways no-one should be treated because we know it of us that it would be wrong if we were subjected to such conduct. I know, for example,

---

4   My indigenous Luo people would respond in a similar manner: "*In ka otimni, d'iyie, koso di ber-ni?* (If the same were done to you, would you agree, or would you like it?)"

that I should be accorded fair treatment in all circumstances when I am arrested by the police. In particular, for example, I expect the arresting officer to treat an arrested person with due respect because she or he deserves it as a human being, and that they should deserve to be tried fairly under the same laws applicable to all persons who have committed an offence similar to that for which she or he has been arrested. in circumstances similar to their own. I say "due respect" because people differ in some social circumstances that require some minimum differences. Many of us remember, for example, how Prime Minister Patrice Lumumba was treated by the military officers who captured him. He was stripped of his clothes and had his hands tied in his back in the back of a military lorry as they drove him away to his murder. Or many of us heard stories of how Emperor Haile Selassie was bundled into the tiny trunk of VW car by members of the military who overthrew him. While no human being deserves to be treated the way either Lumumba or Haile Selassie was treated by their captors, not even criminals, one would expect a difference in respect for these dignitaries from how an ordinary street criminal would be treated.

Thus the principle of sympathetic impartiality and the golden rule contain a standard by which to judge our own conduct by referring us to our judgement of similar conduct by others. In respect to the South African particular discourse, one should ask whether she or he would like it if they were treated with disdain for their humanity: held to be a squatter in her or his own country; treated as a criminal until she or he proves her or his innocense; denied all human rights in respect to white people, and so on. In these senses, the principle of sympathetic impartiality or the golden rule work in conjunction with the idea implicit in the concept of *Utu*, or Ubuntu, to supply proof that there is a law that is irrevocably concomitant with human nature itself. To evoke the latter terms is at once to put out notice that fundamental abominations have been committed in the form of violation of all such laws that are concomitant with human nature, and to open up an avenue for dialogue aimed at rectifying such violations through restitution of the violations and all other wrongs that have led to the breakdown of society. At the hearings of the Truth and Reconciliation Commission, the mother of Siphiwo, one of the many victims of the brutal murders by the apartheid police, asked about the officers who had come forward as the killers of her son: "What if we took guns and started to shoot them as they sit there, would they like it?" In other words, there is a standard way to treat other human beings, and the recognition of that standard starts by asking the question of oneself whether my conduct would still be fine if it were the conduct of the other person toward me. The creation of the Commission itself, and its process, was meant to provide the protection of the law for the perpetrators of apartheid's regime of terror who would come forward to confess their acts. By coming out, they not only applied for the law's protection, they also acknowledged the divide between right and wrong, and thereby admitted that they had been on the wrong. By applying for the law's protection, the perpetrators of apartheid's heinous crimes acknowledged that although the law's protection was a good thing—which was the reason they wanted and applied for it—they themselves had failed to give the same to their victims.

Kagame's metaphysics has an interesting implication for the soio-political and moral world. In his analysis, *Umuntu*'s exercise of reason gives him/her power over nature, and a special moral oversight over the inhabitants with whom he/she shares the category of *Umuntu*. Influenced significantly by Tempels in this regard, Kagame explains that sustaining a balance in nature lies with *Umuntu* just as much as causing misfortune lies with how he/she uses reason in the manipulative management of nature or the moral manage of the co-existence among those of the category of *Umuntu*, his/her fellow humans. The idea of domination and control remains significant in Kagame's conception of *Umuntu*'s special positioning at the top of nature. The idea that *Umuntu* is capable of manipulating nature, or controlling his/her fellow humans to his/her benefit resonates with an understanding of social structures built on inequalities of access to and use of resources for the advancement or sustenance of the position of dominance by those whom such unequal access gives privilege and power. Tempels had explained that the idea of good and evil among the Bantu lies in the ontological hierarchy of forces in which man, by virtue of having intelligence, is capable of manipulating the material world for purposes of controlling the destiny of his fellow men. This, in his view, was where the idea of magic and witchcraft got their explanations. According to Tempels,

> Objective morality to the Bantu is ontological, immanent and intrinsic morality. Bantu moral standards depend essentially on

things ontologically understood. Knowledge of a necessary natural order of forces forms part of the wisdom of primitive peoples. From that we may conclude that an act or usage will be characterized as ontologically good by Bantu and that it will therefore be accounted ethically good; and at length, by deduction, be assessed as juridically just...for Bantu, it is the living "muntu" who, by divine will, is the norm of either ontological or natural law, so equally he is the norm of the customary law [and] by an equally exact logic, that the "muntu" is the norm of language, grammar, geography, of all life and of all that life brings into relationship with the "muntu" (Tempels 1959, 121-122).

To evoke *Utu*, or Ubuntu in the context of post-apartheid corrective discourse, in contrast to Kagame's interpretation of Tempels, and certainly in contrast to the morality of apartheid, is to point to the significance of the fundamental human rights–the basic and inalienable moral goods or guarantees that belong to us all by virtue of being human. The rights teach us, among other things, that the sole purpose for having reason is for humans to use it, so they must be accorded every opportunity to do so. Hence, among human rights, the freedom of thought is among the most basic, or, put another way, most important. Humans must have the right to nurture reason that it may develop appropriately as the means to human flourishing. The primacy of reason and the right to thought are supported by freedom as a condition for the development and use of reason. Therefore freedom is another basic right. Freedom of thought or opinion, freedom of speech are such rights as attached to reason, its development, and use. Although other rights are acquired, their justification go back to those rights that are considered basic and universal. Attaching them to *Utu* implies that they are considered natural, and that although different philosophers and constitutions may have spelled them out at different times in history (John Locke in *Second Treatise of Government* in 1690; U.S. Bill of Rights ratified in 1791; the French Declaration of the Rights of Man and the Citizen, 1789; and the Universal Declaration of Human Rights, formulated by the United Nations in 1948), they reside with the very nature of humanity, *Utu*. To comply with these rights is to treat others with the respect and dignity that belong to them.

The Swahili idea of *Mtu mzima* (a whole, grown or healthy person) carries both descriptive and prescriptive connotations. It means that a person who is grown and is mature, and is in good physical and mental health, is expected to recognize both the theoretical and practical significance of the principle of sympathetic impartiality. She or he ought to comport herself or himself in a particular manner associated with a healthy adult person as a measure of normalcy. She or he is *Umtu omkhulu* in the Nguni languages, and *Umuntu mukuru* in Kinyarwanda. (A physically healthy person is *Umuntu ufite ubuzima bwiza* in Kinyarwanda. An *Umuntu mukuru* is understood to be also generally healthy, meaning both physically and mentally.) Taking all these variations into account as essentially concordant in their meanings, a *mtu mzima* can now be said to be one who is regarded to be in their right mind, and so is expected to be able to make good judgement and to reason well generally, but especially in matters of the right moral choices or conduct where these involve other people's interests. A person who is possessed by *juogi* is not an Umuntu in this sense of possessing the powers of reason and moral judgement. The general abstract form *Utu*, or *Umuntu* in Kinyarwanda, or Ubuntu in the Nguni variant farther south, bears these moral connotations, and illustrates what the Tanzanian philosopher Shaaban bin Robert (1969) means when he writes about *Utu bora*, perfect humanity or human nature. Among the characteristics of human perfection are moral qualities like honesty, doing the right things for self, for others, and for community, especially doing service to those in need or who are disadvantaged. In *Koja la Lugha*, Shaaban writes as follows about doing good and avoiding evil:

Panda mbegu ya wema, yaote mapendeleo,
Panda mbegu ya heshima, ili uvune cheo,
Uovi si mbegu njema, zao lake machukio,
Tena hupata lawama, apandaye mbegu hiyo.

Panda ungoje majira, usivune mbio mbio,
Hapati mazao bora, mwenye pupa na choyo,
Haraka ina hasara, wamesema wasemao,
Wengi wamedorora, kwa kupuuza yapasayo.

(Sow the seeds of good, so they may yield favors,
Sow the seeds of respect, so you may earn status in society,
Evil is not a good seed, its fruit is hatred,
He gets blame, he who plants such a seed,

29

Sow and wait patiently for the right season, do not look to harvest in a hurry,

He never gets the best yields who has haste and covetousness,
Haste brings regrets, so it has been observed,
Many have been ostracized for ignoring to do what is right)
(Robert 1969, 53).

It is obvious now that African thought uses the ideas of "person" and "personhood" in only the human sense. A person must be a human being. A good society or community is the result of the good deeds of its members, and the right *utu* is cultivated only in the right conditions made possible by the right and good deeds of the members of the community, so everyone is called upon to help create that environment by doing that which is both right and good, namely by being virtuous. According to Shaaban, virtuosity does not come automatically to people like natural inclinations do. It is taught and learned, so people have to be reminded continuously to know the values of right conduct so they may adhere to the kind of conduct that produces the desirable society or community. These are the expectations of a *Mtu mzima*, *Umtu omkhulu*, or *Umuntu mukuru* as explained above. It is his or her responsibility to live in accordance with the ideals that define a desirable society, namely one in which everyone is treated with respect and dignity as required by their rights. To treat any person in a manner that degrades their *Utu* is to degrade one's own *Utu*, because it is to conduct oneself in a manner contrary to the expectations of a *Mtu mzima* (*Umtu omkhulu*, or *Umuntu mukuru*). In other words, the idea of Utu spells out the complementarity between rights and responsibilities, between claims and duties.

The recognition and observance of rights is the foundation of a reciprocal moral relationship between citizens, and the democratic practices of a nation. Thus accounts of *Utu*, or Ubuntu, are descriptions of rights and critiques of the problems associated with their violations. Unwarranted arrests and incarceration, restrictions of movement, or of thought and speech, unfair or other forms of discriminatory treatment are all violations of rights in accordance with the understanding of the basic tenets of *Utu*. They are also violations of the democratic principles of governance which depend on the freedom of choice to be exercised by all citizens who are in the category of *Mtu mzima* (*Umtu omkhulu*, or *Umuntu mukuru*). The basic attribute of rationality, and the right to freely use reason for the furtherance of one's well-being require that everyone has the right to contribute to putting in place the best government of their choice, and that, subsequently, they have the right to democratically take the government out of office by popular vote when such a government fails to, or no longer serves the interests of the people. When these rights are enshrined in the constitution, they become constitutional or civil rights of all *Watu wazima* (plural of *Mtu mzima*). In other words, a *Mtu mzima* is not only a moral agent, she or he is also a political agent.

According to Tempels,

> The tenacity of the "muntu" in the defence of his rights is the consequence of his attachment to his fundamental wisdom and to his philosophy... The deeper his thought, the more his arguments are rooted in his philosophical beliefs, in his wisdom and in his ontological behavious, the more tenacious he will be and the more he will rise tot defend his precious human rights. It is in defence of their rights that [the Bantu] peoples show their personalities to best advantage, because their rights...are built upon the ultimate essence of their humanity, upon their conception of the world, and upon their philosophy.
>
> In African eyes, to renounce one's philosophy is to renounce ethics and law. His deepest obligations, founded on the unalterable principles of his philosophy and on his concept of humanity and plenitude of life, condition both the profound consciousness which he has of his rights and the sacred character that he attributes to them... [He] is very conscious of his rights as man (Tempels 1959, 123-124).

Although Africans may not be unique in emphasizing the emergence of the self in social and cultural contexts[5], African modes

---

5   I have shown elsewhere—in *Self and Community in a Changing World* (Bloomington: Indiana University Press, 2010), pp. 228-229—that German philosophy shows a significant exception in Western philosophy in developing a stratum of the social self. G. W. F. Hegel, Karl Marx, and George Simmel emphasized the inter-dependency between individuals while opposing the individualism prevalent in Immanuel Kant and in post-Enlightenment French philosophy. I can now add that leading figures in American pragmatism too, especially

of thought and practices place an even greater premium on the accomplishment of self-awareness in the dynamics of social and moral relations. According to African modes of thought, and in the practices built thereupon, it is not enough to be merely a *mtu* or human being. Rather, it is the expectation that as one grows and matures into being a *mtu*, she or he manifests her or his *utu* in the kind of thought and practices expected of a *mtu mzima*, which implies that she or he grows to exhibit the capacity for due diligence while striving always, in living according to those expectations, to become a *mtu bora* (a perfect person). Thus Mauss's *moi*, the self-aware subject, the "I", emerges in encounters with other "Is" or selves where, in the practice of reciprocity, it becomes a *personne morale* and, one would add, a *personne politique*.

The transition from *moi* to *personne morale* (Wiredu's "person") starts early—probably from birth. The first stages of a child's life are focused on the *moi* which is characterized mostly by instinctive needs and demands which are met by the mother or care givers. As the child grows, the demands get to be controlled and the child begins to encounter limitations. The experience of tension and limitation, or loss of monopoly sets in as a new and long-lasting phase of the development of selfhood. One's own "I" finds itself in constant competition, and sometimes in conflict with other "Is", and Mauss's transition into *la personne morale* is about to take off from an idiosyncratic experience of self, or self-awareness into the experience of the presence of other, competing selves. The development process teaches the child that she or he is not right all the time, nor is she or he right about everything. She or he is fallible, and must learn the rules of discourse and negotiation.

The agency-based view of personhood, such as is also suggested by Kagame's ill-motivated interpretation of Tempels's ontological hierarchy, proposes that "a person is someone who can be a citizen, that is, a fully cooperating member of society over a complete life." There are two major problems with it. First, because it suggests to leave aside people with grievous or permanent physical disabilities or

---

John Dewey and George Herbert Mead, emphasized the socialization of the individual through education (Dewey) and social roles (Mead). Still, the doctrines of the centrality of the individual as the arbiter of moral, epistemological and political values remain the dominant Western stand. There are different versions of these general doctrines.

mental disorders so severe as to prevent them from being normal and fully cooperating members of society in the defined sense, it has evoked criticism for suggesting that disabled people cannot be persons, or at least citizens. The concern is about who defines what counts as handicap, and what degree of it qualifies one for exclusion from being a moral agent. From an agency-focused moral perspective, an individual's status will be relativized to whatever physical, sensory, or cognitive performances are designated as "normal" for the expression of moral activity, meaning the degree to which any of such disabilities make it possible, or impossible, for an individual to understand and execute moral acts. But who defines disability, and how is it measured? Also, the definition suggests that one is a person only when they are cooperative and not when they rebel or think and act contrarily to what is acceptable to the dominant group in society. In this case, the category of personhood could be withdrawn from, and used to justify persecution of opposition parties by dominant social or political groups such as was the case in the apartheid era in South Africa, or in the socio-ethnically hierarchized society in Rwanda or other places where people have been victimized on the grounds of having beliefs or practices different from those of dominant groups.

Secondly, because of its restrictiveness to agency as a factor for personhood, the position has been used as the post-factum basis for racism as the ideology of exclusion since the eighteenth century. The denial of agency and corresponding rights to those politically and juridically designated as "non-persons" in all white dominated nations and states became coterminous with their perceived non-personhood. The category of "subpersons" was created by the Enlightenment idea of a (racial) contract from which non-white people were excluded. The contractarian views of states of perfect freedom and equality of all men from which their agency is understood and envisaged was never conceived by the architects of the so-called "social contract" theory to be applicable to non-white people. According to Charles Mills "the color-coded morality of the Racial Contract restricts the possession of this natural freedom and equality to *white* men" (Mills 1997, 16). In other words, the idea of personhood in "all men" as possessing certain attributes which warrant them to be considered in a certain moral manner does not apply to "all men", but only to "all white men." "It is this [racially specific] language of equality," says Mills, which echoes in the

American and French Revolutions, the Declaration of Independence, and the Declaration of the Rights of Man. And it is this moral egalitarianism that must be retained in the allocation of rights and liberties in civil society" (Mills 1997, 16). This view of agency as a factor of personhood is therefore less replete or less flexible, and therefore less inclusive. Wiredu's idea of agency, however, is universal by virtue of being based on the universal biological similarity of all human beings.

When the idea of *Utu*—or Ubuntu in its southern variant—is evoked in the context of the post-apartheid national discourse in South Africa, it resonates with Charles Mills's critique of the creation of white spaces and systems from which non-white people would be systematically excluded. The evocation is critical because it seeks to interrogate, and to subvert, the moral grounds of the exclusion as a violation of the expectations of the fundamentals of what human rights and equality as grounded in what Wiredu calls the principle of sympathetic impartiality. In other words, the ideal *utu* or Ubuntu is to be found as the moral character of he or she–*mtu mzima*–whose treatment of others is grounded in the principle of the golden rule which is, among other things, the expression of the recognition of the moral equality of all people, "at least, so long as he himself has a practical respect for the rights of his neighbour on the same grounds as those which he claims for his own rights," Tempels (1959, 124) writes of the Bantu. The rational maturity and good reasoning of a *mtu mzima* enables him or her to appreciate the moral value of the principle of sympathetic impartiality as the basis of a society in which everyone is accorded due respect, equal freedoms and rights. Negatively, to say of someone that she or he lacks *Utu* or Ubuntu is to claim that they lack the mastery of the principles of good moral reasoning—such as the principle of sympathetic impartiality, or the golden rule—that hold society together in accordance with acceptable principles of "law, civil, economic, or social rights" (Tempels 1959, 124). It is to claim, in other words, that they lack what morality does in prompting man to go beyond him-or herself by stimulating him or her to realize his or her basic social nature, *Utu*, by being mindful of others' interests in a world in which all are morally equal.

CONCLUSION: THE SELF, AGENCY, AND THE PUBLIC SPHERE

The fears of defining personhood based on agency are legitimate, as they have driven political policies in assigning groups of people their stations and allowing violence to sustain inequality by containing sections of society within the politically-driven discriminatory boundaries to keep them separated from self-designated "normal" groups. Thus the definition of citizenship based on agency carries with it the dangers of the use of whims in the definition of incapacitation, thus leaving every door wide open to exclude anyone or any group from citizenry, that is, from enjoying human and civic freedoms and rights. Anyone, according to that prescription, is susceptible to a whimsical classification of deficits in powers to perform roles or to receive the goods that are the preserve of "normal people." In reading Shaaban bin Robert's *Utubora Mkulima*, however, one learns that the fundamental goal of humanity is indiscriminately to improve the human condition for all, and that this arises in part from the collaborative efforts of all people to create those conditions in which individuals will be able to prosper through engagements in different sectors of the economy. Among these activities, Shaaban emphasizes, agriculture, or farming, must be accorded attention and given priority as Africa is primarily an agricultural continent. Furthermore, Shaaban argues, priority needs to shift from personal to collective improvement, because participation in the production of the common good by people who function in the public sphere in a dialogic mode should be the ideal that supercedes the pursuit of material well-being for the individual. Individual moral perfection should be measured by service or contribution to the common good. As Shaaban says in the passage from "Good against evil" cited above, the motivation to do the good is the status or social standing which our conduct earns us in the eyes of society. He believes that it is natural for people to aim at having a standing in society, to earn honor, or status as he calls it. In *Utubora Mkulima* the leading character Utubora earns his honor for being selfless, especially for helping those in need yet helpless. Motivated by honor to be earned as a result of doing that which is good for other people rather than as motivated by personal material gain, Utubora chooses to perform communal service in secrecy so that his satisfaction should come primarily from the knowledge that he has done the right thing, not for gain, but because it is the right thing to

35

do. He acts in a manner contrary to the expectations of many by sowing the seeds of good and earns honor, but he has to wait patiently for recognition to come to him.

BIBLIOGRAPHY

Carrithers, Michael, Steven Collins, and Steven Lukes. 1985. *The Category of the Person: Anthropology, Philosophy, History*. Cambridge: Cambridge University Press.

Descartes, René. 1979. *Meditations on First Philosophy* (English translation Donald A. Cress). Indianapolis: Hackett Publishing Company.

Giddens, Anthonly. 1991. *Modernity and Self-Identity: Self and Society in the Late Modern Age*. Stanford, CA: Stanford University Press.

Griaule, Marcel. 1965. *Conversations with Ogotemmêli: An Introduction to Dogon Religious Ideas* (English translation). London: Oxford University Press.

Hallen, Barry and J. Olubi Sodipo. 1997. *Knowledge, Belief, and Witchcraft: Analytic Experiments in African Philosophy*. Stanford, CA: Stanford University Press.

Hume, David. 1978 [1739]. *A Treatise of Human Nature*. Oxford: Clarendon Press.

Kagame, Alexis. 1956. *La Philosophie bantu-rwandaise de l'Être*. Bruxelles: Académié Royale des Sciences Coloniales.

Kant, Immanuel. 1978. *Anthropology from a Pragmatic Point of View* (English transl. Victor Lyle Dowdell). Carbondale and Edwardsville, IL: Southern Illinois University Press.

Kiros, Teodros, ed. 2001. *Explorations in African Political Thought*. New York and London: Routledge Publishers.

Godfrey, Lienhardt. 1985. "Self: Public, Private, Some African Representations". In *The Category of the Person: Anthropology, Philosophy, History*, 141-155. Cambridge: Cambridge University Press.

Locke, John. 1956. *Essay Concerning Human Understanding*. Chicago: Gateway Editions, Inc.

Locke, John. 1980 [1690]. *Second Treatise of Government*. Indianapolis, In: Hackett Publishing Company, Inc.

Másolo, D. A. 2001. "Critical Rationalism and Cultural Traditions in African Philosophy". In *Explorations in African Political*

Thought, 81-95. New York and London: Routledge Publishers.

Masolo, D. A. 2010. *Self and Community in a Changing World.* Bloomington: Indiana University Press.

Mauss, Maurice. 1985. [1938]. "A category of the human mind: the notion of person, the notion of self" (translated by W. D. Halls). In *The Category of the Person: Anthropology, Philosophy, History*, Michael Caruthers, S. Collins, and S. Lukes (eds). Cambridge: Cambridge University Press.

Mills, Charles W. 1997. *The Racial Contract.* Ithaca and London: Cornell University Press.

Robert, Shaaban bin. 1968. *Utubora Mkulima* (Diwani ya Shaaban). London: Evans Brothers Limited.

Robert, Shaaban bin. 1969. *Koja la Lugha*, Nairobi: Oxford University Press.

Rorty, Amelie O., ed. 1976. *The Identities of Persons.* Berkeley: California University Press.

Rorty, Richard M. 1989. *Contingency, Irony, and Solidarity: Lectures on language, selfhood and politics plus interpretations of other writers.* Cambridge: Cambridge University Press.

Temples, Placide. 1969. *Bantu Philosophy.* Paris: Présence Africaine.

Wiredu, Kwasi. 1980. *Philosophy and an African Culture.* London: Cambridge University Press.

Wiredu, Kwasi. 1983. "Morality and Religion in Akan Thought". In *Philosophy and Cultures*, 6-13. Nairobi: Bookwise Publishers.

Wiredu, Kwasi. 1996. *Cultural Universals and Particulars: An African Perspective.* Bloomington: Indiana University Press.

CHAPTER 2. BECOMING A PERSON:
PERSONHOOD AND ITS PRECONDITIONS

Anke Graness

INTRODUCTION

Personhood, meaning the status of being a person, is a basic concept in philosophy that is widely debated. In the European tradition of philosophy, the concept of personhood is closely tied to concepts such as autonomy and self-determination, equality and liberty, as well as legal issues regarding possession of rights, accountability, or legal liability. Historically, during the period of slavery and colonization, it was hotly debated whether the concept of personhood could be applied to all human beings regardless of their origin and skin colour. Currently, it is still a contentious issue for example in debates about abortion and foetal rights, which question the beginning of human personhood, or on animal rights, which question the scope of the concept of personhood's application.

In the Euro-American context, personhood is defined in a variety of ways, the earliest formulated in the sixth century by Boethius, who defined a person as 'an individual substance of a rational nature' ('*Naturæ rationalis individua substantia*'). Today, the broad variety of definitions ranges from an understanding of personhood as human essence or substance (here the category personhood is applied to the foetus) to personhood as self-awareness (in which case personhood can be applied to other species, too).

Generally, two main approaches can be identified in the Euro-American context.

The first approach is an ontological personalism which considers personhood as an immortal essence of all human beings. This position underlines the unique status of humans among all other beings. In this view, personhood is associated with an inviolable dignity that merits unconditional respect. This stance is predominantly found in Christian theology.

A second view considers personhood a specific quality or ability which is not given merely by membership in the species *homo sapiens*. The quality of personhood has to be acquired by moral and cultural education. A famous representative of this approach is Immanuel Kant. For him the notion 'person' is inextricably linked with an autonomous moral and cognitive agent. It manifests only in the social practice of human thought and action. Or as Kant puts it in his *Prolegomena*:

> **Person; Imputation**—A PERSON is a Subject who is capable of having his actions *imputed* to him. Moral Personality is, therefore, nothing but the Freedom of a rational Being under Moral Laws; and it is to be distinguished from psychological Freedom as the mere faculty by which we become conscious of ourselves in different states of the Identity of our existence. Hence it follows that *a Person is properly subject to no other Laws than those he lays down for himself*, either alone or in conjunction with others (Kant 1785, 31-32).

The antonym to person as a rational being is, according to Kant, the thing.

> **Thing**—A **THING** is what is incapable of being the subject of Imputation. Every object of the free activity of the Will, which is itself void of freedom, is therefore called a Thing (*res corporealis*) (Kant 1785, 32).

For Kant being a person means by definition to be a rational being[1] and a moral agent. It assumes the accountability for actions and a capacity for self-determination by moral and legal principles, i.e. rational agency. It is—in the Kantian sense—not a property of a

---

1   "vernünftiges Wesen" Kant *Metaphysik der Sitten* AA IV, 428.

40

human being qua member of the human species, but a trait linked to specific characteristics and abilities. Kant's concept of personhood turns away from substance ontology and is the beginning of a new approach to the concept of a person on the basis of action theory and moral philosophy. Being a person is a result of an individual process of moral and educational formation which cannot be achieved by every member of the human species. In consequence, certain members of the human species might not possess personhood. Human beings who cannot be considered rational beings would not be moral agents, and thus do not qualify for personhood. According to this definition, Kant considers neither children, who as emerging personalities are still powerless, immature and subject to parental will[2], nor women, who are directed by emotions rather than rationality (see Kant's *Observations on the Feeling of the Beautiful and Sublime*, 1764) to be persons in the full meaning of the term, namely moral agents.[3] Thus, the Kantian concept of person contains a considerable potential of exclusion.[4]

---

2   In his *Metaphysics of Morals* Kant discusses the rights and obligations of parents towards their children as an 'acquisition of a human being *as of* a thing, but only formally so.' (Kant 1996, 128) And he clarifies: 'From the child's personality it also follows that the right of parents is not just a right to a thing, since a child can never be considered as the property of his parents, so that their right is not alienable (*ius personalissimus*). But this right is also not just a right against a person, since a child still belongs to his parents as what is theirs (is still in their *possession* like a thing…). It is, instead, a right to a person *akin to a right to a thing*.' (p. 65)—until the time of the emancipation of the child.

3   Moreover, Kant strongly doubts that members of 'races' other than the 'white Caucasian race' have the ability to acquire the education and autonomy necessary for moral agency. In particular, the black 'race' is for him incapable of achieving the required level of rationality necessary to attain personhood (in the sense of free, autonomous and rational agency). (see for example Kant, 'On the different Human Races', 1775)

4   The intrinsic worth of all human beings, i.e. their dignity, and that they should be treated as an *end* in themselves and not as a *means* to something else, can be better justified on the basis of Kant's concept of rights. Here Kant pronounces as an imperative that everyone has to respect everyone else's <u>innate right</u> to freedom. As an innate right, it does not require any other precondition than being human.

THE DEBATE ON PERSONHOOD IN AFRICA

In African philosophical discourse, the concept of personhood also plays an important role, for example, in the debate between advocates of ethnophilosophy and their critics and in discussions of various concepts of African socialism and African humanism. Currently, personhood is a central category in the broad debate on the concept of Ubuntu in southern Africa. Two general tendencies can be identified in the discussion on personhood in contemporary African philosophy:

In one view, the African conception of the person is a kind of counter-concept to various other conceptions of person found in 'Western' thought. The Kenyan theologian and philosopher John Mbiti is a central proponent of this approach. In his well-known *African Religions and Philosophy* (1969), Mbiti states the now-classic phrase, 'I am because we are, and since we are, therefore I am' (Mbiti 1969, 108-09), claiming that the relation between individual and community in Africa takes a particular form that distinguishes it from 'Western' or 'modern' societies. By setting up a dichotomy, this approach distinguishes between 'Western' views, which—it is argued—generally hold that a person is a 'lone individual'[5], and 'African' views, which define a person by reference to the community, which always takes precedence over the individual life.

---

5   European philosophers and social scientists like Aristotle, Marx, or Georg Herbert Mead are clearly counterexamples to such an assertion. For them, human beings are essentially 'social animals'; thus they consider the society not as something accidental but as the essence of being human. See for example Marx's expression the 'socialized man', or his 'Theses on Feuerbach', where he states: 'But the human essence is no abstraction inherent in each single individual. In its reality it is the ensemble of the social relations.' (K. Marx, 'Thesen über Feuerbach' VI, MEW 3, 534). According to Marx, man is the totality of his social connections, and modern civil society [today's neoliberal society], based on individualism, violates man as a social being. (See e.g. Karl Marx 'Zur Kritik der Hegelschen Rechtsphilosophie', MEW 1, 285) Thus, what certain African philosophers' critiques call 'Western' or 'modern' society mainly targets a specific neoliberal model of society which emphasizes the pursuit of self-interest and the protection of individual rights—a model which presently reigns supreme worldwide.

The community-centric view of personhood has been contested by several African scholars (see Kaphagawani 2006, 332ff), who have performed a linguistic analysis of the concept of personhood in various African languages, such as Akan or Yoruba, and studied the philosophical derivations of such understandings. Representatives of this approach are among others, the Ghanaian philosophers Kwame Gyekye and Kwasi Wiredu (Gyekye 1995, 85–103; Wiredu and Gyekye 1992). Kwame Gyekye, who strongly opposes Ifeani Menkiti's views (introduced below), has analysed the Akan concept of personhood and found in it a kind of 'moderate or restricted communitarianism', which includes communalistic as well as individualistic values. Gyekye's approach, which shows that strict dichotomies do not exist between 'Western' and 'African' concepts of personhood, is worthy of deeper exploration than can be conducted in this paper. His 'moderate communitarianism' calls for a dialectical view of individualism and communitarianism.

Interestingly, the community-centric view—even though often presented as antithetical to Kant's ethic—shares some aspects of Kant's concept of personhood, as I will show below.

A famous representative of the community-centric view is the Nigerian philosopher Ifeanyi Menkiti. His articles on the African concept of personhood are well known (Menkiti 1984 and 2006). In his discussions Menkiti reflects Mbiti's theory of a fundamental difference between 'African' and 'Western' conceptions of the person. While 'Western' worldviews consider the community to be formed of individuals, in 'African' thought the community forms and gives meaning to the individual. The community —understood in an organic sense and not as a unit constituted by atomic individuals (Menkiti 1984, 180) —is acknowledged to be the source of one's humanity. The primacy of the community over the individual postulated here applies not only ontologically (i.e. the community is seen as the root and nature of the individual and not vice versa) but also cosmologically, spiritually, normatively, and epistemologically. Menkiti argues that it is "in rootedness in an ongoing human community that the individual comes to see himself as man" (Menkiti 1984, 172). A certain individual's rootedness in a group reflects the group's biology (its gene pool) and language, which is a major determinant of mental disposition and attitude. Menkiti summarizes his view:

A crucial distinction thus exists between the African view of man and the view of man found in Western thought: in the African view it is the community which defines the person as person, not some isolated static quality of rationality, will, or memory (Menkiti 1984, 172).

Today, this kind of approach to an 'African' concept of personhood is reflected in the South African debate on the concept of Ubuntu, which is described as a community-oriented African worldview or ethic in contrast to the individualistic worldview of 'the West'. The central feature of the concept—regardless of whether it is considered a traditional philosophy of life, a moral quality of a person, or an ethical framework—is the interconnectedness of all human beings. The deep relational character of Ubuntu is frequently expressed using the Zulu-Xhosa aphorism *'umuntu ngumuntu ngabantu'*—'A human being is a human being through other people', which means that every human being needs other people in order to be human; every person is part of a whole, integrated into a comprehensive network of mutual dependencies. The aphorism expresses "the African idea of persons: persons exist only in relation to other persons. The human self ... only exists in relationship to its surroundings; these relationships are what it is. And the most important of these are the relationships we have with other persons" (Shutte 2001, 23). The aphorism emphasizes the existence of a universal bond that connects all people to each other and to all other types of existence in the universe, including currently living human and nonhuman beings, ancestors[6], the yet unborn, and the natural world.

On a moral level, Ubuntu is seen as a fundamental mindset that values mutual respect and recognition of the rights of others in order to promote human dignity and harmonious, peaceful coexistence. The South African philosophers Augustine Shutte and Mogobe B. Ramose explicitly refer to an Ubuntu ethic (Shutte 2001; Ramose 2003, 324-30). Characteristic features of an Ubuntu ethic are compassion for others, respect for the rights of minorities, conduct

---

6   Menkiti (Menkiti 1984, 174ff.) and Ramose (Ramose 1999, 2nd. ed. 2005, 59ff) discuss the applicability of the notion of personhood to the ancestors or 'living dead' broadly, an idea which cannot be elaborated here.

that aims at consensus and understanding, a spirit of mutual support and cooperation, hospitality, generosity, and selflessness. Moreover, Ubuntu refers not only to the relationship between people, but also to the relationship between human beings and the entire universe. As Ramose emphasizes, this concept considers individual human beings inseparable from an all-encompassing universe. And thus most Africans understand the earth to be a source of life that deserves respect (Ramose 2004, 203-06; Ramose 2009, 308-14).

For Ifeanyi Menkiti its deep relational character is only one important feature of the 'African' conception of the person. The second important feature is that personhood in African thought has a processual nature.[7] Menkiti argues that personhood is not something given at the beginning of one's life, but "something which has to be achieved, and is not given simply because one is born of human seed" (Menkiti 1984, 172). To obtain personhood, one must undergo a lengthy process of social and ritual transformation, learning the social rules by which the community lives, an undertaking which can fail. Thus, not every individual is capable of attaining personhood. In Menkiti's view—and here parallels to the Kantian approach to personhood become obvious—children, for example, are potentially able to attain personhood, but still in the process of doing so. They will complete the development of their personhood only after passing through the process of education and social transformation. Thus there is a qualitative difference between the personhood status of old and young individuals, which is reflected not only in their ethical maturity, but also in the degree of their obligations to and social incorporation in the community.[8] But the possessor of duties and rights cannot be other than a person (Menkiti 1984, 177). Since

---

7   Unfortunately, Menkitis reflections on an 'African' conception of personhood are not based on linguistic or hermeneutical explorations, but rather general assumptions. Thus, he states: "The various societies found in traditional Africa routinely accept this fact that personhood is the sort of thing which has to be attained..." (Menkiti 1984, 176).

8   In his critique of Mbiti, Kaphagawani stresses that the distinction between the elders and the young can only be an epistemological difference and that the young are not ontologically less human than the elders. He considers it a 'most serious problem of the Communalism Thesis ... that it conflates the epistemological with the ontological status of a human being' (Kaphagawani 2006, 339).

the capacity for moral sense is a precondition for having rights and duties, only a person can possess rights and duties.

Participants in the debate on Ubuntu concur about the processual nature of personhood. In a direct reference to Menkiti, Mogobe Ramose states,

> In order to be a person the human individual must, according to traditional African thought, go through various community prescribed stages, and be part of certain ceremonies and rituals. Only at the completion of all prescribed stages does the human individual acquire the status of a person (Ramose 1999, 58).

Augustine Shutte pronounces that personhood is not a trait that exists at the beginning of a human being's life. Shutte argues that "because I depend on relationships with others for being the person I am, in the beginning, at the start of my life, I am really not a person at all. Or put it another way and say that I am a potential person. I only become fully human to the extent that I am included in relationships with others. So I must see my life as a process of becoming a person"[9] (Shutte 2001, 24). He also emphasizes that the process of becoming a person could result in decrease or disintegration, that is, it can fail. Shutte argues that a person is constituted solely by his or her social relationships, beginning with the first relationship between mother and child. Therefore, not only education, but also community and dialogue have a constitutive function. Consequently, in his attempt to draft a new ethic for South Africa, the chapter 'Education' (from early childhood to lifelong education) plays a central role.

I would like to emphasize that an understanding of personhood as a certain quality which has to be acquired and is only potentially inherent in the child, a quality which has to be acquired in a process

---

9   On the other hand, Shutte's assumption that 'I am not a person at the beginning of my life' and that a person is constituted by the relationships to other persons, contradicts his statement on abortion later in his book. There he writes, 'As regards the question of abortion it would be safest to base one's considerations on the supposition that human persons come into being at the moment of conception.' (Shutte 2001, 134) This position, mainly the view of the Catholic Church, clearly contradicts a concept of personhood which considers personhood as an ability or quality which has to be acquired.

of educational and cultural formation, is fully consistent with Kant's view on personhood—although the first precondition of becoming a person (in Menkiti's view), social incorporation, does not play a role in Kant's concept, which focuses on the moral agency of the individual alone.

However, what Kant, Menkiti, and some representatives of the Ubuntu discourse do not take into consideration (or perhaps take for granted) in their reflections on the preconditions for becoming a person are the material preconditions. At this point, the concept of personhood detailed by the late Kenyan philosopher Henry Odera Oruka (1944–1995) might provide valuable enrichment of the theory.

HENRY ODERA ORUKA'S CONCEPT OF PERSONHOOD

The notion 'person' is a basic category for Odera Oruka, particularly in his concept of global justice.[10] For him, the problem of world poverty is not just a moral question of charity or humanitarian assistance, not even a question of restitution, but a matter of justice, and ultimately a question of enforceable law. He considers the protection of a minimum standard of living for everyone, which he calls the 'right to a human minimum', a basic requirement for global justice. The right to a human minimum is founded on the inalienable right to self-preservation. Since a human being's right to self-preservation is the first and fundamental necessity for making use of all other rights, denial of it causes the loss of essential functions of a human being. In his essay 'The Philosophy of Foreign Aid: A Question of the Right to a Human Minimum' (1989) Odera Oruka states,

> For all human beings to function with a significant degree of rationality and self-awareness, they need a certain minimum amount of physical security, health care, and subsistence […] Below this minimum one may still be human and alive. But one cannot successfully carry out the functions of a moral agent or engage in creative activity. Access to at least the human minimum is necessary (even if not sufficient) for one to be rational and self-conscious (Odera Oruka 1989, quoted from A. Graness and K. Kresse 1997, 53).

---

10   For further exploration of Odera Oruka's concept of global justice see Graness 2011, 2012, 2015.

Odera Oruka argues that the denial of the human minimum renders the affected individual incapable of exercising the essential functions of a person. For according to Odera Oruka's definition, a person is a rational, confident, self-conscious, morally acting being capable of making a fair deal (Odera Oruka 1989, quoted from A. Graness and K. Kresse 1997, 51-53). Thus, personhood includes the power of self-determination, a quality that goes beyond merely belonging to the species *homo sapiens*. To obtain the status of a person, a human being must have free and rational self-determination at one's disposition. But a human being in danger of death by starvation exercises neither free and rational self-determination nor autonomy. Facing one's own physical extinction, a human being will grasp at any straw that will increase the chances of survival, even if in the long run one's action is against one's own interest (for example accepting unfavourable contracts). Thus, Odera Oruka seeks to define the threshold between pure survival (a life of sheer existence) and full development of human potential. He states,

> All I am concerned with here is to point out those needs whose fulfillment liberates human beings from the life of sheer existence to that which offers a possibility for creativity. And I am also suggesting that this liberation is a necessary condition for one to function as a person, whatever meaning we attach to this concept (Odera Oruka 1989, quoted from A. Graness and K. Kresse 1997, 59).

In his view (and similar to Menkiti), only persons are holders of rights and duties. Individuals who do not obtain the status of a person are unable to act ethically. They stand apart from the ethical community, are no longer subject to community rules, and take no responsibility for their actions.

Thus, his concept of personhood, which closely links being a person to the qualities of rationality, moral agency, and autonomy, obviously follows the Kantian tradition. Personhood is, in Odera Oruka's view, a quality or development in a human being which requires certain preconditions, which has to be acquired—and can be lost. The basic prerequisite for personhood is the 'human minimum', which Odera Oruka defines as physical security, health, and subsistence (Odera Oruka 1989, quoted from A. Graness and K. Kresse 1997, 53). In his book *The Philosophy of Liberty* (1991), he expands this definition of basic needs to a certain extent (including amongst other things not only food, shelter, and health, but also knowledge and the freedom of expression and assembly), but still limits it to life-sustaining factors (Odera Oruka 1991, 64). For Odera Oruka, the fulfilment of the three basic human needs (physical security, health, and subsistence) is the precondition for obtaining the status of person. Without the human minimum, a human might still survive, but is unable to participate as a rational and reasonable actor in social interactions. For this reason,

> ... the right to a human minimum is absolute. It is absolute from the standpoint that to deny it is to deny one the status of personhood since, as we have tried to argue, this right is a composite of the three basic inherent rights of a person. And a right is inherent if its denial or non-fulfilment eradicates the essential function or creative power of its claimant. Hence, to deny someone the right to a human minimum is to deny him necessary conditions for a decent definition of a person (Odera Oruka 1989, quoted from A. Graness and K. Kresse 1997, 54).

Consequently, Odera Oruka concludes that the right to a human minimum is a universally valid absolute; every moral agent is obliged to ensure that other human beings are afforded the same right. On this basis, every human being can hold the entire world responsible for insuring his or her right to a fundamentally healthy life. On a global level, Odera Oruka draws the following conclusions: foreign aid for economically weak nations is not a kind of charity; it is the right of poor nations to receive and a duty of rich nations to help provide every human being with the human minimum. Moreover, Odera Oruka suggests the redistribution of what he calls 'national supererogation'. In respect to the concept of rights, he distinguishes between absolute rights (fundamental rights above all other rights) and *prima facie* rights (which can be overridden by rights of greater moral significance). Since national supererogation is based on property rights, and property rights are *prima facie* rights, the claim for redistribution of national wealth or supererogation can be justified by the morally more important absolute right to a human minimum (Odera Oruka 1989, quoted from A. Graness and K. Kresse 1997, 53-54).

Odera Oruka's definition of personhood adds another component to the debate on the concept of personhood. Kant's or

Menkiti's definitions, and those of all who follow their line of argumentation, exclude certain human beings (e.g. children) from personhood on the grounds of not having fully developed their potential to become a person. Moreover, according to this view, individuals like patients with severe mental illnesses (either congenital or acquired later in life) or patients in a coma can be excluded from the concept of personhood. Such individuals might have achieved personhood once but lost this quality by accident, illness, or trauma. In addition, Odera Oruka seems to suggest that personhood cannot be applied to humans starving and dying of thirst. Thus, Odera Oruka considers not only individual factors like the physical and mental state of a human being a precondition of personhood, but also material and structural conditions. In this context it is useful to examine Odera Oruka's concept of punishment as developed in his book *Punishment and Terrorism in Africa* (1976). Here he argues that crimes are a symptom of social disharmony, for example, those poor who steal in order to survive. Odera Oruka argues that so-called criminals do not commit their crimes out of their own free will, but always do so because of social, economic, or psychological conditions and constraints. Thus, they are not responsible for their acts. Consequently, instead of punishing them, the state should ensure each person's basic needs. To prevent criminal acts and to secure social harmony, the state has to remove "the conditions that cause people to adopt criminal behaviour" (Odera Oruka 1985, 84). A first step in this direction would surely be to secure the human minimum.

For Odera Oruka extreme or absolute poverty[11] and personhood are interrelated concepts such that extreme poverty is an obstacle to achieving the status of personhood, that is, to acting as a free moral agent. More recent concepts of poverty support Odera Oruka's approach (e.g., Nussbaum & Sen 1995; Sen 1999 and 2009). In these concepts, poverty is seen as a phenomenon that denies the affected the chance to develop his/her inherent capabilities and potential as a human being. In this respect, the elimination of poverty is the precondition for any capacity for acting as a moral agent.

---

11   Absolute poverty was defined by the United Nations in 1995 as 'a condition characterized by severe deprivation of basic human needs, including food, safe drinking water, sanitation facilities, health, shelter, education and information. It depends not only on income but also on access to services.' See United Nations 1995.

Since poverty is a structural and not an individual problem, at this point we return to the embeddedness of personhood in a social community. However, the dimension which unfolds in Odera Oruka's approach is rarely taken into consideration in debates on personhood, where family issues, education, religion, and politics are considered to be, besides individual preconditions and capabilities, the main relational factors in the process of the formation of personhood. But Odera Oruka's approach strongly suggests that the concept of personhood cannot be discussed from an ontological, normative, and epistemological perspective alone, but has to include a material, i.e. bodily or physical aspect of personhood too, which is the foundation of all other dimensions of being a person. To take this dimension of personhood seriously, one must question all social conditions which fail to guarantee the provision of basic needs to every human being.

UBUNTU AND THE HUMAN MINIMUM

The current broad debate on Ubuntu centres on a certain aspect of the concept, namely the dimension of interrelatedness, harmony, forgiveness, and reconciliation. In this context, Ubuntu is considered to be the basis for an alternative 'African' way of conflict resolution and peace building after massive human rights violations and deep social conflicts, a method which focuses on restorative justice instead of retributive justice. Here the relational aspect of being a person— the inseparable interrelatedness of each individual and his or her respective community—and thus, the need to restore harmony in the community are central concerns. Such concerns as the material preconditions for creating a harmonious community and for attaining personhood (including socio-economic conditions) are generally marginalized or even neglected.

However, the value of harmonious human relations at the core of Ubuntu has a distributive dimension, too, for a truly shared humanity includes more equitable sharing of resources and securing the (material) preconditions of personhood for all human beings. Few scholars have explored the distributive dimension of Ubuntu to date (Shutte 2001; Metz 2007 and 2011; Metz and Gaie 2010; Praeg 2014). One of them is Augustine Shutte, who explicitly includes the bodily or physical aspect of a person in his discussion of the concept of Ubuntu. Shutte devotes an entire chapter of his book to the issue

51

of healthcare. Here he acknowledges that health is a central requisite that allows human individuals and communities to develop and flourish, and a precondition for acquiring personhood. Therefore, health must be central to an Ubuntu ethic, for "all my abilities, physical, psychological and intellectual, are what enable me to live a complete human life", and health includes the bodily, emotional, and intellectual dimensions of one's being (Shutte 2001, 128). Moreover, Shutte recognizes that an individual's health status depends to a certain degree "on where and how we live, the work we do and the food we eat" (Shutte 2001, 129); that is, our health status depends on our living conditions, which are determined (not alone but to a high degree) by material (i.e. socio-economic) conditions. Consequently, Shutte argues, an Ubuntu ethic calls for "equitable access for all members of society, and a basic provision of health-care that is adequate for normal needs" (Shutte 2001, 150). He points out that a government has the duty to ensure that there is sufficient professional health care to meet the people's reasonable need and the duty to create living conditions that will keep people as healthy as possible by, for example, securing a supply of clean water, safe sanitation, a good diet, and proper housing (Shutte 2001, 140-41). In the distribution of the means to ensure health and access to healthcare systems, an Ubuntu ethic can be a fair and human guide. Moreover, arguing that "the goods of the earth are the common property of all" (Shutte 2001, 151), Shutte advocates a just distribution of resources. His following chapter on work amplifies his reflections on the social setting of Ubuntu and the preconditions for becoming a person. Like Odera Oruka, who considers property rights *prima facie* rights, Shutte argues,

> In an ethic of UBUNTU ownership and property, whether private or public, individual or communal, only get their meaning and purpose from their relation to work as a means to personal growth and community. The resources of the world are there for common use for the common good. All systems of ownership and property are secondary to this. They are justified insofar as they enable productive work for the common good, unjustified insofar as they prevent it (Shutte 2001, 159).

In this, Shutte shows that the value of personal growth and community—the core of an Ubuntu ethic—has serious implications for the socio-economic conditions of a society which plans to live according to an Ubuntu ethic, for example with regard to property rights. Ownership and property have to be used to strengthen the personal growth of every member of the community in order to guarantee the growth and harmony of all individuals and the community as such.

Thaddeus Metz approaches questions of distribution and responsibility in the context of an Ubuntu ethic in a different way, addressing them not via the concept of personhood but by examining the meaning of poverty for relationships within the community. Metz argues that the central aspect of Ubuntu is the community as an ideal form of relationship that features the core values of friendliness and respect. According to him, in any African moral theory an act is regarded as morally right if, and only if, it honours beings in virtue of their capacity for being the subject and object of relationships of identity and solidarity. Otherwise, an act is morally wrong, especially insofar as it prizes division and ill-will. Alienation or isolation is the opposite of a shared identity, and poverty is an example of this kind of alienation. According to Metz, from an Ubuntu perspective, poverty is understood not only as a lack of material resources, but as an obstacle preventing people from living their social relationships. For example, a lack of financial means, appropriate clothes, or education prevents people from taking part in social events. And thus, poor people find themselves at variance with or isolated from other people. From this perspective, poverty manifests itself as a form of social alienation or isolation. Consequently, the distribution of economic goods has to be organized in a way that gives people the opportunity to 'live well'. Metz defines 'living well' and 'the good life' as being able to live in harmony with one's community. The focus here is not the autonomy of the subject, but the capacity to live a harmonious communal life. For the sake of social harmony, opportunities and resources must be distributed in a balanced manner, argues Metz. Thus, an Ubuntu ethic deals with the significance of issues of distribution and representation within a network of relationships in the community. Consequently, drastic differences in property ownership are as much to be rejected as property waste, for property is always associated with a commitment to the preservation of all members of the community (Metz and Gaie 2010, 277–78).

Such analysis of an Ubuntu perspective on poverty and the distribution of resources is indeed of great importance, particularly for the South African debate on Ubuntu. As Leonhard Praeg (2014) emphasizes in his analysis of the Ubuntu discourse in South Africa, there is a big gap between a prevailing rhetoric of a shared humanity on one side, and the neoliberal order institutionalized by the government after the end of the Apartheid system on the other. During the negotiation process between the ANC and the former South African government in the early 1990s, questions of ownership and property relations did not play a central role. The need for changes in the ownership of major corporations and land was not raised, so the governmental transformation of South Africa went without a thoroughgoing economic transformation. Or as Issa Shivji writes, "South Africa's "independence" was born into neoliberalism" (Shivji 2014, 148). This might be one of the reasons why Ubuntu has mainly been seen as an abstract ethic, unconcerned with politico-economic issues and their consequences. The focus on a single aspect of an Ubuntu ethic—the dimension of harmony, forgiveness, and reconciliation, central concerns in South African politics and education during the last twenty years—cemented existing economic inequalities and poverty. The Mozambican philosopher Severino Elias Ngoenha, who shows great sympathy for the concept of Ubuntu, which he regards as one of the first important philosophical contributions of the African continent with global relevance, at the same time points to the risk of a new split along the lines of economic and social differences—and thus of an economic apartheid (Ngoenha 2006 and 2008).

The division between the ideal of a shared humanity and socio-economic realities is according to Praeg the

> ... success with which a neoliberal order has managed successfully to quarantine the very logic of our shared humanity within the domain of ideas–that is, within the parameters of the division that the ANC government has made and institutionalised between the ideal and material, the political and the economic, between the priority of political freedom (first transition) and the realisation of the material conditions for the meaningful exercise of that freedom (second transition). But, of course, this is what capitalism has always done. It quarantines the economic, political and cultural domains because only on the basis of such a separation can the

supremacy of the economic imperative be sustained (Praeg 2014, 68).

According to Praeg, the principal challenge for the discourse on Ubuntu is "how to square the logic of *unity* with a neoliberal modernity that promotes the relentless pursuit of interests conceived in terms of its *individualist* a priori, while criminalising, delegitimising or struggling to reduce to mere *difference* any pursuit of interests articulated, formally or informally, as attempts to honour, recognise and sustain the value of *unity*" (Praeg 2014, 44).

However, when used to create a comprehensive social critique—and not as a tool to suppress critical voices in the name of social harmony—the concept of Ubuntu offers an approach which might provide substantial solutions to crucial social problems (see Praeg 2014; Praeg and Magadla 2014). Underscoring the interconnectedness of all human beings, the relational characteristics of an Ubuntu ethic—'I am because we are'—and the concept of personhood in its social and bodily dimension, demand a project of human emancipation that requires recognition, education, political freedom, and certain material and structural preconditions. In this sense, the concept of Ubuntu can serve not only as an ideal for reconciliation and social harmony, but also as a means to formulate a profound critique of prevailing social conditions that would provide an antidote to unbridled neoliberal notions of individual freedom.

CONCLUSION

At present, the predominant focus of the broad debate on Ubuntu is a single aspect of personhood: the inseparable interrelatedness of a human being and his or her community. As a result, Ubuntu is taken mainly as an abstract ethic of communal harmony, unconcerned with politico-economic issues and their consequences. Such a one-sided approach runs the risk of affirming the economic inequalities and poverty that prevail in most African countries. Since a human being's physical well-being is the first precondition of personhood, an Ubuntu ethic cannot neglect socio-economic conditions, for as long as human beings are dehumanized by their living conditions, they cannot acquire moral agency in the full sense, and thus, will be unable to fulfil their expected social role in our shared humanity.

To summarize the ideas of thinkers like Odera Oruka or Augustine Shutte: As a universal human potential which can be attained only through the development of such faculties as rationality, responsibility, and moral agency, personhood has two preconditions for its full development:

(1) In order to act as moral beings, humans must fulfil bodily needs, including subsistence and health care;
(2) Human beings must be incorporated into a community through a process of social and cultural formation.

Odera Oruka and Augustine Shutte clearly point to the importance of a holistic view of personhood, which takes both aspects into consideration. In addition, they call attention to the social consequences of such a view, for example, regarding distributive relationships. Moreover, Thaddeus Metz and Leonhard Praeg underline the distributive aspect of an Ubuntu ethic, an approach which posits Ubuntu as a comprehensive social critique and, at the same time, an *imaginaire* or guiding principle for an equitable society.

BIBLIOGRAPHY

Coetzee, P.H., and A. P. J. Roux, eds. 2003. *The African Philosophy Reader*. New York/London: Routledge.

Graness, Anke. 2011. *Das Menschliche Minimum: Globale Gerechtigkeit Aus Afrikanischer Sicht: Henry Odera Oruka*. Frankfurt am Main: Campus Verlag.

Graness, Anke. 2012. "What is Global Justice? Henry Odera Oruka's Contribution to the Current Debate." *Journal on African Philosophy* 6: 31–46.

Graness, Anke. 2015. "Is the Debate on "Global Justice" a Global One? Some Considerations in View of Modern Philosophy in Africa". *Journal of Global Ethics* 11 (1): 126-40.

Graness, Anke and Kai Kresse, eds. 1997. *Sagacious Reasoning: H. Odera Oruka in Memoriam*. Frankfurt am Main: Peter Lang.

Gyekye, Kwame. 1995. *An Essay on African Philosophical Thought: The Akan Conceptual Scheme*. Philadelphia: Temple University Press.

Kant, Immanuel. 1996. *The Metaphysics of Morals*. Edited by Mary Gregor. Cambridge: Cambridge University Press.

Kant, Immanuel. 2002 [1785]. "Prolegomena. General Introduction to the Metaphysic of Morals." In *The Philosophy of Law: An Exposition of the Fundamental Principles of Jurisprudence as the Science of Right*, edited by Kant, Immanuel. Union, NJ: The Lawbook Exchange Ltd.

Kaphagawani, D.N. 2006. "African Constructions of a Person: A Critical Survey." In *A Companion to African Philosophy*, edited by Wiredu, Kwasi, 332–42. Oxford: Blackwell.

Marx, Karl. 1973. *Karl Marx, Friedrich Engels Werk* (MEW), Vols. 1 and 3. Berlin: Dietz Verlag.

Mbiti, John S. 1969. *African Religions and Philosophy*. London: Heinemann Educational Books.

Menkiti, Ifeanyi A. 1984. "Person and Community in African Traditional Thought." In *African Philosophy: An Introduction*, edited by Wright, Richard, 171–82. Lanham, MD: University Press of America.

Menkiti, Ifeanyi A. 2006. "On the Normative Conception of a Person." In *A Companion to African Philosophy*, edited by Wiredu, Kwasi, 324–331. Oxford: Blackwell.

Metz, Thaddeus. 2007. "Toward an African Moral Theory." *Journal of Political Philosophy*, 15 (3): 321–41. doi: 10.1111/j.1467-9760.2007.00280.x.

Metz, Thaddeus. 2011. "Ubuntu as a Moral Theory and Human Rights in South Africa." *African Human Rights Law Journal*, 11 (2): 532–59.

Metz, Thaddeus. 2013. "The Western Ethic of Care or an Afro-communitarian Ethic? Specifying the Right Relational Morality." *Journal of Global Ethics*, 9 (1): 77–92. doi: 10.1080/17449626.2012.756421.

Metz, Thaddeus. 2014. "Harmonizing Global Ethics in the Future: A Proposal to Add South and East to West." *Journal of Global Ethics*, 10 (2): 146–55.

Metz, Thaddeus and Joseph Gaie. 2010. "The African Ethic of Ubuntu/Botho: Implications for Research on Morality." *Journal of Moral Education*, 39 (3): 273–90.

Murove, Munyaradzi Felix, ed. 2009. *African Ethics: An Anthology of Comparative and Applied Ethics*. Pietermaritzburg: University of KwaZulu-Natal Press.

Ngoenha, Severino Elias. 2006. "Ubuntu: New Model of Global Justice." *Indilinga: African Journal of Indigenous Knowledge Systems*, 5 (2): 125-34.

Ngoenha, Severino Elias. 2008. "Ubuntu: Novo modelo de justiça glocal?" In *Begegnung der Wissenskulturen im Nord-Süd Dialog: Dokumentation des XII. Internationalen Seminars des Dialogprogramms Nord-Süd/The Encounter of Knowledge Cultures in the North-South Dialogue/Las culturas del saber y su encuentro en el dialogo norte-sur*, edited by Raúl Fornet-Betancourt, 95-105. Frankfurt am Main: IKO-Verlag für Interkulturelle Kommunikation.

Nussbaum, Martha, and Amartya Sen, eds. 1995. *The Quality of Life: A Study Prepared for the World Institute for Development Economics Research (WIDER) of the United Nations University*. Oxford: Clarendon Press.

Oruka, Henry Odera. 1985. *Punishment and Terrorism in Africa*. 2nd. ed. Nairobi: Kenya Literature Bureau.

Oruka, Henry Odera. 1989. "The Philosophy of Foreign Aid: A Question of the Right to a Human Minimum." *Praxis International* 8 (4): 465-75.

Oruka, Henry Odera. 1991. *The Philosophy of Liberty: An Essay on Political Philosophy*. Nairobi: Standard Textbooks Graphics and Publishers.

Oruka, Henry Odera. 1997. *Practical Philosophy: In Search of an Ethical Minimum*. Nairobi: East African Educational Publishers.

Praeg, Leonhard. 2014. *A Report on Ubuntu*. Pietermaritzburg: University of KwaZulu-Natal Press.

Praeg, Leonhard, and S. Magadla, eds. 2014. *Ubuntu: Curating the Archive*. Pietermaritzburg: University of KwaZulu-Natal Press.

Ramose, Mogobe B. 2005. *African Philosophy through Ubuntu*. 2nd. ed. Harare: Mond Books.

Ramose, Mogobe B. 2003. "The Philosophy of *Ubuntu* and *Ubuntu* as a Philosophy". In *Philosophy from Africa: A text with Readings*, edited by Coetzee, P.H. and Roux, A.P.J., 230-38. Oxford: Oxford University Press.

Ramose, Mogobe B. 2003. "The Ethics of Ubuntu". In *Philosophy from Africa: A text with Readings*, edited by Coetzee, P.H. and Roux, A.P.J., 324-30. Oxford: Oxford University Press.

Ramose, Mogobe B. 2004. "The Earth "Mother" Metaphor: An African Perspective". In *Visions of Nature: Studies on the Theory of Gaia and Culture in Ancient and Modern Times*, edited by F. Elders, 203–06. Brussels: VUB Brussels.

Ramose, Mogobe B. 2009. "Ecology through Ubuntu". In *African Ethics: An Anthology of Comparative and Applied Ethics*, edited by Munyaradzi, F. Murove, 308-14. University of Kwazulu-Natal Press.

Sen, Amartya. 1999. *Development as Freedom*. Oxford: Oxford University Press.

Sen, Amartya. 2009. *The Idea of Justice*. Cambridge, MA: Belknap Press of Harvard University Press.

Shivji, Issa G. 2014. "Utu, Usawa, Uhuru: Building Blocks of Nyerere's Political Philosophy." In *Ubuntu: Curating the archive*, edited by Leonhard Praeg and S. Magadla, 137–49. Grahamstown: University of Kwazulu-Natal Press.

Shutte, Augustine. 2001. *Ubuntu: An Ethic for a New South Africa*. Pietermaritzburg: Cluster Publications.

United Nations. 1995. Report of the World Summit for Social Development, March 6–12, 1995. http://www.un.org/documents/ga/conf166/aconf166-9.htm.

Wiredu, Kwasi. 2006. *Cultural Universals and Particulars: An African Perspective*. Bloomington: Indiana University Press.

Wiredu, Kwasi and Kwame Gyekye. 1992. *Person and Community: Ghanaian Philosophical Studies I*. Washington, DC: The Council for Research in Values and Philosophy.

CHAPTER 3. PERSONHOOD WITHOUT UBUNTU

~~~~~~~~~~~~ ✹ ~~~~~~~~~~~~

Mpho Tshivhase

INTRODUCTION

In this article I aim to challenge the African conception of personhood by means of critically evaluating the constitutive relation that is spontaneously drawn between the concepts of Ubuntu and *personhood* in African thought. The African view of personhood is characteristically communal, and so, it is relational. Similarly, Ubuntu, whose defining principle is captured by the famous adage 'muthu ndi muthu nga vhathu'[1] (a person is a person through other persons), is also communal and relational. Ubuntu is commonly understood as an African principle of humaneness, but it is also used to express humanness. This sense of humanness that is derived from Ubuntu expresses personhood. In this way, it follows that Ubuntu and personhood derive from the same maxim; *muthu ndi muthu nga vhathu.*

The fact that one maxim is used to capture both Ubuntu and personhood begs the question: what kind of relation really exists between Ubuntu and personhood? The general assumption seems to be that Ubuntu is constitutive of personhood so that we cannot talk of personhood without Ubuntu. Understood in this way, what it

---

1   This is the TshiVenda version of the Nguni expression *umuntu ngu muntu nga bantu,* or the Sotho *motho ke motho ka bathu.* I use the Venda expression simply because TshiVenda is my mother tongue.

means to be a person is captured by Ubuntu, where a lack of Ubuntu is indistinguishable from a lack of personhood.

I contend with the view that one's personhood is fundamentally defined by Ubuntu so that one cannot be considered a person if one is found lacking in Ubuntu. I want to argue that personhood can exist without Ubuntu, and so, what it means to be a person is not essentially defined in terms of the way one relates to other people, at least not in the sense championed by the African conception of personhood. I think that the principle of Ubuntu speaks to the moral worth of an individual's actions, when viewed in terms of assessing an individual's moral praiseworthiness or blameworthiness. I will use the idea of moral worth to argue that there is a mistake in thinking that Ubuntu fully accounts for an individual's personhood.

Undoubtedly, Ubuntu is useful in guiding our moral actions, and so, it gives us the tools to assess one's moral worth by indicating actions that invoke blame or praise. My overarching aim is to show that although Ubuntu could be related to personhood, we may be stretching it beyond its means when we appropriate it to defining personhood. It is possible that personhood is not necessarily moral, and I am skeptical of a theory that limits the nature of personhood to the moral sphere. I am also doubtful of a theory that depends on the same maxim to describe moral conduct and the nature of who one is. In my mind, these concepts refer to two different aspects about individuals—standards of behavior and the nature of being a person—and, so, they deserve to be explicated in a manner that illustrates this difference.

I dedicate the first section of this paper to the African view of personhood. Next, I will discuss the principle of Ubuntu with the view to show that Ubuntu is not identical to the concept of personhood. Thereafter, I will construct my argument against the idea that personhood is derived from Ubuntu. I will argue that Ubuntu is crucial to guiding our assessment of whether a person's actions are deserving of moral praise or blame. In other words, Ubuntu works better as a normative moral theory that prescribes right actions. I will argue that personhood is distinct from moral goodness, and that it is a mistake to define personhood based on a principle that is fundamentally aimed at guiding moral actions. At best, Ubuntu provides us with a framework for the means to acquiring a favorable kind of personhood, but I am not convinced that it tells us what the nature of personhood is. I hope to defend the view that personhood can exist even if it is devoid of the kind of moral concern prescribed in Ubuntu. In other words, one can have personhood without Ubuntu.

AFRICAN CONCEPTION OF PERSONHOOD

The question of personhood is important for personal and social (or political) reasons. Social structures and laws or rules that govern such structures are often built based on some view of what a person is. In most cases it is the idea of personhood that enables us to realize certain goals pertaining to society or social arrangement. The idea of personhood also influences our view of rights—we often ask whether a person is a being with rights that cannot be overridden by anything else? We also consider personhood when we are concerned about the common good and we often ask whether a person's role in society involves an obligation to the welfare of others. Consequently, the issues of individual rights and moral duty relate the person to his/her community.

One view of personhood stemming from the Western tradition, involves viewing a person as a rational entity whose individuality is independent and not predetermined by anyone (Zagzebski 2001, 405-410). On this Kantian view, personhood lies in one's rational capacity, which enables one to act and deliberate autonomously as a self-determining being (Kant 2002, 43-55). It is when an individual acts autonomously that the individual becomes deserving of respect, where such respect is the recognition or praise of that individual's dignity. Furthermore, a person is an entity with the capacity to act for ends (*ibid*). In short, the Western view of personhood, or at least the Kantian version of it, cites rationality as the feature that accounts for the nature of personhood. Although the African view of personhood also defends human dignity and holds no disregard for rationality, it does so in a manner that is communal rather than individualistic.

The African view champions the idea of a communally defined personhood. That is to say persons are products of their community (Kaphagawani 1991, 173). One becomes a person through the relationships one fosters with other people in one's community. Personhood is relationally constituted and so the cultivation of personhood is largely a communal process (Kaphagawani 2006, 332, 337-338; Wiredu 1992, 200). African thinkers, like Ifeanyi Menkiti (1984, 2006), accept John Mbiti's (1969, 108-109) maxim "I am because we are, and since we are, therefore I am" as the fundamental maxim in understanding the interdependent and relational character of a communal view of persons. Menkiti (1984, 171) uses this expression to defend the ontological primacy of the community in relation to the individual, so that we come to understand the community as having the authority to confer personhood on an individual.

Implicit in Menkiti's unrestricted communitarian view of personhood are three assumptions: (1) community defines personhood, (2) personhood does not derive from our biological nature as human beings, and (3) personhood is something one can fail to achieve (1984, 172-174; 178-179). Menkiti accepts that the community is the sole determinant of one's personhood, and so, one's personhood cannot exist outside one's relationship with other people. Individuals are born into communities, which makes persons inherently interdependent—never to be viewed as isolated atomic beings. Here, Menkiti rejects the view that there is one static feature, such as rationality, that defines personhood in favor of a communal view that takes into account the relations one has with other members of his community, as well as the common goals, hopes, values and interpersonal bonds that form part of what it means to live with other people.

The first assumption aims to illustrate the relation between persons and their community. Herein personhood is understood to involve an acceptance of one's obligations to the welfare of others (Prinsloo 1991, 42). Didier Kaphagawani explains that communal life is very important to the creation of one's personhood because one is not really considered a person until one enters into relationships of interdependence with other members if his/her community (1991, 173). Personhood then, is a derivative of living with other people and building good relationships with them. When one lives well with others, the community confers personhood upon one.

The second idea that personhood is not derived from the biological status of being human shows that there is a distinction between persons and human beings. Human beings are biological entities. In his treatment of the Yoruba concept of a person, Segun Gbadegesin described being human as a physico-material state that has internal and external components such as bone, heart, skin, blood and so forth. This physical component is called *ara* in the Yoruba language. *Ara*, is the body, whose function includes housing the

64

senses which enable the person to experience the external world (Gbadegesin 1991, 150). According to Gbadegesin, there is more to a person than the body. He notes that what differentiates being human from being a person is that personhood has a normative dimension while the biological status of being human is descriptive (Gbadegesin 1991, 149-151). A person is considered a combination of the body and ratiocinative activities. The point made in Mentiki's view of personhood is that although personhood is derived from the biological and physical appearance of a human being, it is not the same thing. Personhood involves more than just the human body—it takes into account the moral concern for oneself and others.

The third assumption regarding the possibility of one failing to become a person follows from the idea that personhood is an achievement and not a natural characteristic about a person. That is to say that one has to work at becoming a person, and, on the communal sense of it, one has to buy into the preset communal goals and values with the aim to contribute positively to the wellbeing of others so as to enable communal unity and harmony. Gyekye notes that a problem with the idea that one could fail to become a person is that it excludes children and newborns from the status of personhood (1991, 322). Given that personhood is something one has to consciously work on in order to arrive at a satisfactory state of being that is accepted by society, it is not possible to imagine that children and newborns can do this, and so, community would not be able to confer personhood on them, thus meaning that children and newborns cannot foster personhood. Nonetheless, the positive thing about the possibility of failing is the fact that it illustrates personhood as a processual aspect about a person, and not a static unchanging one.

Overall, the logic of the African view of persons can be understood in two ways. On the one hand, the view aims to address the nature of persons; on the other hand, the view addresses the moral means to acquiring personhood. In this way, I find the African view of personhood to be both descriptive and evaluative. Its evaluative feature is evident in its prescription of the acceptable moral attitude that should be cultivated to maintain the community's welfare. Its descriptive feature has to do with the criteria that is key to the nature of personhood.

Elsewhere, I have outlined the morality and expectations models of the African view of personhood to illustrate the difference between the evaluative and descriptive features of personhood (Tshivhase 2011, 124-135). Briefly, I think that the morality view of personhood, which I think coincides with the nature of personhood, encourages people to accept that their behavior ought to be guided by the concern to improve and maintain the welfare of the community. Herein, one should always behave in a manner that noticeably shows concern for the welfare of others (Masolo 2010, 172). The expectations model, which I find fitting with the means to acquiring personhood, asserts that personhood is arrived at through abiding by the expectations that the society puts forward with regard to whom one should become.

Masolo asserts that the person whom one should become is one who abides by the community's expectations, which typically function to keep the community united (2010, 217). In this way, one can understand the means to becoming a person as closely tied to one's commitment to maintaining group solidarity within a community. I will not delve any deeper into this argument. For the purpose of this paper it suffices to establish that personhood, according to the African perspective, is morally loaded, and so, places more value on communal construction of personhood, which is characterized by relationality and interdependence among individual members of a community.

The African view of personhood is socio-centric and, in Gyekye's perspective (1991, 320), assumes firstly, that one's membership to a community is not optional. The idea seems to be that individuals do not voluntarily choose to become a part of the community. Furthermore, one cannot live apart from other people. A character like Tarzan may not be granted personhood given that he was part of a community of wild animals, as opposed to human persons. The strong assumption that the African view of persons makes is that one's life must not unfold in isolation from other persons. A further postulation involves the belief that one is naturally oriented towards others and must form relationships with them. Introverts may be excluded from personhood since they are loners who are not enthusiastic about forming relationships with others, and according to the African view of persons, social relationships are necessary. In short, for one to become a person, one necessarily has to be relational and interdependent in one's encounters with other persons.

The idea that one's personhood is acquired through communal processes is extremely important because it seems to set aside any other attributes of a person besides the fact that s/he is inescapably bound to his/her society. This has implications for the individual person as communal personhood gives complete moral power to the community and, as Kwame Gyekye (1991, 322-323) indicates, confuses the real nature of personhood. In a way, the communal view of personhood misrepresents the purpose of a community. While it is true that an individual with all his talents and skills is not self-sufficient enough to meet all of his/her basic needs, it is not necessarily the case that the function of the community is to define one's personhood. Gyekye also admits the functional significance of society for practical purposes since one person cannot be a cook, a tailor, a midwife, a builder, a doctor and so forth. In this way we do necessarily depend on each other to flourish and so we use our different talents and skills to support and complement each other's needs.

In sum, the idea that runs through the African conception of personhood has to do with personhood being a communal process that one can fail at. Personhood is determined by one's relationships with other people in a community. This idea of personhood is based on assumptions that take it for granted that a person is naturally communal and interested in forming caring relationships with other people. In the next section I will discuss Ubuntu, and move on to draw the connection between Ubuntu and personhood. This is necessary for the charge I plan to lay against a kind of personhood that is determined by Ubuntu.

THE PRINCIPLE OF UBUNTU

Ubuntu is generally interpreted as humanness, personhood and morality (Letseka 2012, 48 and Bennett 2011, 30). Ubuntu promotes certain virtues as necessary for a kind of human excellence that involves respecting, caring, and being compassionate toward others (Letseka 2012, 48; Prinsloo 1991, 41-42). Ubuntu, simply understood, is a virtuous regard for others. Ubuntu is an other-centered principle that promotes relationality between persons in a community. It is this relationality that sits at the heart of humanness. To be regarded a full human; one must always consider the wellbeing of others, and act in ways that are directed at bringing about others' welfare (Gyekye 1991, 325-326; Metz 2007, 330-331).

Humanness, in the abovementioned sense, is dependent on other people, hence the proverb *muthu ndi muthu nga vhathu.* According Thaddeus Metz (2007, 323), this proverb expresses the idea that the nature of an individual's being is caused by other people, and so, it is causally and metaphysically dependent on other members of the community. It is in the way that he treats other people that his character is shaped and assessed. In short, Ubuntu expresses the relationality among persons (Murove 2014, 42; 44). Ubuntu expresses one's deep rootedness in his community.

Thinkers like Letseka (2012, 54) and, Metz and Gaie (2010, 275-276) seem to share the conviction that Ubuntu is a moral theory that serves to bring about cohesion and solidarity in a community, especially in the face of trouble. In such cases, what brings people together in the spirit of care and compassion is a common goal, which, in the face of trouble, is maintaining the peace in community. Herein, there is a requirement to help others, where such consideration for others comes to be viewed as an obligation one owes others by virtue of being a member of that society (Gyekye 1991, 331; Metz 2007, 326). What is articulated in the principle of Ubuntu, when applied to moments of conflict and crisis and need, is a principle of goodwill (and cooperation) aimed at remedying the problem and restoring the welfare of one's fellows (Metz 2007, 336). Ubuntu has to do with the interconnectedness and fellow feeling among people where these values are deemed important for the maintenance of harmonious living within a society.

A person is supposed to understand her human condition as interrelated with other people's welfare, and she is expected to always put other people's interests ahead of her own. When she understands that it is expected of her to ensure the welfare of others, it is then that she will reach full humanness. Without other people one is considered incomplete, and so, unable to develop into a full human (Munyaka and Mothlabi 2009, 67). Implicit in this statement is a need for a sense of belonging, which leaves almost no room for individualism.

Ubuntu can also be viewed as a theory that exposes reverence for human life, wherein valuing human life requires right action in order to promote social harmony and justice (Metz 2007, 340; Bennett 2011, 35). Ubuntu has to do with a collective consciousness of people in a community, where such consciousness can be explained by a network of terms such as sympathy, conviviality, care, etc. (Prinsloo 1991, 41-43). All these concepts are indicative of the interpersonal character of Ubuntu, whose aim involves fostering and maintaining group solidarity. Such group solidarity reveals the "existential condition of bondedness with others, where full humanness is attained through [this] interconnectedness" (Murove 2014, 37). Understood in this way, Ubuntu (or humanness) is deeply relational.

Furthermore, Ubuntu means treating other people with kindness, compassion respect and other virtues. Failure to treat others well indicates lack of humanness (Murove 2014, 37). In this way Ubuntu can be understood to exclude certain behavior or actions that do not promote harmony and unity in a society. Acts such as forcing someone to have sexual intercourse with you, stealing, lying, killing, selfishness, are regarded to be negative and thus hinder the process of becoming a full human being (Metz 2007, 324; Metz & Gaie 2010, 275). Ubuntu is a non-racial and non-sexist ethic and so it does not discriminate—"…every person is a social being who can realize his Ubuntu in the company of, and in interaction with, other human beings" (Bhengu 1996). The point is Ubuntu is a positive ethic that aims to promote goodness among people in the way they regard one another, and direct their own relational self-realization.

Ubuntu claims to regard a person as a self-defining value where only the self-definitions that are aimed at fulfilling the purpose of the community are considered to be legitimate (Bhengu 1996). One purpose of the self-realization is maintaining solidarity or unity among people in a society. As relational beings, persons are expected to help foster and maintain cohesion and so any self-definition that deviates from this goal is rejected. I argued elsewhere that self-definitions that are individualistic are often rejected, as they do not primarily aim to serve the community. A full person or an individual with full personhood should, at all times, be considerate towards others, and so, never act for selfish reasons. In this way, one can understand persons as causally determined by their relation to others (Metz 2007, 323).

Moreover, Ubuntu tells us that a person is a person through (or because of) other people. The dependence of one's personhood on other people is also captured in Mbiti's "*I am because we are, and since we are, therefore I am*". What we should take from this dictum is the idea that for one to recognize and be recognized as a person, one must necessarily maintain relationships with other people; relationships that are built on compassion, generosity, love and care for others. In this way Ubuntu determines the African view of personhood. Ubuntu states that a person is a person through other persons. It is this idea that one's personhood is necessarily dependent on other people's wellbeing that bothers me about the African view of personhood that is derived from Ubuntu

If a person is a person through (or because of) other people, and Ubuntu is defined by the maxim that asserts that a person is a person through (or because of) other people, then it follows that Ubuntu is personhood. I mentioned earlier in this section that Ubuntu has been defined, among other things, as personhood (see Letseka 2012). I contend with the idea that Ubuntu accounts for personhood, in addition to humanness and morality. In this case, I think Ubuntu goes beyond its scope. Moreover, I disagree with the view that personhood is a matter of Ubuntu. I will argue that Ubuntu, understood as a moral ethic, is more useful in guiding our behavior, rather than defining personhood.

OBJECTIONS TO UBUNTU AS PERSONHOOD

So far I have explained the African view of personhood and illustrated that it is a communal process that is morally laden. I also described Ubuntu as an ethic that guides people's actions, where the right or preferred actions are motivated by virtues that contribute to the welfare of people in a community and ultimately breed unity in the community. Furthermore, I illustrated that Ubuntu is also understood to define personhood. According to Ubuntu, one is a person in so far as she accepts obligation to care for the interests of others, and does not upset harmony and solidarity in society. Viewed in this way, personhood is about the welfare of other people and cohesion of a community.

In this section I want to level my charge against the idea that personhood is derived from Ubuntu. I am skeptical about the use of one maxim *'muthu ndi muthu nga vhathu'* to explain both personhood and Ubuntu. In my mind this dependence makes the distinction between personhood and Ubuntu murky. We use this maxim to express the moral virtues that should guide our actions, and we use the same maxim to define what a person is. This use of Ubuntu as a moral theory, and at the same time the defining feature of personhood worries me as I think that we may be relying too heavily on Ubuntu to explain humanity. Along similar lines, Bernard Matolino and Wenceslaus Kwindigwi are concerned that the application of Ubuntu on every social concern could lead to the bastardisation of Ubuntu (2013, 204). To avoid such bastardisation, my recommendation is that we should accept Ubuntu as a moral theory so that it may become most useful in guiding people's actions and motivating people to always pursue goodness. In this way it becomes possible to argue that Ubuntu tells us what the means to acquiring personhood entail, but it cannot define personhood.

I think that Ubuntu goes beyond the function of moral principles when it states that one's personhood is a matter that is wholly determined by other people; that it is only in treating other people well and putting their wellbeing ahead of one's own, and thus contributing to ensuring the general cohesion of the community that one attains his personhood. I understand ethics to provide guiding principles for our interactions with other people. Ubuntu can be defined as a moral principle that guides our actions. However, it is quite another thing to argue that Ubuntu defines what a person is. Defining one's personhood and guiding one's actions are two separate concerns and I think that defining a person is beyond the scope of Ubuntu, especially when it is understood as a moral guiding principle.

Although, there are some unique elements of Ubuntu, the ethic shares some features with Kantian deontology[2] in that it emphasizes one's obligation to others, which is based on the recognition of another's dignity and then channeling one's behavior towards maintaining that dignity, whether it be by feeding the person, giving them money or helping them in ways that will produce happiness.

One also finds elements of utilitarianism[3] in Ubuntu. To become a full human, an individual is expected to suspend his interests in order bring about the general wellbeing of others and maintain solidarity in the community. Herein, it is not impossible to infer that Ubuntu implores us to allow our behavior to be guided by the consequence of ensuring utility and solidarity. In this sense Ubuntu

2   See Kant's Groundwok for the Metaphysics of Morals, Second Section: Transition from popular moral philosophy to metaphysics of morals
3   See J.S. Mill's Utilitarianism, 1863.

has a consequentialist tone because there is an aspect of it that focuses on prioritizing securing the general welfare of people in a community over that of the individual. Furthermore, there are traces of Aristotelian virtue ethics[4] in Ubuntu. We are to judge a person's moral character based on the virtues he displays towards others. In addition, persons are denied personhood if they neglect to cultivate their virtues thus fattening their vices, and so disrupting the unity and harmony of the community. From a young age, individuals are trained to develop their personhood to display features of goodness that are developed to appreciate the value of their community (Metz & Gaie 2010, 280). Ubuntu dictates that one's personhood is based on her capacity to show sensitivity to the needs of others and advocates for such sensitivity to become habitual.

I illustrate the parallels between Ubuntu, deontology, utilitarianism and virtue ethics not for the purpose of affirming the legitimacy of Ubuntu as an ethical principle that guides our actions. There are thinkers, like Murove (2014, 36-40), who are concerned to defend Ubuntu from charges that trivialize it, but this is not my concern here. The point of drawing these parallels is to show that Ubuntu belongs to a family of principles that aim to clarify the right way to be with other people, where such theories comment on assessing a person's moral worth, but do not claim to define one's personhood so that we come to believe that personhood is defined by our duty to others or by the consequences of our actions. Nonetheless, the rightness of our actions is assessed by these utilitarian and deontological ethics in the same way that we can apply Ubuntu to assess the rightness of an action.

A possible response to my view could indicate that the way we treat other people is crucial to our moral development. That without forging relationships without others we cannot understand what it means to be a person. How we interact with others reveals something about our character. It is this character that Ubuntu considers pertinent in defining one's personhood. Supporters of Ubuntu could argue that without a good character, one cannot be understood as a person since personhood should involve being good to others by recognizing and respecting their existence as persons. Furthermore, without such regard for the value of others, it would be difficult if

---

4   See Aristotorle's *Nicomachean Ethics*, transl. Roger Crisp, Book II.

not impossible for a society to become harmonious. Therefore, consideration for the wellbeing of others is good for the society, which is ultimately good for the individual. In other words, being good to others is the same as being good to oneself since one becomes part of the reciprocal circle of goodness. The danger in thinking that personhood is about treating other people well is the assumption that personhood is always already good. Herein one imagines personhood as moral goodness. However, this is a mistake, since who we are as persons is not fundamentally a prescriptive matter but a descriptive one about the qualities that make us persons. As Gyekye explains, a morally laden view of personhood defines personhood in normative terms, so that when we say she is a person, we mean she has a good character (1991, 324). The underlying assumption is that personhood is inherently good. In viewing personhood as inherently good, we suppress the idea that persons can be inherently bad.

In defending Ubuntu further, supporters of Ubuntu could argue that the moral guiding aspect of Ubuntu together with its description of personhood could be the very thing that makes it unique to other theories. Utilitarianism and the like do not tell us what a person is, but focus on how to judge the rightness of an action, and so, lack the unique feature that Ubuntu has, which involves a description of the nature of personhood. Having Ubuntu as a foundation for personhood allows Ubuntu to ground personhood as a moral way of being, which makes morality a natural human capacity. In this way morality ceases to be something we learn, and so, becomes the natural way of being. In a word, in guiding our actions and defining the nature of personhood, Ubuntu does what no other moral theory does, that is, it naturalizes moral behavior.

The problem with trying to naturalize moral behavior is that moral behavior and personhood address two different aspects about human beings. Gyekye points out that moral behavior or good behavior is a kind of self-expression that forms part of the capacities one has as a person (1991, 326). In other words, when a person fails to express Ubuntu it does not diminish his personhood since Ubuntu is a matter of social status. The appropriate consequence of which should be loss of social respect, not denial of personhood as Menkiti suggests. Understood in this way then we should say, contra Menkiti, that one fails at securing a favorable social status, not personhood (see Gyekye 1991, 326). A display of Ubuntu is a sort of performance that is praised by society thus giving a person the social recognition as a good person. Failure to display Ubuntu is judged with disdain. The point is that personhood is not a matter of social status whereas moral behavior endorsed by Ubuntu is. Personhood can be defined outside of morality, but Ubuntu's concern is a purely moral one. As a moral principle, Ubuntu can also guide our assessment of a person's moral worth. What I refer to as moral worth involves the level of an agent's praiseworthiness or blameworthiness (Arpaly 2002, 224). When a person performs an action, we judge the agent's moral worth based on the rightness and wrongness of that action. A person is usually blameworthy when she performs an action that is not motivated by moral reasons. Such an individual is then thought to be deficient in good will, and so, unresponsive to moral reasons for action. What counts as a moral reason includes a concern for rightness. When a person's behavior stems from ill will, or a deficiency in good will, we judge that person to be blameworthy. On the other hand, when a person's actions are motivated by good will and a concern for moral rightness, we tend to think that the agent performing those actions is deserving of praise (Arpaly 2002, 266-231). I think that the ethic of Ubuntu fits with this formulation of moral worth, and so, is useful precisely in that it provides us with a framework for assessing an agent's moral worth.

Moral worth and personhood are not the same things, and so, to say that Ubuntu defines a person is a mistake. We do not define people based on moral praise or moral blame; we do not say of Munei that he is a person because his actions are always morally praiseworthy. We generally do not define a person primarily in terms of their relationship to others and their commitment to improving their welfare. We consider those relationships to matter to a person and to influence one's self-understanding or self-realization, but we do not say that your personhood is defined by your virtue.

In much similar ways, we do not say you have full personhood because you practice deontology or utilitarianism. It does not seem to follow that morality defines what persons are. It seems more fitting to say that moral views, like Ubuntu, give us the tools to judge moral worth, not define a personhood. We can say of one's personhood that it is more admirable when it is moral, but we should not set out to prescribe actions based on the desire to obtain personhood.

A person should be understood as a bearer of value, whose personhood is informed by concerns and desires that direct his reflective processes (Singer 2002, 133; 193). One's reflective process should be free and directed towards cultivating one's personhood. Personhood can be informed by many other shared concerns and desires, but even with the existence of such shared concerns, one's personhood should separate her from other people. Such separation should not simply be accounted for by the idea that a community is made up of individuals (Buscaglia 1978, 100-103). It is not enough to recognize a person as an individual only in terms of him being a part of a sum. This accounts for a quantitative individuality where one is a single entity that is recognized to be part of a community only when counted in with others.

What a person is cannot be accounted for by the principle of Ubuntu, at least not fully so. Even if we reformulate the relationship between Ubuntu and personhood, it would remain that we would be claiming that moral character or moral worth accounts for what a person is. This does not sound right. Logically speaking, there are many qualities and values that constitute a person, whether personhood is understood metaphysically or normatively.

Interconnectedness seems to me an inescapable position of a person; one is born into an existing community, and grows to reproduce thus bringing other people into that community—and the cycle goes on. It is true that Lebo would not exist if Mulalo and Lufuno had not procreated, and Mulalo and Lufuno would not exist if their parents did not exist, and one could go on tracing relations centuries back. The point is that it is questionable to say that a central criterion of personhood necessarily involves one's relationality, something that includes being born of one's person. Surely if this is the case, then every human being is a person by virtue of being related to someone by blood, marriage or otherwise, and so the view that personhood is something that is achieved is weakened, since relationality in the above sense is naturally given.

Ubuntu clarifies the moral qualities necessary for becoming a good person. It shows us what the desired moral character should involve. To say a person is a moral agent does not prevent a person from ignoring his moral obligations and choose to be immoral instead. It merely indicates that a person is a being with the capacity for moral behavior. Although there is something both admirable and desirable about a personhood that is morally directed, personhood in itself, is not defined by moral concerns espoused in Ubuntu. In short an individual can attain full personhood without Ubuntu, it is just that personhood lacking in Ubuntu is generally not admirable, as it indicates a disregard for others. The prescription for moral conduct is important as it enables individuals to be good persons who can flourish in the presence of others without necessarily violating the rights of others. It is in molding persons into good persons that Ubuntu (and by implication the community) relates to personhood.

CONCLUSION

Ubuntu champions a personhood that is morally loaded, where the right kind of personhood is not individualistic, but rather communal. Ubuntu, as moral view, endorses a kind of personhood that is subsumed by the concern to always put the interests of others ahead of your own. Ubuntu seems to me to have an underlying anthropology that aims to explicate something of what is entailed in a dignified personhood, but it does not, at least in my view, define the nature of a person. In trying to define the nature of personhood, Ubuntu's scope becomes stretched in such a way that it limits the nature of Ubuntu to moral concern, so that personhood is as good as moral worth. I reject this view and recommend that the view of Ubuntu be revised in view of the distinction between the means to acquiring personhood and the nature of personhood.

However, my rejection of Ubuntu as the central feature of personhood is not a rejection of the principle of Ubuntu in totality. Ubuntu is an important principle as it aims to promote goodness and right action to preventing heinous behavior that violates the welfare of other persons. A society filled with bad persons hinders human flourishing, and so it should be avoided. My point is that a person is simply not caused by other people, but rather, a person comes to understand the value of oneself and another person, and responds to that value with an attitude that reflects unpretentiousness and a concern for the continued existence of the other, whose existence reflects one's own reality.

BIBLIOGRAPHY

Arpaly, Nomy. 2002. "Moral Worth". *The Journal of Philosophy*, 99: 223-245.

Bennett, Thomas W. 2011. "Ubuntu: An African Equity". *Potchefstroom Electronic Law Journal, 14:* 30-61.

Buscaglia, Leo F. 1978. *Personhood: The Art of Being Fully Human.* New York: Ballantine Books.

Gbadegesin, Segun. 1991. "*Ènìyàn:* The Yoruba Concept of a Person." In *Philosophy from Africa: A Text with Readings,* edited by Coetzee, P.H. and A.P.J. Roux, 149-168. Cape Town: Oxford University Press.

Gyekye, Kwame.1991. "Person and Community in African Thought Identities." In *Philosophy from Africa: A Text with Readings,* edited by Coetzee, P.H and A.P.J. Roux, 317-336. Cape Town: Oxford University Press.

Khaphagawani, Didier N. 1991. "African Conceptions of Personhood and Intellectual Identities." In *Philosophy from Africa: A Text with Readings,* edited by Coetzee, P.H. and A.P.J. Roux, 169-176. Cape Town: Oxford University Press.

Kaphagawani, Didier N. 2006. "African Conceptions of a Person: A Critical Survey". In *A Companion to African Philosophy,* edited by Wiredu, Kwasi, 332-342. Oxford: Blackwell Publishing.

Letseka, Moeketsi. 2012. "In Defence of Ubuntu". *Studies in Philosophy & Education,* 31: 47-60.

Masolo, D. A. 2010. *Self and Community in a Changing World.* Indiana: Indiana University Press.

Matolino, Bernard and Wenceslaus Kwindingwi. 2013. The End of Ubuntu. *South African Journal of Philosophy,* 32: 197-205.

Mbiti, John. 1969. *African Religions and Philosophy.* London: Heinemann Educational Books Ltd.

Menkiti, Ifeanyi A. 1984. "Person and Community in African Traditional Thought." In *African Philosophy: An Introduction,* edited by Wright, R. A., 171-181. New York: University Press of America.

Menkiti, Ifeanyi A. 2006. "On the Normative Conception of a Person". In *A Companion to African Philosophy,* edited by Wiredu, Kwasi, 324-331. Oxford: Blackwell Publishing.

Metz, Thaddeus and Gaie, Joseph B.R. 2010. "The African Ethic of Ubuntu/Botho: Implications for Research on Morality". *Journal of Moral Education,* 39: 273-290.

Metz, Thaddeus. 2007. "Toward and African Moral Theory". *Journal of Political Philosophy,* 15: 321-341.

Munyaka, Mluleki and Mokgethi Mothlabi. 2009. "Ubuntu and its Socio-moral Significance". In *African Ethics: An Anthology of*

Comparative and Applied Ethics, edited by Murove, F.M., 62-84. Pietermaritzburg: University of KwaZulu Natal Press.

Murove, Munyaradzi F. 2014. "Ubuntu". *Diogenes*, 59: 36-47.

Prinsloo, E. D. 1991. "African Conceptions of Personhood and Intellectual Identities." In *Philosophy from Africa: A Text with Readings*, edited by Coetzee, P.H. and A.P.J. Roux, 41-51. Cape Town: Oxford University Press.

Singer, Peter. 2002. *Unsanctifying Human Life*, edited by H. Kuhse. Oxford: Blackwell Publishers Ltd.

Tshivhase, Mpho T. 2011. "Personhood: Social Approval or a Unique Identity?" *Quest: An African Journal of Philosophy*, 23-24: 119-140.

Wiredu, Kwame. 1992. "Moral Foundations of an African Culture." In *Person and Community: Ghanaian Philosophical Studies*, I. edited by Wiredu, Kwasi and K. Gyekye, 193-206. Washington DC: The Council for Research in Values and Philosophy.

Zagzebski, Linda. 2001. "The Uniqueness of Persons". *The Journal of Religious Ethics*, 29: 401-423.

Chapter 4. The Primacy of the Personal

≈≈≈≈≈≈≈≈≈≈ ❊ ≈≈≈≈≈≈≈≈≈≈

Augustine Shutte

> Cat at the window
> Bird in the tree
> Notice each other
> But don't really see
> That one has a home
> And the other is free

The two deepest needs, and desires, of our human nature are these: to have a home and to be free. We need to belong, and we need to be free to be ourselves. And the truth is that it is only in certain kinds of interpersonal relationships that these apparently contradictory but in reality complementary desires can be fulfilled. In this paper I am going to argue as carefully and as rigorously as I am able for this truth. I am doing this not merely as an academic exercise but because I think that insight into this truth can throw healing light into the gathering darkness in the global village in our time. The culture that is at present dominating the world has forgotten the primacy of the personal.

I speak of darkness because the 'global village' is presently in a state of crisis. It would be more accurate to describe this state as a state of war, but by that I don't mean war in the military sense, a third World War. The world is full of armed conflict, refugee camps and displaced people. But the war I am speaking of is a cultural war, a war between the dominant Western culture and the rest, between the culture of the 'developed' and the 'undeveloped'. And it is this conflict that underlies and inspires all the rest.

From my philosophical point of view, the dominant Western culture is founded on an inadequate and mistaken conception of human freedom as independence. It is from this that all the problems inherent in liberalism, capitalism, the free market and the global financial system flow. In this connection even such notions as human rights make for individualism, alienation and the loss of the sense of responsibility for the common good.

It is my view that the traditional African conception of Ubuntu, though developed in a tribal context, embodies an insight which if formulated in a manner appropriate to our scientific and secular culture, could well function as a corrective to this. The essence of the African notion is that human persons can only realise their humanity in dependence on personal relationships with others. In the context of tribal society these relationships were, and in some cases still are, limited to the members of the tribe. And individual freedom was seen as essentially subordinate to the common good.

I do not think these historical limitations affect the truth and universality of the essential insight of Ubuntu. And as I have already said I intend to argue that authentic freedom can only be realised in dependence on certain kinds of interpersonal relationships, that in fact self-determination and such intersubjective dependence grow together in direct and not inverse proportion to each other. This argument is the heart of this paper. Before setting it out I will give a brief description of the predicament in which I see the contemporary world, and especially Africa, involved. And having presented what I think a possible remedy might be I will give two examples of how I think a contemporary understanding of Ubuntu can be applied in specific spheres of life. The two spheres I have chosen are those of gender relations and health-care.

It is the primacy of the personal and interpersonal that has disappeared from the culture that is dominant in the global village. We can see this in all the important spheres of human life. Perhaps it is at its clearest in the way in which the electronic media have become central to our lives. To a large extent electronic contacts have replaced interpersonal ones. And electronic media now play an increasingly dominant role in education and character formation. Think of the infant seated in front of the cartoon channel of the TV rather than in the lap of a parent listening to a story. And information during schooling comes more from the internet than from a teacher.

The most important sphere however where the primacy of the personal has disappeared is that of family life. Few families now enjoy the personal presence of both parents and children for any significant amount of time. Financial factors ensure such loss of contact.

Money-power is in fact one of the chief causes of the loss of the primacy of the personal. The way in which the world of work and business has developed in the modern era means that a person's, or a family's, security depends more on their money-power than on the supportive relationships of other persons, friends or fellow-workers. Marx's critique of the alienating power of money is even more accurate today when the 350 wealthiest people own as much as the 65% poorest members of the world's population, than it was when the industrial revolution in Europe was just beginning.

The way society itself is organised also contributes to a loss of the personal and interpersonal. I am thinking of the exponential growth of bureaucracy in all our institutions, espccially in businesses and government. Even universities are no longer run by academics but systems experts and managers. There is also another side to this depersonalisation of institutions that one can clearly see in the sphere of health-care. Here there is a similar escalation in specialisation with its focus on specific diseases rather than on patients. In our huge omnicompetent hospitals it is often the case that there is no single person who knows the whole health-history of a specific patient who has been seen by several different specialists. All their findings are on an electronic file but not in any single person's mind.

Last but not least in this symbolic list of spheres from which persons and personal relations have disappeared is that of religion. Too often in the major religions it is the religious establishment itself, whether expressed in the authority of the religion's officials or the authority of its doctrines or scriptures, that is the religion's chief concern rather than the needs of its followers. This is a loss of the sense of the primacy of the personal in the sphere where it is most damaging and dangerous. We are now witnessing a connection between religion and violence that is a something new in human history.

I hope I have done enought to indicate what I mean by a loss of conviction as to the primacy of the personal in the dominant contemporary culture. I now want to give a sketch of the different ways in which personhood is understood in European and in African culture. By European I am referring to the culture that originated in Europe but has since spread far beyond it, going wherever European science and technology has gone. It is the culture usually referred to (in an equally misleading way) as Western. In my paper I am using the terms 'person' and 'personhood' in a quite specific way. As I use them they do not refer simply to human individuals and their individuality but to something that is distinctive about human nature, something that is recognised in different ways in every known culture but which I will illustrate by that of Europe and of Africa.

In Europe the distinctive feature of human personhood has come to be seen as our capacity for self-determination. The development of this insight in Europe culminated in the modern period that saw the rapid growth of science and secularisation. In spite of all the determinisms discovered by science and the materialistic view of reality produced by secularisation, individual freedom came to be seen both as the most important fact about human beings, and also as their highest value, that which gave persons a unique dignity and made them worthy of respect. This idea of the dignity of free individuals also led to the idea of fundamental human rights possessed by all people and which all authorities, religious or political, had to respect. The spirit of the new age brought about by science and secularisation is beautifully expounded by the Rennaissance poet, philosopher and painter, Pico della Mirandola. In his "Oration on the Dignity of Man" he depicts God speaking to Adam in this way:

> Neither a fixed abode nor a form that is yours alone nor any function peculiar to yourself have we given you, Adam, to the end that according to your longing and according to your judgement you may have and possess what abode, what form, what functions you yourself shall desire. The nature of all other beings is limited and constrained within the bounds of laws prescribed by Us. You, constrained by no limits, in accordance with your own free will, in whose hand We have placed you, shall ordain for yourself the limits of your nature. We have set you at the world's centre that you may from there more easily observe whatever is in the world. We have made you neither of heaven nor of earth, neither mortal nor immortal, so that with freedom of choice and with honour, as

though the maker and molder of yourself, you may fashion yourself in whatever shape you shall prefer (Taylor 1989, 199-200).

The traditional African view of what is distinctive about human persons is very different. European culture has taught us to see the self as something private, hidden <u>within</u> our bodies. Of course we don't think that the self is literally within us, as our brain and heart are. But because we think of ourselves as <u>things</u>, that is the image we have, and it determines how we see ourselves and relate to others.

Because traditional African thought sees reality as consisting of force, vital force rather than things, its understanding of human personhood is very different: the self is seen as <u>outside</u> the body, present and open to all. This is because the self is the result and expression of all the forces acting upon us. It is not a thing, but the sum total of all the interacting forces. So we must learn to see ourselves as <u>outside,</u> in our appearance, our acts and relationships, and in the environment that surrounds us. These are the manifestations of the life-forces that make me me.

If we can see ourselves in this way, we will have grasped the key insight in the African idea of persons: persons exist only in relation to other persons. The human self is not something that first exists on its own and then enters into relationship with its surroundings. It only exists in relationship to its surroundings; these relationships are what it is. And the most important of these are the relationships we have with other persons. This is why, in all African languages, there is a local variant of the Zulu saying *umuntu ngumuntu ngabantu-* a person is a person through other persons. As African philosophers are fond of saying, "I am because we are." This is the most important consequence of seeing ourselves as living centres of vital force.

This insight into our personhood finds its full expression in the African conception of community. African thinkers are at pains to distinguish the African idea of community from both the individualist conception that underlies liberalism and capitalism as well as the collectivism of socialism and communism. Both of these see society as something artificial, a product of human design. The famous African philosopher, poet and statesman, Leopold Senghor, has coined the term "communalism" and speaks of a "community society" in order to distinguish the African conception from European collectivist theories such as socialism and communism. A community society is, he writes, "a community-based society, communal not collectivist. We are concerned here not with a mere collection of individuals, but with people conspiring together, conspiring in the basic Latin sense (literally "breathing together"), united among themselves even to the very centre of their being." (1963, 16)

The idea that a community is like an organism, a natural rather than an artificial whole, is closer to the African conception, which does indeed see society as a natural growth. But it is still insufficient to do justice to the way in which Africans see *umuntu ngumuntu ngabantu*, persons depending on other persons to be persons. An organism, a plant or animal, is a natural whole but it is not personal. Each part gets its character, its identity, only from the role or function it has in the organism as a whole. The heart, for instance, is the pumper of blood. So the important thing about each organ is what makes it different from the others. In the African conception of community each part is the same—a person. The important thing about each person is what they have in common, namely that they are persons.

In fact, although, it may sound strange, one can only do justice to the African conception of community by visualising it as a single person. Each individual is then related to the community, not as a part to the whole, but as a person is related to themselves. Each individual member of the community sees the community as themselves, as one with them in character and identity. Each individual sees every other individual member as another self. Thus there is no room for a separation between the individual and the community, and all the relationships and transactions between individual members and the community as a whole remain fully personal.

The European and African traditions thus present us with different insights into the personhood of human nature. The African insight is into our communal nature: persons depend on persons to be persons. The European insight is into the freedom of the individual. I hope I have done enough to suggest the truth and importance of both these insights. The question must now be asked as to whether they contradict each other or whether they are compatible. There is in fact a third possibility: that the two insights are complementary, and can be married to provide an even deeper and richer conception of our personhood. I aim to show that this is the truth of the matter.

PERSONS ARE UNLIMITED

At first sight the two insights indeed appear contradictory. European self-determination looks the exact opposite of African dependence on others. But if one takes a closer look one will notice something, a feature that they share, which could provide a link between them and a way of combining the two in a unified approach. They both see human persons as possessing a certain kind of unlimitedness.

We have seen that the African idea of community is very different from the dominant European ones that underlie contemporary liberalism or socialism. To say that persons depend very much on the community, as Africans do say, is something that liberals and socialists would certainly agree with. But liberals would see such dependence as potentially dangerous and in need of careful limitation by government. Socialists, on the other hand, would see this dependence as the foundation of society and as something the government should have complete control of. And this shows that both understand the nature of this dependence in a very different way from traditional African thought.

In African thought the individual is dependent on the community not because he is in some way less than it or only a part of it but because he is identical with it. As long as we think in our customary materialistic way we are bound to think of the individual person as a single unit and the community as made up of many of the same. But the African tradition invites us to abandon this habit and to view the matter from the heart of our own experience of being a person. Then we will see that whether we are thinking of one person or many we are thinking of the same identical thing, the humanity we share. Whether we are thinking of individuals or of the community, the humanity of the individual or of the community is one and the same. There is no more humanity in the community than in the individual. According to the African way of thinking humanity is that field of force in which all individuals live and move and have their being. It is the same force that is present in each of us and in the community as a whole.

So to the extent that I identify with this common humanity I develop my own humanity, my own identity, and I enter into the hearts and minds of others. This is demonstrated by human experience in any culture. It is insofar as I come to know and love others for their own sake that I grow in self-knowledge and genuine self-esteem. Insofar as I am open to others and give myself in service for the good of the community I myself am strengthened and built up. This is why real generosity and unselfishness—even to the point of self-sacrifice—are realistic and creative attitudes, and not illusory or neurotic. They express and confirm my true humanity as something that transcends the limitations of my physical, social, economic and political individuality. It is something unlimited and all-inclusive and can be shared in by all without being divided or diminished. Being human is being unlimited in this special way.

Let us now consider the European insight into the freedom of the individual. As we have seen this is the freedom we have because we are able to do and believe things for reasons of our own making, rather than simply being caused to think and act by external forces of some or other kind. And so we are self-conscious and self-determining, transcending the influence on us of our whole physical or social environment in our deliberate judgments and decisions. Being self-conscious and self-determining thus means being in a certain way unlimited. We are free from the limitations of our physical and social environment. They are not ultimately responsibile for who we are.

This unlimitedness of human beings shows itself in a central and familiar feature of our lives. Being self-conscious and self-determining involves being continually present to oneself and in charge of oneself. Each of us is not only the hero of our life-story. Each of us is also writing it. We are each actually in the process of composing, constructing, inventing ourselves. And this is being unlimited in a special way, not just in the negative sense, of being free from outside control, but in the positive sense of being free to be who one chooses to be, the person one is creating.

So it seems that the European idea of freedom and the African idea of community do have something in common after all, albeit something mysterious, namely the idea that human beings are unlimited in a certain way. Of course this being unlimited is expressed in different ways in African and in European thought. In African thought it shows itself in openness and inclusiveness, in self-transcendence. In European thought it shows itself in self-determination. But it is such an unusual idea that the fact that it occurs in both of them could be a sign that at a deep level their different insights into human nature are compatible, even complementary, and taken together can provide a deeper understanding of our personhood.

This in fact is what I want now to show: that self-determination and depending on other persons for being a person need not be opposed to each other, but are in fact the very opposite of that. You can't have one without the other. It all depends on the kind of relationship between the persons, the attitude they have to each other.

What I am going to do in order to demonstrate this is to outline a phenomenology of intersubjectivity. I am going to do this with the help of three models. Each presents us with a simple story of an interaction between persons. But I have chosen them to illustrate features that are fundamental and universal in all persons and personal relationships. It must be remembered that I am using the models to demonstrate the *necessary* intersubjective relationships for the exercise, development and fulfilment of our personhood. As such they are ideal; they are not intended to be realistic: persons actually develop their personhood (or don't: it is not alas inevitable) in relation to a number of partially undeveloped persons and not only in relation to one fully developed. Nor is what I am doing a kind of pseudo-science, though I do not think any scientific findings would contradict it. In this sense it is abstract (as all philosophy must be) but it is intended to reflect our inescapable experience of being a person.

MOTHER AND CHILD

The first model is that of a new-born baby and its mother. The baby, I want to say, has the capacity for being self-determining. That is what makes it human and different from, say, a baby chimpanzee. Of course it is not able, at birth, to exercise this capacity, as it is able, for instance, to exercise its capacity to scream. It does not have the ability to be self-determining. It is not even conscious of being a self. What then does it need to gain this ability?

The answer is the presence of another person. In our model this is the mother. It is only insofar as she treats the baby as a person, with a capacity for self-determination, that it can become conscious of itself as such and actually begin to exercise this capacity. We know this to be true because we know what happens in the case of "wild children". These are those children who, for whatever reason, were left to die at birth or soon after, but who did not die. Instead they grew to physical maturity quite outside human society. In the few cases where we have reliable records they seem to have been kept alive by animals. But in all these cases these human children had not developed in any way as human persons. They were not conscious of themselves as self-determining, as in charge of their own lives and actions.

In normal human life the mother acts as a kind of mirror in which the child can discover itself. The wild children had no such mirrors in the wilds. When they gazed into the eyes of their wolf or ape foster-mothers they did not see someone who saw them as a person. When a normal child looks into the eyes of its mother it does not just see white and coloured lash-fringed orbs. It sees a person looking at a person. And because its mother treats it as a person it soon discovers that the person who is looked at is itself. It begins to be self-conscious.

So self-awareness comes to us as a gift from another person who makes themselves present to us. And this is just the beginning of the development of our capacity for self-determination. In our story the mother does not only look at the baby. She values it, cares for it, loves it. She doesn't just recognise that the baby is a person. She affirms it and treats it as a person. This makes the baby happy. After all it has the natural capacity to be a person and it craves to exercise this and grow. So it responds to the mother's love with joy. And this, because she loves her baby, makes the mother happy too. And she shows it. Bit by bit the baby begins to discover that, weak and helpless though it is, it has a kind of power, a power capable of producing important results in the real world. It has the power to make the mother happy. Or not. It is now conscious of itself as a being who can choose to act. It is self-determining.

It is only because the mother loves it that the child has this power. If she did not love it, its desire to be recognised and valued would not be satisfied and it would not be happy. And it is only because she loves it that the child's happiness makes her happy too. So the development of the child's capacity for self-determination comes to it as a gift from the mother's love. But it is really the child's capacity that develops. The child becomes really self-determining.

This truth, that persons can only develop their capacity for self-determination, if they are empowered to do so by certain kinds of attitude towards them of other persons, is proved beyond doubt by seeing what happens when these attitudes are lacking. This happens in the case of babies in institutions where there are too few nurses and too many babies for there to be genuine human contact between them. The exhausted nurses can often do no more than care for the bare physical needs of the child. They have no energy left to relate to them as persons, cuddling them and playing with them as a normal mother would. Studies of such institutions have shown that in every case the personal development of these children is retarded almost to a standstill. They become confused, disorientated, deeply disturbed.

This model has shown us the attitudes essential to personal growth. They are those that most fully express the personal nature of the mother and child. The mother has to open herself up to the child as the person she is, putting herself at the service of the child's own growth as a person. She must identify with it, valuing it and affirming it as a person, as she does herself. Only then will the transference of power from her to him take place unimpeded. This active affirmative openness to the child is answered by the child's own receptive openness to such an influence. Human babies, unlike those of other species, have very few built-in instincts. This is why they are and remain so much more helpless than the young of other species. And why they have so long a period of immaturity. Instead they have an apparently limitless desire for and openness to the presence of another person.

The attitude required of the mother if the child is to develop its capacity for self-determination is in fact that which we have identified as Ubuntu, the whole-hearted identification of the self with the other. We have therefore in this model a dramatic example of how Ubuntu and the freedom of the individual are not opposed. In fact it is that very kind of influence of the mother on the child that makes it free. There is indeed something paradoxical here, that self-determination can only be achieved in dependence on the power of another. That should not however be taken as a sign that we are mistaken, but rather as a sign of something unlimited in human life and in the ordinary relationships between human persons. The self-determination of the child and the self-transcendence of the mother are just two ways in which the unlimitedness of persons shows itself.

This model of the mother and the child is however itself rather limited. It is very good for showing us how radical our dependence on other persons is for developing as a person. But it is not a very good model of self-determination. A child's capacity for self-determination is largely undeveloped. Not only is not very much of a self, but the self it is is full of conflict and confusion. Crowds of conflicting emotions come and go. Confusing new impressions enter its consciousness at every moment. Every act, every gesture, is an experiment that can succeed or fail.

Without inner unity or harmony, proper self-determination is not possible. Self-determination means self-control, knowing what you really want to do and choosing to do it. And this is impossible in a state of confusion and conflict.

And yet a state of confusion and conflict is normal in the life of human beings, not just in children. Not only are we pulled this way and that by conflicting emotions. We also acquire mistaken beliefs about what we really want and what will make us happy. Our ideas don't fit our true needs. And our decisions and actions often don't fit in with either. We do things we don't really want to do. We even do things we have decided not to. We build up habits of thinking and feeling and choosing that are opposed to each other and to our own deepest desires.

GURU AND NOVICE

So we need another model that will better depict the situation in which the struggle to develop our capacity for self-determination usually takes place. The capacity and the desire for self-determination is so central to human nature that it can never be quite extinguished, but will persist in making itself felt in all sorts of disguised ways. I am going to take as my model for the kind of interpersonal relationship in which it is able to be developed to the full, that of the relationship between a beginner in monastic life and his spiritual director, a novice and his guru.

I must stress that this is just a model. I am not suggesting that everyone ought to join a monastery. The model is a model of something that is going on all the time in ordinary life, not just in monasteries. We all have a desire for personal growth. And this means we all desire to develop our capacity for self-determination to the full. The model of the novice and the guru can help us to see that it is only in dependence on certain kinds of relationship with other persons that this can happen.

What is it that I, a novice, want from my guru? I am a normal person with a normal confused and conflicted inner life. I want above all to discover what I really want, what will make me happy. And once I know that, I want to commit myself to it, to choose it and do it and live it, with my whole heart. In short I want a certain kind of self-knowledge and a certain kind of inner strength or power, a power of self-dedication or self-affirmation. Self-knowledge and self-affirmation are in fact the two basic elements in self-determination as it actually takes place in adult human life. And acquiring them will enable me to overcome the inner disunity of my life (since that arose from mistaken beliefs and choices) and choose—and be—myself.

What is it that the guru has to give me? He has grown as a person to a certain fulness and maturity. His inner life is no longer a place of confusion and conflict but of integration and integrity. He is truly happy, smiling a Buddha smile, his face radiating the beauty of goodness. What is his secret? He has self-knowledge. He is self-affirming. And he can give what he has to me. Why is this?

He knows me better than I know myself. And he affirms me more completely than I am able to affirm myself. This needs explanation.

Firstly, he knows me better than I know myself because he knows what I really want. In his argument for the unbanning of his novel *Lady Chatterley's Lover*, D H Lawrence wrote as follows: "All that matters is that men and women should do what they really want to do. Though here as elsewhere (he is discussing our sexual life) we must remember that man has a double set of desires, the shallow and the profound, the personal, superficial, temporary desires and the inner, impersonal, great desires that are fulfilled in long periods of time. The desires of the moment are easy to recognize, but the others, the deeper ones, are difficult. It is the business of our Chief Thinkers to tell us of our deeper desires, not to keep shrilling our little desires into our ears" (1931, 52-53).

It is these "deep desires", desires I may know nothing of, that the guru recognises in me. What could they be? Lawrence was talking about sex. And he contrasted superficial, trivial desires in this sphere, the kind of desires that supported a huge population of prostitutes in Victorian England, with a profound and life-changing desire for intimate and enduring sexual friendship with one other person. But there are all sorts of other deep desires: the desire to understand, the desire to create, the desire to play, to laugh, to worship... the list is endless. They are deep because they come from our human nature.

91

They are not desires we have been taught to have or picked up from our society, like the desire to hang-glide or to go to the moon. They aren't desires that are peculiar to this or that country or culture. They come from our common humanity. And that is why my guru can recognise their presence in my life even when I do not. Because he has discovered them in his own.

Knowledge of these deep desires is the most important part of self-knowledge because it is knowledge of my own humanity. And it is only when I know what my deep desires really are, that I have any chance of fulfilling them. And that is the next step. I must come to affirm these deep desires, in spite of all the other desires I may have. The deep desires are the most fundamental and far-reaching. If I don't recognise and affirm them, and try to live so that they are fulfilled, I will remain alienated and dissatisfied. They will persist in any case, in a state of war with all the other desires which I do recognise and try to satisfy. Like an underground movement in an enemy-occupied country, they will cause chaos and confusion until they are recognised and given the vote.

How then do I come to know what my deep desires, my true needs, are? By entering more fully into my relationship with my guru so that I come to know him better as a person and find out what he truly values. These values are his deep desires, not unconscious in his life but fully known and affirmed. But since these are the deep desires of the humanity we share, getting to know them in him is the way to knowing them in myself. In him they are not hidden, but fully conscious and expressed in all he does.

So now our question is "How does the novice, so lacking in self-knowledge, come to share deeply in the self-knowledge of the guru?" The answer is "The guru enables him."

It is impossible to gain intimate knowledge of a person unless the person wants to be known and gives themselves to the knower to be known. And this is what my guru does to me. He does not only know me better than I know myself; he also affirms me more whole-heartedly then I am capable of affirming myself, in something of the same way as the mother did the child. In fact he affirms me as he affirms himself, since what he is affirming, whether in himself or me, is identically the same—the deep desires of our common humanity. And he, being fully developed as a person, is fully self-affirming. So his affirmation of me is just as complete.

In the welcome security of this complete affirmation I am empowered to respond. Fear and anxiety are defeated and I am able to see him as he is. What is more I see him as valuable, valuable to me as someone who affirms me completely, makes me feel valuable, gives me hope. And so I affirm him. And, as we should now have no difficulty in seeing, when I do affirm him in this way I am affirming the deep desires of the common humanity we share. And this is true self-affirmation.

This model of the novice and the guru shows in a much fuller way than that of the mother and child how it is our shared humanity that enables the guru to empower me to become more fully self-determining. In him this humanity has reached fulfilment. In me it exists only as a dynamism for growth. The deep desires that form its nucleus have been fulfilled in him and seek fulfilment in me. They are the same desires, and the paradox is that the more they are fulfilled in me, the more I become like my guru, the more I am truly myself, more truly self-determining.

This knowledge and affirmation of the humanity that we share, but which is also the most intimate possession of each of us, is of course the attitude of Ubuntu. We must not fail to recognise the traditional idea in contemporary clothing. And what the second model shows is that the community formed by Ubuntu is no enemy of individual freedom but its absolutely necessary condition. The monastic model may seem strange—and I have chosen it partly for that purpose—but the interpersonal relationship it depicts is universal in ordinary experience. All of us have had the experience of being able to be more oneself in the company of certain people. And this is an experience of increased freedom. We feel empowered to do things we have never dared to before. Often there is a sudden breakthrough of insight into oneself. Or a surge of confidence and hopefulness that makes one's carefully built-up systems of security seem unnecessary. What the model shows is what is really happening: that one is becoming more self-determining because one is becoming a more integrated personality, more authentic in one's choices, more self-possessed. The model also shows that it is the attitude of Ubuntu that is the source of this power.

Of course in ordinary life one develops as a person in relation to many others who themselves are at very different stages of personal growth. And the process is lifelong, never complete. But here too the monastic model is a good one. For it presents the process of personal growth as a process of initiation, a two-way process of invitation and response, in which the initiative is always with the more developed person.

In this second model we also see more clearly the underlying reason for the complementarity of the African insight into community and the European insight into the freedom of the individual. The idea that persons develop as persons the more they are subject to a certain kind of influence of others (Ubuntu) would not be true if persons were not possessed of the kind of unlimitedness that the European idea of self-determination contains. For if persons were limited in the way that physical things are limited then the more they were under the influence of other things the less self-determining they would be. Seeds need water in order to grow, carts need horses in order to move. But in the case of persons, the more the novice comes under the influence of the guru the more he is self-determining.

FRIEND AND FRIEND

If one is to grasp the full extent of the way in which the African and the European insights complement each other, and also provide a more adequate understanding of personhood, one needs a further model of interpersonal relationships in which both persons have developed to the full. Only then can one see what the process of personal growth is aiming at all the time, and so understand it at its deepest level.

Just as we depended on other persons for acquiring the bare ability to exercise our capacity for self-determination, and need them for its continuing growth, so too we need them for its full expression, though perhaps "need" is the wrong word to use in this context. We can see this by taking a closer look at the deep desires that we have been speaking of.

These deep desires are those that well up from the human nature that we all share. We have named a number of them. But there are two we have deliberately not mentioned. They are the "deepest" and most comprehensive of all. The first is simply the built-in desire that all our deep desires find fulfilment. This is in fact the desire for the fulness of personal growth, which is, as we have seen, growth in self-determination, with the self-knowledge and self-affirmation that that involves. This is the central desire of our human nature, which can never be obliterated, although it can be buried or forgotten. The second of these "deepest of the deep" desires is the desire for community with others.

It is not difficult to see that these two desires are two sides of the same coin. The other person is the source of my personal growth, and I naturally desire that. But to put it simply like that is misleading. Because it suggests that personal growth is my goal and community with the other merely the means to it. And that is a mistake. Because the desire for the other is a desire that is for their sake as well as for mine. This needs explanation.

Think back to the second model. It was only because I came to affirm my guru that I was able to affirm myself. But my affirmation of him was valuing him for his own sake not just as a potential source of personal growth in me. I saw something in him that was valuable and affirmed it as valuable. If I hadn't, then I wouldn't value his affirmation of me. If I had seen he was arrogant and self-seeking, for instance, his affirmation of me would give me no satisfaction.

It was only because I really affirmed him that I was able to affirm myself as he did. So the more I am able to affirm myself, the more I will in fact be affirming him, since it is only through affirming him that I am able to affirm myself. This sounds very complicated but it is not in fact. The whole matter can be put more simply.

What I really desire is a form of community with the other in which my personal growth and his are both complete. I desire this not as a means to an end but as an end in itself. Part of this comprehensive desire is the desire for my personal growth. This is, as I have said, a desire natural to my human nature. Every being desires its own fulfilment. But I desire personal growth for another reason too: so that I can enter into community with the other, something I can only fully do if I have grown to completeness as a person. My overall desire for community thus includes the desire for personal growth. And, finally, it also includes the desire that he too be fully developed as a person—for my sake, but also for his.

This desire for community, which includes the desire for personal growth, is the desire for friendship. It goes beyond the desire for self-knowledge and self-affirmation to a desire to know and affirm my friend for his own sake. The model I have in mind for such a community of persons is that of two friends. In this model both friends are fully developed as persons, that is, they have full self-knowledge and are fully self-affirming. Of course this model is even less realistic than the two previous ones. But that doesn't matter. It is a model of something that is present in the whole process of personal growth and the interpersonal relationships in whch it takes place. The model represents the ideal goal at which the process aims. To say the goal is ideal is not to say it is not really aimed at. It is, and it is the most powerful aim in human life. To understand it is crucial for our conception of human personhood.

One can perhaps get a clearer idea of this kind of community if one visualises it as a sexual friendship. In such a case it is clear that I want my friend to love me for my own sake, for myself, rather than selfishly, merely as a means to his own satisfaction. It is no less clear that I want my friend to be someone whom I genuinely love as well. If I didn't really love him for himself, I wouldn't really want him to love me. Our desire for love is as much a desire to give love as to receive it. And this is what the model of a community of friends is trying to depict.

Real sexual desires and relationships are so ambiguous that the word "love" in that context is as well. But if we substitute the word "value" we can make the same point with regard to any relationship between true friends. I want my friend to value me for my own sake, not just for what I can give him. Of course he will also value me for that. But in addition he must be glad that I exist and want me to flourish even if he doesn't benefit in any way from my happiness. And I want to value him in that way too. I want him to be the sort of person whom I genuinely value for his own sake and not just because he values me. So the desire for friendship, although it includes the desire for self-fulfilment, also includes the desire for another whom one can truly value for themselves. It is an expression of our desire for full self-determination, for full self-knowledge and self-affirmation. But it is also an expression of the desire for self-transcendence and self-giving, in the intimate knowing and loving of another.

We have here another example of the unlimitedness of persons that both traditional European and African thought recognise. In the community of friends neither is limited by the life or activity of the other. On the contrary, the more one friend influences the other, the more self-determining the other becomes. And because of the community between them, each friend is able to transcend his separate individuality and live in the life of the other as though it were his own. All the riches of my friend's life are known and affirmed as my own.

Nor is personal community of this kind something that is limited to relationships between two people. Or just to relationships that we have with our friends, in the usual sense of that word. As I have described it it is the goal and full expression of personal growth and the relationship between fully developed persons of whatever number and in whatever sphere of life—marriage, family life, work, recreation, politics.

The model is a two-person model because two is the minimum number for a relationship between self and other. The term "personal community" defines a relationship between persons that is fully and mutually personal, namely one in which each knows and affirms themselves and the other. The community created by such mutual knowledge and affirmation is potentially unlimited. There is no built-in limitation regarding whom one can enter into community with in this way. The other person can be one's spouse, one's child, one's servant, one's boss, one's president, a fellow South African, anyone. This is because the attitude that creates community, Ubuntu, is an attitude towards humanity as such, the humanity that makes each of us who we are.

Having said that, it is important to prevent a misunderstanding. To say that we can create community with anyone, because community is the result of knowing and affirming our common humanity, could be taken to mean merely that we recognise that every person is human and treat them with the same standards as we treat ourselves. But it means something different from—and more than—that. As we saw from the last model community is only created when I know and affirm my friend as I know and affirm myself! The attitude that is being described is not just the knowledge that we are both human and as such equally valuable and so to be equally affirmed. The knowledge I have of myself is not this sort of commonsense or even theoretical knowledge. It is a knowledge by contact or familiarity with the unique person that is me. This is the primary self-knowledge that I affirm when I affirm myself. I affirm my own existence as valuable, as good. And this is the knowledge and affirmation I extend to my friend.

Such knowledge does not depend in knowing any particular details about a person. I know myself more certainly than I know even the most intimate details of my life and character. So I can

97

extend this familiarity to strangers as well as to close acquaintances, even to people I have never met. When one puts matters like that it is not difficult to see that this kind of affirmation is much more personal and demanding an attitude than merely deciding to treat another with the respect due to a human being. It is not the kind of attitude that one can simply decide—or be commanded—to have. It can only be developed in us by the difficult process of personal growth. And as we have seen that comes to us as a gift in the personal relations we have with others.

If one takes the personal community achieved by personal growth as the ultimate standard for ethics then one is able to overcome the apparent conflict between self-love and love of others that other understandings of personhood find so difficult to deal with. Genuine self-love turns out to be love of precisely that in myself that I most deeply share with others, our personhood. This is the attitude of Ubuntu. So *eros*, the desire for personal fulfilment, and *agape*, desiring the fulfilment of others for their own sake, are seen as two sides of the same coin rather than as enemies.

This is the attitude I have identified as Ubuntu. Rich and complex though it is, it is essentially a knowledge and affirmation of the humanity we all share—and so it is properly translated humanity. It is the power that produces personal growth in individuals and at the same time creates personal community between them. This is the twofold ultimate goal of Ubuntu. It gets its specific content from the various circumstances, the different spheres, in which human life is lived. In each different sphere persons will be involved in different kinds of community (educational, sexual, political and so on) and so *ubuntu* will aim at different concrete goals. This will require different abilities in people, and so personal growth will take a different form in each (being a good teacher, a good health-care worker, a good father and so on). In this way our moral life will get a specific concrete shape. It is not a system of abstract rules or principles. Rather animating the whole will be the same basic attitude of Ubuntu, which will be what makes for personal growth and community in each sphere.

We are dealing with the actual attitude and outlook of people. Nothing less will do. Political and social changes without changes in interior habits of feeling and thinking will never work. Nevertheless political and social changes are crucial. In each sphere of life we have to identify impediments to Ubuntu if we are to promote personal growth and community in a way appropriate to that sphere. If, for instance, certain aspects of our health-care system—say the size and inefficiency of our hospitals—make Ubuntu difficult or impossible there, then they are enemies of personal growth and community.

We are also concerned with what needs to be done to promote personal growth and community in each sphere of life. And this means discovering ways in which Ubuntu is properly expressed in that sphere. The spirit of Ubuntu will take different forms in us in the different spheres of our lives, in child-raising or in politics. And these different attitudes will find expression in different ways of behaving and different projects in the different spheres. We shall need a great deal of imagination as well as good-will to envisage how our country can be transformed

The desire for the fulness of personal community is at the heart of human life. The model of a community of friends shows what is involved in it, what sort of a community it is. And here, even more than in the other models, we can see how European self-determination and African dependence on others go together. This model also shows in a fuller way the unlimitedness of persons. And finally, it is the fullest model of all for the attitude of Ubuntu. Though personal community as we have described it is always only an ideal, it is an ideal that is rooted in our human nature and so something that reveals most clearly what that nature is and what will bring it to fulfilment.

What I now intend to do is to give a sketch of how the notion of Ubuntu as I have analysed it in the above models can give specific guidance in our attempts to transform society so as to make it a more hospitable home for humanity in the twenty-first century. I will take the spheres of gender and gender relations and of health-care as examples. In each case I will indicate both the impediments to personal growth and community and also ways in which the attitude and practice of Ubuntu can help to overcome them.

GENDER

The sphere of gender and gender relations is perhaps the most basic in human life. It is after all the sphere from which all human persons originate. And in our contemporary world it is probably the sphere in which Ubuntu is most threatened. By gender I mean everything that distinguishes women from men, physical and mental alike; by sex I refer simply to the erotic—as in sexy! This is because I believe, with every known culture except sections of our own, that this distinction of gender is a natural and not simply a cultural one. And this is in no sense a denial of the absolute equality of the personhood of women and men. It is precisely because their complementarity is denied that real a real personal equality will never be achieved.

Because gender difference is part of human nature this means that the distinction between self and other is also real in each human being. Each of us is both male and female and personal growth entails the development and integration of both. The work of people like Carol Gilligan (1983) has made this quite clear. The problem is to realise this truth in society as a whole. And the conception of Ubuntu as I have analysed it is thus the perfect guide as to what changes have to be made.

Complementarity as well as equality is our guiding light in using Ubuntu as our guide in the sphere of gender. It must be achieved within the individual, as an integration and balancing of the different gender characteristics. It must also be achieved in the relationships between individuals with each gender enabled to offer what is uniquely theirs. Finally it must be achieved in the institutions of society in which people live and grow. These must promote rather than impede the development of persons of the different genders. And promote the development of persons of different genders equally.

And here we come face to face with a real problem. Our society doesn't do this. And what is true of South Africa is also true of the dominant culture of the whole contemporary world. Women are subordinated to men. This has the effect of preventing the proper personal growth of women, but also that of men. It also makes true personal community between persons of different gender difficult if not impossible. And the result is that every sphere of society is dehumanised and dehumanising because of this.

Let us investigate this by looking first at the most obvious and external manifestation of gender inequality, namely that in society as such. This is the inequality in social authority and power of men and women. Consider the sphere of work. In pre-industrial society work was centred on the home. Economic power was in the hands of women. Men were concerned with security and defence. They had political power. Then came the development of cities and industrialisation. Work and home were separated. And those with political power used it to assume economic power too. It was the development of modern science and technology that forged the link between economic and political power. It changed both the nature of tools and of weapons and put them in the hands of men. So in the world created by science and technology economic and political power go together. And they are in the hands of men. This is also the world of modern democracy, in which everyone is equal. Democracy is the appropriate ideology for this world because all are equally producers, equally consumers. And hence have equal value, equal rights. That is the rhetoric. But the truth is different. As Ivan Illich has so brilliantly revealed in his penetrating analysis of the phenomenon of "shadow work", most of the work, the overwhelmingly larger part in fact, is done by women. That is because most of the work done in any society is domestic work. And that is mostly done by women. This work is the time and energy spent in keeping and caring for the "worker" who goes to work outside the home for eight hours a day. Illich has shown how much more it costs to get the nutrition from the beans in a can in a supermarket into the blood-stream of a worker than it cost to get those beans into the can in the supermarket in the first place. But we don't think of the second process as work because it is unpaid.

Of course, since the enfranchisement of women in a democratic society, increasing numbers of women work outside the home. But all studies show this means simply that they do even more work than before. They don't relinquish their work in the home because they are working outside it. They just do two jobs instead of one. And what is more, other studies show, is that most of the productive work (as distinct from managerial and administrative work) even in the recognised economy is also done by women. Think of the number of clerks and secretaries in any firm. Think of the number of workers in factories. Think of the number of nurses in the health care service. As productive workers women far outnumber men. But as managers, directors, heads and owners they are in a tiny minority.

So the work of the world is still mainly done by women. But economic power is in the hands of men. The ratio of women's wages to men's wages in America is 3:5. It was that a hundred years ago as well. This situation is not only unjust. It prevents the full development of women in the sphere of work. And it does something to men as well. It is dehumanising. The world of work has become dehumanised because of this inequality. It won't become human again just by making sure that women can have equal power in the same dehumanised world. That is not the goal of Ubuntu. The more power women have, the more the world of work will change its whole character to reflect the character and abilities of both genders equally. That is the goal.

Who can doubt that all our social arrangements, our law, our institutions, our customs and practices would be different if in living memory women had had as much public power, power in the major institutions that form our society, as men have. Imagine a society in which men and women were present in roughly equal number in all the highest positions of authority in government, the police and army, in education, in law and health-care and religion. It is difficult to imagine what it would be like, but it would certainly be radically different. And can one doubt that it would be more humane?

If one looks at the way in which inequality of gender affects the sexual relationship between men and women, and at the way in which it affects the personal growth and integration of children in relation to their parents' one will find a similar situation. The global imbalance of power skews the sexual relationship of men and women, making one the master the other the slave. And the phenomenon of the absent father and the omnipresent mother prevents the integrated development of the child. Of course it wouldn't be sufficient simply to have this equality. One is not concerned here just with justice. One is concerned with creating a different, more humane, society. To do this one requires a revolution in thinking about society and its goals. And this is what the concept of Ubuntu enables us to do.

In our dominant contemporary culture society is thought of as an artefact, an artificial entity created by human science and technology. The goal of social organisation is to produce more of what science and technology is capable of producing. The use of this huge new social product can be left to individual whim. The only constraint is some or other principle of equality. But this whole conception is a dangerous myth, justified by an equally dangerous ideology. It cannot fail to create an inhuman world. And it is inherently sexist. Instead we must see society as a natural growth and organism different from other natural growths only in this: that it is composed of beings with the capacity for freedom. So though it is natural it is also, and must remain, personal. Nature and freedom are not opposed but inextricably connected in human persons. The in-built natural goal of society on this understanding is the development and fulfilment of persons, and the personal community that is the natural result of this. Society exists to produce and perfect persons. We are its essential product. Our science and technology are subordinate to this end. They can be a great help in this process, but they can also prevent it. The absolutely essential thing is the quality of personal relations between persons, in every sphere of life. Nothing can take the place of this.

If we think of society in this way, we will see gender with new eyes. Gender difference is the necessary condition for the production of persons and their development as persons. Gender difference is thus the root of human society and must be reflected in every sphere as the necessary condition of its humanity and of the possibility of personal growth and community for its members. This will mean that the equality and complementarity of the different genders must be realised in every sphere.

If this is the truth of the matter, then we can see how important will be the character of the institiutions that embody and facilitate this process of personal growth. And most important of all is the institution in which this growth begins and gets its basic orientation. I am referring to the family, in which human persons are born and begin to grow. This is by no means an artificial institution, though the forms it takes in different societies are different. It is as natural a reality as gender itself.

If the production of persons is the purpose of society then the family is its most important institution. All other production, all other institutions, must gain their purpose in relation to this: political arrangements, ways of working, the sort of products we concentrate on in our technology, the sort of research we do in science, the kind of education we favour. And the equality and complementarity of genders must be realised in the family more securely than anywhere else. No longer will there be a division of labour with the woman in the home and the man at 'work' outside it. The equal presence and activity within the home and family of both men and women will have far-reaching effects on the personal and sexual relationship between husband and wife and on the personal development of children. The inequality of husband and wife will disappear and this will change their sexual relationship to one between two of equal power, and allow true complementarity to flourish. The phenomenon of the 'absent' father and the 'omnipresent' mother will also disappear, to the benefit of a balanced growth of the child.

Equality of gender participation will also exist in the most important professions, such as the police and army, education, law, government, health-care and religion. In all of these the two genders must be equally represented and equally powerful. This should be obvious in theory. But because of the state of our contemporary world it is not realised in practice. In fact it is probably true to say that the devaluing and disempowering of the female is the greatest threat of all to our humanity in the contemporary world. Overcoming it is thus one of the most important goals of Ubuntu. "It is perhaps not too much to say that the Achilles heel of human civilization, which today has reached global genocidal and ecocidal proportions, resides in this false development of maleness through repression of the female" (Ruether 1975, 11). The liberation of women is the most important, and the most far-reaching, form of liberation that there is.

HEALTH-CARE

The World Health Organisation defines health as "a state of complete physical, mental, emotional and social well-being, and not merely the absence of disease or infirmity" (WHO 2. No.100). This definition is echoed by the words of a Zulu practitioner of traditional as opposed to scientific medicine: "Whites have failed to see that in Africa a human being is a single entity, not divided up into various sections such as the physical body, the soul and the spirit. When a Zulu is sick it is the whole man who is sick" (Buhrmann 1984, 32). In this sense health is almost equivalent to our account of the goal of Ubuntu as the attainment of the fulness of personal growth and community. But here I am considering health in a more restricted sense as the concern of a particular sphere of life amongst others, that in which the recognised professionals are doctors and nurses assisted by various departments of government such as those concerned with water affairs, waste disposal, sanitation and so on.

From the point of view of Ubuntu even health-care in this restricted sense must have as its ultimate goal the personal growth and community we have identified. And this does involve our personhood as a whole. But it contributes to this by focussing on the impersonal and unconscious aspects of human persons, the bodily and psychic factors that can impede or prevent this. And in our contemporary world it uses everything that scientific medicine as well as complementary medical traditions can provide. That it does so in the spirit of *ubuntu* depends on two things: that the self-determining individual themselves bears the ultimate resonsibility for their health-care, but, secondly, only in the appropriate relationship to family and friends as well as society as a whole, which of course includes the government and the provision it makes for its people's health. Thus in the sphere of health care the two basic principles will be individual autonomy and community care. Care in this context is the attitude of Ubuntu to a person, whether oneself or another, to a person in need. Here I will only consider the care of health-care professionals for other persons, although of course doctors and nurses have a duty to care for their own health—as do their patients.

I use the term 'professional' deliberately in connection with the responsibility for my health assumed by health-care workers themselves. Health-care, because it is so closely connected to the ultimate aim of human life, has to be an interpersonal affair. It requires that health-carers are present to those they care for as persons and not simply as functionaries. They have to acquire moral virtues as well as purely technical skills. They must be committed to those whose health they care for. This in fact is contained in the meaning of the word "profession". It means "vow". This refers, in the first place, to the vow made by members of a religious community when they join a monastery or a convent. They take a vow of poverty, celibacy and obedience. From then on they are considered "professed" religious. At "solemn profession" they take "final vows", which means they are professed for life. Their aim is a complete commitment. Medical professionals also take a vow, the "Hippocratic oath". And this has a similar meaning, though a more restricted application. And just as professed religious, monks and nuns, are supposed to have a "calling", a deep inner motivation, in order to sincerely take the vows, so too are those involved in health-care. It can't be 'just a job', a way of making a living, if it is to be an expression of Ubuntu.

Thus if one considers health-care work as team work (which is what it should be from the point of view of Ubuntu) the patient is to be seen as the leader of the team and the health-care professionals as there to serve with care the patient's health. They do this by their knowledge of the patient (including and especially their expert knowledge of their state of health) and by their affirmation of the patient's autonomy. Such knowledge and affirmation usually takes the form of enabling the patient's informed consent to whatever procedures the professionals recommend. On the patient's side the responsibility is exercised in trust in the care offered and commitment to its exercise. It is important to note that in the context of health-care authentic care of necessity involves the aim of competence. The object of care is to successfully remove the bodily and psychic impediments to the patient's personal growth. Care thus regards the end of health-care, the fostering of personal growth through promoting health. Competence regards the means, which comprise both the science and the technology of medicine, aimed at the maintenance or restoration of the bodily and psychic integrity of the patient. Care is thus the foundation of health care, from which all else follows. It is a total attitude involving the intellect, the will and the emotions. Within it one can distinguish certain subsidiary virtues of special importance for health-care.

One such virtue could be called the "rescue" virtue. This is the willingness to drop all else, including thought of one's own rights or safety, for the sake of the patient in an emergency situation. Obviously such a refusal to "count the cost" (including the financial cost) must be balanced by a commitment to justice if it is to count as a virtue. But the preparedness for self-sacrifice it involves establishes it as a genuine aspect of Ubuntu in health-care that can lift the whole sphere of health-care above the merely practical and utilitarian.

An opposite, but equally significant, virtue in health-care could be called "medical modesty". Because of the inherent threat in ill-health there is a temptation to make extravagant claims or promises concerning treatment, and to encourage false hopes. Health-care professionals occupy a position of immense power in their field and it is easy to misuse it. Medical modesty brings the health-carer down to the human level and establishes a deeper than merely professional solidarity with the patient. Medical modesty will also moderate the tendency—so very prevalent in commercial health-care—to over-treatment.

The activity that most fully expresses the attitude of care is that of nursing, which is the active service of the patient's health-care needs as a whole. The nurse is thus the definitive health-care professional. Other functions of a more specialised nature can be fulfilled by workers with more limited competence, but these will only serve the purpose of a humane health-care service to the extent that these workers are also skilled in the practice of nursing and animated by the virtue of care.

Care is essentially the overall attitude of a person to a person in need, but since it also entails the aim of competence it will show itself in a whole host of particular activities, procedures and practices in the sphere of health-care. It is not merely an inner feeling

Nursing theorists, such as Patricia Benner in her work *From Novice to Expert: Excellence and Power in Clinical Nursing Practice*, provides an extremely rich vision of how care will show itself in practice.

Benner lists seven "domains" of nursing care:

1. The helping role
2. The teaching-coaching function
3. The diagnostic and patient-monitoring function
4. Effective management of rapidly changing situations
5. Administering and monitoring therapeutic interventions and regimens.
6. Monitoring and ensuring the quality of health-care practices
7. Organizational and work-role competencies.

In each of these domains she distinguishes a number of different activities and interpersonal transactions requiring different qualities and skills from the health-carer. So, for instance, in "The Helping Domain" there are the following:

1. The healing relationship: creating a climate for and establishing a commitment to healing.
2. Providing comfort meansures and preserving personhood in the face of pain and extreme breakdown
3. Presencing: being with a patient
4. Maximizing the patient's participation and control in his or her own recovery
5. Interpreting kinds of pain and selecting appropriate strategies for pain management and control
6. Providing comfort and communication through touch
7. Providing emotional and informational support to patients' families
8. Guiding a patient through emotional and developmental change: providing new options, closing off old ones; channeling, teaching, mediating

It is not difficult to see what a rich and complex picture of the expert health-carer emerges. Health-care is an interpersonal transaction. But it takes place in a social setting. The forms of personal community that support the practices of care are determined by the institutions that society provides. Apart from the fundamental institutions of the family and government, institutions such as hospitals, hospices and clinics, as well as schools and adult-education programmes, universities and training colleges, determine the shape and the spirit of health-care in a country.

Here as elsewhere, if we are to achieve Ubuntu in our institutions, the principle of subsidiarity is important. The autonomy of the local, the grassroots, must be preserved. This does not mean that there must be no centralisation. In health-care it is especially important that there be central planning and funding to meet certain needs. But the overall emphasis must be to help families and their members to help themselves. Nor does subsidiarity imply increased privatisation of health-services. Privatisation of health care can be the enemy of autonomy in health-care in a society in which there are great differences in wealth. It increases the range of possible choice for those with money, but it can decrease the range of effective choice for the whole population because it "locks up" resources and skills in the private sector

Subsidiarity will mean trying to make each home as far as possible a centre for health-care. The hospice movement provides a good model for this. In addition to the actual hospice centre, with wards and resident staff, there is a day-care centre with its own resident and travelling staff of doctors, nurses, occupational therapists, social workers and counsellors. The vast majority of patients live at home, being treated there or visiting the day-care centre according to their need. From time to time they may be taken into the wards for special treatments. A central teaching hospital with its specialist departments and wards servicing a spread-out field of satellite clinics is another example.

It is very difficult to achieve and maintain Ubuntu in a huge omnicompetent hospital. Central insititutions of that kind are necessary, as well as specialised hospitals (psychiatric or paediatric or whatever), but the less time patients spend in them the better. This is particularly true in a country of cultural pluralism. Scientific medicine has its own culture and patients need to be educated in it in order to be able to 'take' it. It can otherwise be a source of of terrible alienation and a factor in producing iatrogenic disease, making the hospital a cause of ill-health rather than its cure.

When it comes to achieving Ubuntu in the sphere of health-care, traditional cultures and alternative health-care systems have a lot to offer. Vera Buhrmann (1984, 42) has a compelling account of the traditional treatment of a psychological disorder in Xhosa culture which could complement Western approaches to psychotherapy. This is just one example of how the community, in the family and beyond it, can play an active part in health-care. But the community as a whole also has an unavoidable responsibility, and authority, in the regulation and distribution of a country's health-care. As far as possible, for the sake of Ubuntu the aim must be to empower each person and to locate health-care in the home. But the government is also bound to develop, finance and administer a health-care system that is country-wide and open to all. Two qualities should characterise such a system if it is to be an expression of Ubuntu: equitable access for all members of society, and a basic provision of health-care that is adequate for normal needs.

Obviously these two qualities are difficult to identify in practice. They are also difficult to achieve in a setting of scarce resources. But they are a good test of the overall humanity of a society with respect to justice and respect for human life. Health is such a clear and definite need—even more so than education—that the way a country manages its health-care system is a good indicator of its peoples' values. Justice and respect for persons should characterise every aspect of government but it is often difficult to tell whether policies in other spheres of life are just or humane. In the sphere of health-care it is not.

More clearly in this sphere than in any other it can be seen that the basic goods of life are the common property of all. Impartiality and solidarity are natural values when it comes to health-care. In order to decide on how health-care resources should be distributed, and what the basic health-care entitlement should be, the demands of Ubuntu can be a fair and humane guide. We need to ask ourselves what we think is fair to want for ourselves or those we love if we were in need of health-care. And we need to ask ourselves this question both from the point of view of a patient and from the point of view of the health-care provider. An honest answer will help us to decide how best to use the available resources of money and

109

expertise. Anthony Fisher puts this well when he formulates the test as follows: "Would I think the healthcare budget and principles of allocation were fair if I (or someone I loved) were in healthcare need, especially if I were one of those excluded from provision or were among the weakest in the commnunity (i.e. sick with a chronic, disabling ailment, poor, illiterate etc.)? Would I think them fair were I (etc.) a healthworker, healthplanner, taxpayer and/or insurer?" (1994, 135). The fundamental criterion for the distribution of resources in a health-care system animated by Ubuntu is need. All have an equal right to share in the health-care system but not all have equal need. "Need" is a difficult notion to apply. As technology makes more and more goods and services available, humanity has more to choose from to satisfy the important inclinations of our nature. What one considers basic needs will depend on what is available, subject to the proviso that the goods of the earth are the common property of all. And "all" here means all, not just all Americans or all in the First World. In a particular country however it means everyone for whom the government is responsible. The public opinion and the prevailing values of the people will determine what are considered basic health-care needs. Anthony Fisher calls this the community's "life-plan". In South Africa it is what I am suggesting should be Ubuntu.

Fisher sums up this requirement as follows: "Subject to the constraints of other duties, virtues and the community's life-plan, access should as far as possible be provided to healthcare appropriate to every person's healthcare needs. Sometimes there will be too much need or too few resources to achieve this goal. A nuanced healthcare requires a criterion that can provide some guide to eliminating false needs and prioritizing true ones: needs can be more or less urgent, more or less crucial. Healthcare should be allocated according to healthcare need, irrespective of factors such as race, religion, age, consciousness, provider-whim, ability to pay, social contribution and quality of life; but with a certain preference in favour of the disadvantaged, those to whom one has particular responsibilities, and those upon whom others crucially rely" (1994, 188).

When it comes to deciding what the basic health-care needs are in a particular country two factors must be taken into account, the values of the people, the "community life-plan", and the facts concerning health-care science and technology as provided by health-care professionals. Because the question of health-care provision is so important and equally important to all, all should have a say in how these two factors are to be combined to establish a basic health-care provision.

A most original, imaginative and humane attempt to do this was that of the state of Oregon in the USA. It is known as the Oregon plan and is a model of democratic decision-making. The plan was to draw up an ordered list of health-care priorities so that it could be measured against the state's health-care resources in order to decide on a basic package of health-care that would be available to everyone, as well as providing a measure for deciding on state spending between different medical procedures.

First of all a list of (745) health-care services and procedures was drawn up. Then country-wide community meetings were arranged (at 47 venues, 1048 citizens attending) to prioritize these. These small groups then produced a list of the values that underlay these choices. They were asked "to think and express themselves in the first person plural, namely as members of a statewide community for whom health care has a shared value" (Garland 1994, 218). They produced a list of thirteen values for health-care. In summary here it is: prevention, quality of life, cost effectiveness, ability to restore function, equity, effectiveness of treatment, benefits many, connecting mental and physical health, personal choice, community compassion, impact on society, length of life, personal responsibility. A government commission then measured the list of services against the list of values to determine ranking.

Michael Garland comments on the process as follows: "In summary, the Oregon Plan is an application of basic democratic principles to the complex field of health care. It stimulates active participation by the general citizenry in declaring the values on which new political choices should be based. It maintains a role for experts in describing the probable outcomes of specific health care interventions that in the aggregate make up a package of benefits. It requires legislators to conduct an open and accountable budget-making process that finally delivers to human services agencies the resources necessary to organize and administer a valued set of health services" (1994, 225).

The Oregon Plan is a wonderful practical manifestation of Ubuntu at the level of the whole people and the government.

There is no reason why its basic principles, and even its methods, should not be used here.

In a country like South Africa where there are huge disparities of wealth the crucial issue in the sphere of health-care is the just distribution of resources. But there is another issue linked to this and if it is not addressed there is no hope of justice in health-care. Unless the different understanding of sickness and health, and the different approach to therapy and care, of the African and the European traditions can be seen as complementary and reconciled in a common health-service, justice has no hope of being done. A welcome step in this direction has been made by a working party in the Department of Medicine at UCT by the publication of a handbook of primary health care that combines the approach and practice of scientific medicine with that of a traditional African one: *South African Primary Health Care Handbook* (Felhaber T (ed) 1999)

In the two examples I have chosen, that of gender relations and of health-care, I have sketched the way in which I think the primacy of the personal can be achieved in these spheres of life. This paper has been written with the conviction that our present society and culture prevent this primacy and that it must be restored if human persons are to flourish and find fulfilment. And this can only happen if the capacity for freedom that defines our personhood is enabled to develop in and through certain kinds of interpersonal relationships, relationships expressive of Ubuntu.

BIBLIOGRAPHY

Barr, Stringfellow. 1949. *The Pilgrimage of Western Man*. New York: Harcourt Brace.

Benner, Patricia. 1984. *From Novice to Expert*. Menlo Park: Addison–Wesley.

Buhrmann, Vera. 1984. *Living in Two Worlds*. Cape Town: Human and Rousseau.

Felhaber, Taryl, ed. 1999. *South African Primary Health Care Handbook*. Cape Town: Copy Cat Communications.

Fisher, Anthony. 1994. *The Principles of Distributive Justice Considered with Reference to the Allocation of Health-Care*. Oxford: unpublished PhD thesis.

Fromm, Erich. 1961. *Marx's Concept of Man*. New York: Ungar.

Garland, Michael. 1994. "Oregon's Contribution to Defining Adequate Health Care." In *Health Care Reform: A Human*

Rights Approach, edited by Chapman, Audrey, 211-232. Washington DC: Georgetown University Press.

Gilligan, Carol. 1983. *In a Different Voice*. Cambridge: Harvard.

Heron, John. 1970. "The Phenomenology of Social Encounter: The Gaze". *Philosophy and Phenomenological Research*, 10: 243 – 264.

Illich, Ivan. 1971. *Deschooling Society*. London: Calder and Boyars.

Illich, Ivan. 1975. *Tools for Conviviality*. London: Collins.

Illich, Ivan. 1982. *Gender*. New York: Pantheon.

Kierkegaard, Soren. 1958. *Journals*. London: Collins.

Lawrence, David H. 1931. *Apropos of Lady Chatterley's Lover*. London: Penguin.

Keller, Helen. 1959. *The Story of My Life*. London: Hodder.

McCormick, Richard. 1981. *How Brave a New World: Dilemmas in Bioethics*. New York: Doubleday.

Mead, Margaret. 1950. *Male and Female*. London: Penguin.

Prozesky, Martin. 1995. *Living Faiths in South Africa*. Cape Town: David Philip.

Sartre, Jean-Paul. 1948. *Existentialism and Humanism*. London: Methuen.

Schumacher, Ernst F. 1973. *Small is Beautiful: A Study of Economics as if People Mattered*. London: Abacus.

Schumacher, Ernst F. 1979. *Good Work*. London: Cape.

Senghor, Leopold S. 1963. "Negritude and African Socialism". In *St Anthony's Papers No. 15*, edited by Kirkwood, K. London: Chatto and Windus.

Sheed, Frank. 1953. *Society and Sanity*. London: Sheed and Ward.

Taylor, Charles. 1989. *Sources of the Self*. Cambridge: Harvard.

CHAPTER 5. MWALIMU JULIUS NYERERE–THE POWER OF HIS MORAL VISION AND LEGACY

Aloo Majola

INTRODUCTION

"The memory of the righteous is a blessing, but the name of the wicked will rot" Proverbs 10.7.

This paper seeks to reflect briefly on the life and work of Mwalimu Nyerere within the context of his moral vision and praxis. In view of the present moral darkness and decadence on the African continent the memory of the life and thought of Mwalimu Julius Kambarage Nyerere is refreshing. It is reminder and a challenge to our youth and all progressive minds to critically and robustly engage the present in the search for viable human alternatives that reflect and restore our humanity (Utu/Ubuntu). While Mwalimu Nyerere was not a perfect human being, he stands out as unique leader by the example of his moral vision, simplicity, honesty, humanity and concrete actions to create a more humane society rooted on his understanding of what it means to be human (Utu/Ubuntu).

Mwalimu Julius Kambarage Nyerere is an unforgettable historical landmark on the African social landscape.[1] He commands widespread respect and global recognition for his outstanding and principled struggle for the cause of human freedom and dignity. It is noteworthy that the Catholic Church has included him as candidate for beatification and canonization, a process launched sometime in January 2006 by Catholic Cardinal Polycarp Pengo that could possibly culminate in Julius Nyerere being declared a Catholic saint! A French author Marie Aude Fouere has questioned this process. She has argued that "The cause for canonization reinforces the current process of extracting Nyerere from the secular realm and elevating him to the sacred: a disconnection which, if it were finally to take place, would definitely erase the historical, political, and intellectual context of the 1950's – 80s that gave birth to the man and the values he defended, producing instead an utterly decontextualized moral figure" (Fouere 2015, 44). On the contrary it could be argued that it is not possible to understand Mwalimu Nyerere the man without understanding the extent to which his moral values and social thought is rooted, immersed and influenced both by his Catholic faith, his traditional African heritage and his internationalist socialist thought. These have to be taken together without dispensing of any of them.

The present African situation for the vast majority Africans could simply be characterized as Hobbesian. It is peopled with many atomistic leaders and a populace whose one and only preoccupation is personal gain and aggrandizement at whatever cost. This in itself is an apparent contradiction in a continent that not long ago was steeped in a communitarian ethos and what could be referred to as Ujamaa values—with a strong emphasis on the extended family. The reality that confronts us now on a daily basis is grand scandal of greed, corruption and looting of public or state resources. This reality

---

1   Among books on Nyerere, the following are helpful and representative—William Edgett Smith, *Nyerere of Tanzania: The first Decade 1961-1971*, Colin Legum & Geoffrey Mmari, eds. *Mwalimu: the influence of Nyerere*, 1995, Thomas Molony, *Nyerere: The Early Years*, 2014, Paul Bjerk, *Building a Peaceful Nation: Julius Nyerere and the Establishment of Sovereignty in Tanzania, 1960 – 1964*, 2015, Marie Aude Fouere, ed. *Remembering Nyerere in Tanzania: History Memory Legacy, Dar*, 2015.

is at the epicenter of what Jean-Francois Bayart has described as the 'politics of the belly' (Bayart 2009). Interestingly, the words of English political philosopher Thomas Hobbes (1588-1679), writing in the mid-seventeenth century in his classic text *Leviathan* (1968), sound familiar to those sensitive to everyday African reality, "The condition of man ... is a condition of everyone against everyone... in such a condition there is no place for industry... no knowledge of the face of the earth; no account of time; no arts; no letters; no society; and which is worst of all, continual fear, and danger of violent death; and the life of man, solitary, poor, nasty, brutish and short"(Hobbes 1968, 1; 13; 186). Characteristic of these sad Hobbesian landscapes "The notions of Right and Wrong, Justice and Injustice have no place ... Force, and Fraud are ... (the) two cardinal virtues" (Ibid, 188). The above depiction of a Hobbesian situation is typical of many an African state and provides the backdrop of Mwalimu Nyerere's Ujamaa and Utu project.

SOCIAL INEQUALITY–A DISTURBING REALITY

Social inequality and injustice are all too familiar themes in our African social milieu. Mwalimu Nyerere agonized and grappled intensely, with these themes. They are pervasive in his recorded speeches as in his published writings. In recent times popular public discourse on the disturbing reality and crisis of social inequality has been at the forefront of global attention and debate. A number of best sellers have helped focus attention on this theme, among them, *Capital in the Twenty First Century* (2014) and *The Economics of Equality* (2015) both by French economist and academic Thomas Piketty[2]. A strong aversion to social inequality lies at the heart of Nyerere's thinking and social philosophy. Swedish Sociologist Goram Therborn

---

2   Among many others could be mentioned such recent titles as Joseph Stiglitz, *The Great Divide*, Raymond Fisman and Edward Miguel, *Economic Gangsters: Corruption, Violence and the Poverty of Nations*, Tim Di Muzio, *The 1% and the Rest of Us: A Political Economy of Dominant Ownership*, Branko Milanovic, *Global Inequality, The Haves and Have-Nots: A Brief and Idiosyncratic History of Global Inequality*, Danny Dorling, *Inequality and the 1%* , Francois Bourguignon, *The Globalization of Inequality*, David Cay Johnston ed., *Divided: The Perils of Growing Inequality*, Chuck Collins, *99 to 1: How Wealth Inequality is Wrecking the World and What We Can Do about It.*

has succinctly captured the kinds of questions that disturb like-minded persons:

> Why shouldn't a new born child in Congo have the same chance to survive into a healthy adulthood as a child in Sweden? Why shouldn't a young Bihari woman have the same autonomy to choose her life pursuits as young white American male, or an Egyptian college graduate the same as a Canadian? Why shouldn't all Pakistani and Brazilian families have the same access as British or French to good sanitation, air conditioning and/or heating, washing machines, and holiday tickets? Why should many children have to work? Why shouldn't a black HIV positive person in Southern Africa have the same chance to survive as a white European? Why should a handful of individual 'oligarchs' be able to expropriate most of the natural resources of Russia, while a large part of the population has been pushed into pauperism? Why should big business executives be able to pay themselves hundreds of times more than the workers they are constantly pushing to 'work harder', more flexibly and at lower cost? In brief, there is inequality in this world because many are denied the chance to live their lives at all, to live a life of dignity, to try out their interests in life, and to make use of their existing potential. The inequalities of the world prevent hundreds of millions of people from developing their differences (Therbom 2006, 5).

Mwalimu sought to engage and tackle these kinds of questions, albeit within his own social context and domain, precisely where he had some leverage. His avowed goal was the creation of an egalitarian human society modelled on the African extended family. He was disturbed by the extreme inequalities that were emerging in Tanzanian Society, and that seemed to be a creation of the educational and economic systems inherited from the colonial regimes. These inequalities were contributing to dividing people along class lines, in separating people from one another, to favor some over others, to undermining mutual respect and humane relationships, and to destroying the values and infrastructure necessary for a fair and egalitarian society. Inequalities of every kind abound in every nation and continent, and they cause much despair and suffering. They undermine many of our cherished values and ideals. Communities are torn apart, polarized and destabilized.

To help us better understand the idea of inequality we draw from the work of Swedish academic and Cambridge don, Goram

Therborn's definition of inequality as "a historical social construction which allocates the possibilities of realizing human capacity unequally" (Alvarez 2016). For Therborn "Inequality is a violation of human dignity, it is a denial of the possibility for everybody's human capabilities to develop. It takes many forms, and it has many effects: premature death, ill-health, humiliation, subjection, discrimination, exclusion from knowledge or from mainstream social life, poverty, powerlessness, stress, insecurity, anxiety, lack of self-confidence and of pride in oneself, and exclusion from opportunities and life-chances. Inequality, then, is not just about the size of wallets. It is a socio-cultural order, which (for most of us) reduces our capabilities to function as human beings, our health, our self-respect, our sense of self, as well as our resources to act and participate in this world." Therborn distinguishes three kinds of inequality as follows: *vital inequality*, which refers to inequality of life and death, "measured through infant mortality, or life expectancy or health expectancy, the number of years you can expect to live without serious health problems"; *existential inequality*, which refers "to issues of dignity, humiliation, recognition, respect or ignorance, and marginalization. Important manifestations of existential inequality are racism, sexism, patriarchy." (Therborn 2006, 1) *Existential inequality* is "based on the unequal allocation of personhood, i.e. autonomy, dignity, degrees of freedom, rights to respect and self-development, etc." (Therborn 2006, 49). The third kind of inequality is *resource inequality*, which includes "one's parents, their wealth, their knowledge and their support" as well as income, wealth, and also includes inequalities of power, social contacts, etc. (Therborn 2006). Evidently inequality kills in many ways. "It starts already in the uterus, before the baby is born—a baby born to a poor mother, or an undernourished mother" (ibid.). And so does unemployment which for example "increases the risk of mortality and the link to social and economic stress which affects the hormones in your body, which in turn weakens your immune system and makes you more susceptible to all kinds of infections and diseases" (ibid.). So also do low status and stressful work. The title of Therborn's book *The Killing Fields of Inequality* highlights the ways in which inequality kills. It violates basic human rights. It leads to stunted lives—"primarily an indicator of undernourishment of children..." (Therborn 2013, 3). It excludes "people from possibilities produced by human development" (Therborn 2013, 21). It puts people asunder, it tears people and families apart, it creates exorbitant squandering, self-indulgent profligacy and other evils and horror stories. Life under inequality is "solitary, poor, nasty, brutish and short" (Hobbes 1968).

Nyerere was disturbed and horrified when he realized that he was becoming an architect of a government sponsored system of inequality! He was moved to do something about it. His Ujamaa system of African socialism offered a response and attempt to remedy this situation. He was of the view that the traditional African family structures and virtues familiar to him, such as those of his own ancestral Zanaki community, contained much of value and could provide a model for breaking the inequality curse. He desperately sought to do something about it. Questions of inequality have gained global dimensions. Figures indicating the widespread nature of inequality worldwide are shocking and worrying. The top one percent control and rule the world, and in almost every nation this top elite continues to amass increasingly more and more. The situation is becoming more and more intolerable and immoral. Nyerere from very early on in his political career could not tolerate this reality, both in his own nation and across the globe. He chose the path of resistance and struggle against this inhumanity and immorality.

THE 1966 STUDENT CRISIS AT UNIVERSITY OF DAR ES SALAAM AS A WATERSHED MOMENT FOR THE NYERERE ERA IN TANZANIA

Mwalimu Nyerere pinned his hopes on education and educational policy as contributing greatly to solving the problem of inequality. He defended an education policy that promoted self-reliance, equity and justice. He understood education to be an instrument of change and transformation, and one capable of bringing about a social order in line with the above principles. His handling of a student crisis at the University of Dar es Salaam in 1966 is eye opening. The students at this university then and now saw and still see education as a means to a better life, to higher position, status and power. These students saw education as providing a ladder to the upper echelons of privilege, prestige and a life of luxury. The students at this University bluntly rejected out of hand a new law by the government to implement a five-month compulsory scheme of para-military national community service for students followed by a two-year period, whereby the students would receive only 40% of their salaries tax free before joining the normal civil or non-civil work force. In October 1966 a group of four hundred students, mostly from the Dar es Salaam University College, marched to the State House in Dar es Salaam to protest against this new law, dressed in their academic gowns. They delivered the following ultimatum to President Nyerere whom they saw as the source of these new demands on the students as follows:

> Your excellency, unless the terms of reference and the attitude of our leaders towards students change, we shall not accept National Service in spirit. Let our bodies go, but our souls will remain outside the scheme and the battle between the political elite and the educated elite will perpetually continue (William Edgett Smith 1972, 27).

The students vehemently protested against the scheme with placards one of which proclaimed that "Life during Colonial Days was Better" (Edgett Smith 1972, 27).

> I've accepted your ultimatum. And I can assure you I'm going to force nobody. You are right. I take nobody into the National Service whose spirit is not in it. Nobody. Absolutely nobody. (hesitant applause) (Edgett Smith 1972, 29).

Nyerere's response to this Student challenge was decisive and reflected his principled and ideological choice for the way forward in Tanzania. He did not look back. Excerpts from his response are given here *in extenso* to help appreciate Nyerere's mood.

> It's not a prison you know. I'm not going to get anybody there who thinks it is a prison camp, no one! But nevertheless it will remain compulsory for everybody who is going to enter government service. So make your choice...
> You are right when you talk about salaries. Our salaries are too high. You want me to cut them? (some applause) ......Do you want me to start with my salary? Yes, I'll slash mine. (Cries of 'No'.) I'll slash the damned salaries in this country. Mine I slash by twenty per cent as from this hour.....
> Do you know what my salary is? Five thousand damned shillings a month. Five thousand damned shillings in a poor country. The poor man who gets two hundred shillings a month— do you know how long it's going to take him to earn my damned salary? Twenty five years! It's going to take the poor man in this country, who earns two hundred shillings a month, twenty-five years to earn what I earn in a year.

The damned salaries! These are the salaries which build this kind of attitude in the educated people, all of them. Me and you. We belong to a class of exploiters. I belong to your class. Where I think three hundred and eighty pounds a year (the minimum wage that would be paid in the National Service) is a prison camp, is forced labour. We belong to this damned exploiting class on top. Is this what the country fought for? Is this what we worked for? In order to maintain a class of exploiters on top?

.....Forced labour! Go, go in the classroom, go and don't teach. This we shall count as National Service for three hundred and eighty pounds a year. You are right, salaries are too high. Everybody in this country is demanding a pound of flesh. Everybody except the poor peasant. How can he demand it? He doesn't know the language. Even in his own language he can't speak of forced labour. What kind of country are we building?

"I have accepted what you said. And I am going to revise salaries permanently. And as for you, I am asking you to go home. I am asking all of you to go home (Edgett Smith 1972, 29-30).

The students were all expelled from the University. This incident no doubt influenced the new conditions and educational policies that followed, notably the radical and revolutionary Arusha Declaration. (Nyerere 1973, 31-250). Looking at this incident in the context of Kenya where parliamentarians have given themselves salaries and all manner of allowances that together makes them among the highest paid in the whole world. To imagine that this is the case in a country where the majority live in abject squalor beats all moral logic! Here leadership is synonymous with privilege. It has become in our African situation the very antithesis of selfless servanthood and service delivery to the populace responsible for placing them in such 'enviable' positions of grabbing and looting of common resources under their care for the common good.

EDUCATIONAL POLICY AND PLANNING AS CENTRAL TO ACHIEVING NYERERE'S AGENDA AND VISION

This incident undoubtedly throws light on Nyerere's radical rethinking regarding the nature of education in the public sphere (Nyerere 1973, 267-290). Nyerere was opposed to an educational system that creates and generates class and economic inequalities, a system designed for the creation of an elite that was "intellectually stronger than their fellows". He was of the view that the "most central thing about the education we are at the present providing is that it is basically an elitist education designed to meet the interests and needs of a very small proportion of those who enter the school system" (Nyerere 1968, 275). Such system, he argued, creates feelings of superiority among such a minority elite and generates feelings of inferiority among the majority (Nyerere 1968, 275-276). This goes against declared ethos and values consonant with an egalitarian society and a clear policy that would block the emergence of a class structure and consciousness in such a society. Nyerere believed that the inherited colonial system of education encouraged "school pupils in the idea that all knowledge which is worthwhile is acquired from books or 'educated people'—meaning those who have been through a formal education. The knowledge and wisdom of other old people is despised, and they themselves regarded as being ignorant and of no account..." (Nyerere 1968, 277). Local and cultural knowledge was despised. Traditional practices and knowledge were looked down upon and the foreign and colonial looked up to and upheld. This situation had to be changed and transformed. For Nyerere: "This is what our educational system has to encourage. It has to foster the social goals of living together, and working together, for the common good. It has to prepare our young people to play a dynamic and constructive part in the development of a society in which all members share fairly in the good or bad fortune of the group, and in which progress is measured in terms of human well-being, not prestige buildings, cars, or other such things, whether privately or publicly owned. Our education system must therefore inculcate a sense of commitment to the total community, and to help the pupils to accept the values appropriate to our kind of future, not those appropriate to our colonial past "(Nyerere 1968, 273). In others words Nyerere championed an education system that stood for and emphasized "cooperative endeavor, not individual advancement; it must stress concepts of equality and responsibility to give service which goes with any special ability... And in particular, our education must counteract the temptation to intellectual arrogance; for this leads to the well-educated despising those whose abilities are non-academic or who have no special abilities but are just human beings." (Nyerere 1966, 82).

Central to Nyerere's Utu and Ujamaa project was a transformative educational policy as outlined initially in the *Education for Self-Reliance* paper issued in March 1967.This paper consequently became a basic tool for forming attitudes, disseminating values and moulding character in Tanzania's educational institutions, both formal and non-formal. For Nyerere this was not empty talk. He had to model the ideas contained therein in his own life and practice. Perhaps it is here that the figure of Mwalimu Nyerere stands out in sharp contrast as the very anti-thesis of the majority of African leaders. These African leaders are well known for empty rhetoric on the one hand, self-aggrandizement and a rapacious greed and clinging onto power on the other hand. The failure of his Ujamaa/Utu project is often used as an argument to discredit Nyerere thinking, his policies and his praxis. Nonetheless the validity and dream of a world where everyone is equal and accepts and treats the other as brother or sister, and where all live in mutual respect and peace remains a common dream. Nyerere cannot be faulted for not trying to achieve this dream in the context of a harsh and cruel international environment. It is widely acknowledged that he practiced an exemplary principled, sacrificial and people-centred leadership. He honestly walked the talk and lived what he preached. Nyerere's state house (*Ikulu*) was a holy space and not a den of thieves. Even though endemic corruption and plunder of public resources by public officials was anathema, it still happened under his watch. On 17th May 1960, speaking on corruption at the very beginning of his reign he had this to say:

> Now sir, I think I would be less than honest if I said that all is well, because it is not. There is corruption. Now sir, I think corruption must be treated with ruthlessness because I believe myself corruption and bribery is a greater enemy to the welfare of a people in peacetime than war. I believe myself corruption in a country should be treated in almost the same way as you treat treason. If people cannot have confidence in their own government, if people can feel that justice can be bought, then what hope are you leaving with the people? The only thing they can do is to take up arms and remove that silly Government (Nyerere 1966, 82).

Subsequent Tanzanian governments as is the case with the majority of African governments, have been plagued with corruption and absolute disregard for their own self-respect, honor or for the basic demands for ethical rules and simple morality. The ruthless and murderous corruption cartels that now run amok on the continent are believed to be protected by the state and the local power mandarins. Very few such heinous governments have been removed or sent home by the citizenry due to corruption as Nyerere thought could happen. Interestingly during his own lifetime, despite this tough talk, the fight against corruption and for justice in Tanzania is believed to have cost the life of his Prime Minister, Edward Sokoine, a dedicated and indefatigable crusader against this horrific vice, whose death in a road accident was probably a planned assassination. The corruption-cartels are known to fight back rather viciously and without any respect for human life. The rise of the current President Magufuli was in large part a reaction against the intolerable and rampant runaway corruption.

THE PRIMACY OF UTU/UBUNTU IN NYERERE'S THOUGHT

Arguably, central to Nyerere's thinking and value system was his firm belief and robust support for the core values of Utu/Ubuntu and human equality. In a speech to the Governor of Tanganyika, Sir Richard Turnbull, Mwalimu Nyerere justified the demand for responsible self- government for Tanganyika as follows:

> Our position is based on the belief in the equality of human beings, in their rights and their duties as human beings, and in the equality of citizens, in their rights and duties as citizens ... We in Tanganyika believe, sir, that only a wicked man can make colour the criterion for human rights. Here we intend to build a country in which the colour of a person's skin or the texture of his hair will be as irrelevant to his rights and his duties as a citizen as it is irrelevant to his value in the eyes of God (Nyerere 1966, 76).

As a firm believer in Ujamaa and as a proponent of the socialist values of human equality and liberation, Nyerere defended his core value, the centrality of humanity as follows: "First and most central of all... Man is the purpose of all social activity. The service of man, the furtherance of human development, is in fact the purpose of society itself. There is no other purpose above this, no glorification of 'nation', no increase in production—nothing is more central to a socialist society than an acceptance that Man is its justification for existence" (Nyerere 1966, 4). Here Nyerere did not have in mind, man or woman in isolation but in community. Rooted and strongly influenced by his African traditional roots and his Ujamaa philosophy, Nyerere naturally has a communitarian view of humanity that is central to Utu/Ubuntu thinking. This has been well captured by Bishop Tutu who cites the African expression *"Umntu ngumtu ngabantu"* roughly translated as "A person is a person through other persons." In further explication of this, Bishop Tutu has written,

> For us the solitary human being is a contradiction in terms. *Ubuntu* is the essence of being human. It speaks of how my humanity is caught up and bound up inextricably with yours... The completely self-sufficient human being is sub-human...We are made for complementarity. We are created for a delicate network of relationships, of interdependence with our fellow human beings, with the rest of creation... *Ubuntu* speaks of spiritual attributes such as generosity, hospitality, compassion, caring, sharing. You could be affluent in material possessions but still be without *Ubuntu*. This concept speaks of how people are more important than things, than profits, than material possessions. It speaks about the intrinsic worth of persons as not dependent on extraneous things such as status, race, creed, gender, or achievement. In traditional African society, *Ubuntu* was coveted more than anything else... (Tutu 2011, 21-24).

The idea of Ubuntu accurately captures Nyerere's commitment to communitarian thinking explicated in terms of his Ujamaa ideology. Ubuntu is however the equivalent of the Swahili term Utu (See Mojola forthcoming, 1976 and 1994).

UJAMAA AND VILLAGIZATION AS THE CONTEXT FOR RESTORING UTU/UBUNTU

African traditional societies have always been grounded on the idea of the extended family and communitarian thinking. This was the basis of Nyerere's Ujamaa philosophy. The tendency was however, traditionally and in some present day African societies, to understand this in ethnocentric terms, a practice that has its negative ramifications in the ugly practice of so-called tribalism or negative ethnicity. A number of African nations have been ruined by the ethnic hegemony and marginalization of non-members on the basis of ethnocentric criteria. Nyerere's Ujamaa ideology sought to extend communitarian thinking beyond the circle of ethnic group ie the so-called tribe, to the wider and more inclusive circle of all humanity. Nyerere strongly promoted the idea of the brotherhood and sisterhood of all humans. All humans are in this way members of the same family. All humans are expected to treat one another as equals and with mutual respect. The idea is for all humans to see each other as members of the same family, or rather "as members of the ever-extending family ...*Binadamu wote ni ndugu zangu, na Afrika ni moja*" (translation—*All humans are my brothers and sisters and Africa is one*). (Nyerere 1966, 170). Nyerere writes:

> '*Ujamaa*', ...or 'familyhood', describes our socialism. It is opposed to capitalism, which seeks to build a happy society on the basis of the exploitation of man by man; and it is equally opposed to doctrinaire socialism which seeks to build its happy society on the philosophy of inevitable conflict between man and man...Modern African socialism can draw from its traditional heritage the recognition of 'society' as an extension of the basic family unit. But it can no longer confine the idea of the social family within the limits of the tribe, nor indeed of the nation... Our recognition of the family to which we all belong must be extended yet further—beyond the tribe, the community, the nation, or even the continent—to embrace the whole society of mankind (Nyerere 1966, 170-171).

The brotherhood and sisterhood of all humans is predicated on the principle of the equality of all humans, men and women, black and white, black and yellow, black and black, etc. Nyerere was committed to this as a matter of faith. He held that it could not be proved empirically or by scientific means. He argued that belief in human equality, the acceptance and support of this core and essential tenet is "a basic assumption of life in society" (Nyerere 1966, 170)

According to Nyerere the purpose of society is to serve humanity and this without discrimination, segregation, prejudice, or unequal justice. He writes: "The service of man, the furtherance of his human development, is in fact the purpose of society itself...The word 'man' ... means all men—all human beings. Male and female; black, white, brown, yellow; long-nosed and short-nosed; educated and uneducated; wise and stupid; strong and weak; all these, and all other distinctions between human beings, are irrelevant to the fact that all are members of the society—all the human beings who are its purpose—are equal" (Nyerere 1968, 4).

ARUSHA DECLARATION AS A LOGICAL CONSEQUENCE OF NYERERE'S MORAL VISION, ITS STRENGTH AND CHALLENGES

The Arusha Declaration has been understood as central to understanding Nyerere's agenda and programme. As interpreted by Nyerere, the Arusha Declaration,

>...is based on the assumption of human equality, on the belief that it is wrong for one man to dominate or to exploit another, and on the knowledge that every individual hopes to live in society as a free man able to lead a decent life in conditions of peace with his neighbours. The document is, in other words, Man-centred...It is a commitment to the belief that there are more important things in life than the amassing of riches, and that if the pursuit of wealth clashes with things like human dignity and social equality, then the latter will be given priority (Nyerere 1968, 316).

Or as he states elsewhere: "For the Declaration is about the way we shall make a reality of human equality in this country, and how our citizens will achieve full control over their own affairs" (Nyerere 1973, 179). The execution and implementation of the Arusha Declaration encountered many challenges and much resistance from many Tanzanians. It was controversially and forcefully enforced. This resulted in many hardships and involved the persecution of those who opposed it or did not agree with its agenda. As it turned out the devil was in the detail. It turned out to be Nyerere's Achilles' heel. This Declaration was nonetheless logically consistent with Nyerere's core beliefs regarding equality, justice, human brotherhood and sisterhood, the Utu/Ubuntu ideals, etc. The implementation process as indicated above encountered not just local and national resistance from capitalist and anti-socialist forces, but also from global and international capitalist reprisals and intrigues. It encountered enormous obstacles and holdbacks. The economic future and success of the Arusha Declaration and its ideals was doomed.

The Arusha Declaration provided a formal mandate for Nyerere's execution and implementation of his avowed Ujamaa policy of villagization and communal living, designed and intended for the common good and for ensuring the dignity and development for all villagers. The Ujamaa villagization project like the Arusha Declaration itself faced humongous encumbrances and hurdles. Nyerere defined an Ujamaa village as "a voluntary association of people who decide of their own free will to live together and work together for their common good. … A group of people must decide to start an Ujamaa village because they have understood that only through this method can they live and develop in dignity and freedom, receiving the full benefits of their co-operative endeavor…" (Nyerere 1973, 67-68). As is well known the practice and reality were different from the theory. The project was not voluntary and the choice to start or belong to an Ujamaa village was not always based on free will. It was not smooth. Its implementation turned out to be complex. Hence forcing people to move to these villages met much resistance and challenges. Indeed some over-zealous civil servants were brutally murdered in the course of duty. The case of a certain Dr Wilbert Klerruu, a doctrinaire communist and overzealous regional commissioner, murdered on Christmas day while on duty in Iringa in the Southern Highlands of Tanzania is much talked about.[3]

"THE PURPOSE OF DEVELOPMENT IS MAN…"

Nyerere's discourse on development was justified in terms of the development of humans. He held that "The purpose of development is man." insisting that "development means the development of people. Roads, buildings, the increases of crop output, and other things of this nature, are not development, they are only tools of development…Development, brings freedom, provided it is development of *people*. But people cannot be developed; they can only develop themselves. For while it is possible for an outsider to build a man's house, an outsider cannot give the man pride and self-confidence in himself as a human being." (Nyerere 1973, 59-60). Modern economics and discourse on political economy is justified in terms of development. Development has become the catchall phrase, the metanarrative for describing the state of humanity and the nations of their domicile as well as the level of their material culture. It is used to distinguish nations, between the so-called developed and less developed, the overdeveloped and underdeveloped. Increasingly the development in question is less about the quality of human life and more about material and industrial development. Questions of

---

3 See Andrew Coulson, *Tanzania: A Political Economy*, 1982, 2013:294. See also Ralph Ibbott, *Ujamaa: The hidden story of Tanzania's socialist villages*, 2014 and also Leander Schneider, *Government of Development: Peasants and Politicians in Postcolonial Tanzania*, 2014.

justice and fairness, of mutual respect, of mutual love and compassion, of levels and types of inequality, of issues of oppression, exploitative practices and man's inhumanity to man, among others are rarely highlighted or focused upon in the development discourses. Nyerere's Tanzania was not favorably rated in terms of its human development index. Characterized by poverty, low household incomes and empowerment, lack or poor access to basic resources such as health facilities, clean water, basic food and nutrition or decent shelter, Nyerere's policies failed to make a dent in alleviating these major social economic challenges. Everyone however agrees that Nyerere left behind a stronger more united nation. Tanzanians as a people are more united than their neighbours. Nyerere succeeded in slaying the ogre of tribalism, which is the bane of countries such as Kenya or Rwanda. It was the root cause of genocide in Rwanda. Tribalism causes a sundering of peoples, denying them an equal share in their common resources and goods. It leads to exclusion and preferential treatment of people on the basis of their ethnicity. His Ujamaa ideology created a community where Tanzanians saw their co-citizens as brothers, sisters, uncles, aunts, grandparents, sons and daughters. Local and regional ethnicity was overtaken by Tanzanian nationhood. Nyerere's pan-Africanist agenda made Tanzania the hub and epicenter of the struggle against apartheid and the liberation of the peoples of Southern Africa. Tanzania made huge sacrifices for this cause. However Nyerere's humanist and Utu/Ubuntu perspective encompassed all of humanity.

In our view Nyerere will be remembered for the values he stood for and for his indefatigable efforts to defend and promote these values, especially in the interests of the weak, the marginalized, the poor, the oppressed, the excluded, the suffering. There are however those like the British psychiatrist Anthony Daniels who worked as a village doctor in Tanzania between 1984-86, who thought of Nyerere that "Despite a poor education... was cultured enough to translate Shakespeare's Julius Caesar and the Merchant of Venice into Swahili". Daniels describes Nyerere not as teacher but "certainly a Professor of Poverty"[4] Of the same feather is the colonial Governor

---

4   Anthony Daniels, "Nyerere the leader who achieved by cunning what Idi Amin achieved by force", Daily Mail, 15 October 1999 quoted by James R. Brennan, "Julius Rex: Nyerere through the Eyes of His Critics", 1953-2013 in Marie Aude Fouere, 144.

Edward Twining (1949-58) from whose perspective "Julius Nyerere, who took a pass degree in history after four years in Edinburgh, considers himself to be a sort of prophet and sees himself a second Nkrumah. He has no business head but undoubtedly has the gift of the gab and a quick brain". Those who see Nyerere from this narrow minded perspective are numerous, not including a host of others whose memory of Nyerere is worse. Our own memory of Julius Kambarage Nyerere is best captured in the words of Trevor Huddleston, who understands Nyerere as possessing:

> The quality of a great human being who has treasured his humanness (his humanity if you like) more deeply than his office; who has always preferred approachableness to protocol, and who in leading his country through the first most testing years of its life as a sovereign independent state has set an example san peur et sans reproche which few others can rival and none surpass. For it is an example not only of humanity, but of humility. And that quality, in politics and statesmanship today, is rare indeed; as rare as truthfulness itself and as desperately needed in this turbulent world (Fouere 2015, 1).

BIBLIOGRAPHY

Alvarez, Maria Jose. 2016. *An Interview with Goram Therborn.* DO1:http:/dx.doi.org/10.7440/res57.2016.10.

Bjerk, Paul. 2015. *Building a Peaceful Nation: Julius Nyerere and the Establishment of Sovereignty in Tanzania, 1960 – 1964.* Rochester, New York: University of Rochester Press.

Chabal, Patrick. 2009. *Africa: The politics of Suffering and Smiling.* London: Zed Books.

Cohen, Herman J. 2015. *The Mind of the African Strongman: Conversations with Dictators, Statesmen and Father Figures.* Washington, DC: New Academia Publishing.

Coulson, Andrew. 2013. *Tanzania: A Political Economy.* Oxford University Press, 1982.

Fisman, Raymond and Edward Miguel. 2008. *Economic Gangsters: Corruption, Violence and the Poverty of Nation.* Princeton: Princeton University Press.

Fouere, Marie Aude, ed. 2015. *Remembering Nyerere in Tanzania: History Memory Legacy.* Dar es Salaam: Mkuki wa Nyota Publishers.

Freire, Paulo. 1973. *Education for Critical Consciousness*. New York: Seabury Press.

Freire, Paulo. 1970. *Pedagogy of the Oppressed*, New York: Seabury Press.

Hobbes, Thomas.1968 [1660]. *Leviathan*. Baltimore: Penguin Books.

Hyden, Goran. 1980. *Beyond Ujamaa in Tanzania: Underdevelopment and an Uncaptured Peasantry*. London: Heinemann.

Jerven, Morten. 2015. *Africa – Why Economists Get It Wrong*. London: Zed Books.

Katare, E.R. 2007. *Julius Kambarage Nyerere: Falsafa zake na Dhana ya Utakatifu*. Dar es Salaam.

Legum, Colin and Geoffrey Mmari. 1995. *Mwalimu: The influence of Nyerere*. Dar es Salaam: Mkuki na Nyota/James Currey/Africa World Press.

Lema, Elieshi; Marjorie Mbilinyi and Rakesh Rajani, eds. 2004. *Nyerere on Education, Nyerere Kuhusu Elimu: Selected Essays and Speeches 1954 – 1998*. Dar es Salaam, Tanzania: The Mwalimu Nyerere Foundation.

Listowel, Judith. 1965. *The Making of Tanganyika*. Zanzibar: Gallery Publications.

Malik, Kenan. 2014. *The Quest for a Moral Compass: A Global History of Ethics*. Brooklyn, London: Melville House.

Milanovic, Blanko. 2016. *Global Inequality: A New Approach for the Age of Globalization*. Harvard, Cambridge, Mass.: Belknap Press, Harvard University Press.

Molony, Thomas. 2014. *Nyerere: The Early Years*. Rochester, New York: James Currey.

Msekwa, Pius. 2012. *Uongozi wa Mwalimu Julius Kambarage Nyerere*. Dar es Salaam, Tanzania: Nyambari Nyangwine Publishers.

Msekwa, Pius. 2013. *A Concise Political History of Tanzania – 50 Years of Independence*. Dar es Salaam: Nyambari Nyangwine Publishers.

Mojola, Aloo Osotsi. 1976. "Nyerere's Social and Political Philosophy". *Thought and Practice*, 3 (2): 1-12.

Mojola, Aloo Osotsi. 1994. "A Question of Values and Basic Assumptions: The Present African Socio-economic Crisis and the search for Development and Justice". In *A Just Africa – Ethics and the Economy*, edited by Viggo Mortensen, 121-132. Geneva: Lutheran World Federation.

Mojola, Aloo Osotsi. 2014. "The African Bantu concept of Ubuntu in the Christian theology and praxis of Bishop Desmond Tutu of South Africa and its implications for global justice and human rights." a paper originally presented at a Research Seminar at University of Pretoria in 2014.

Mortensen, Viggo, ed. 1994. *A Just Africa: Ethics and the Economy.* Geneva: Lutheran World Federation.

Muzio, Tim Di. 2015. *The 1% and the Rest of Us: A Political Economy of Dominant Ownership.* London: Zed Books.

Nyerere, Julius K. 1966. *Freedom and Unity, Uhuru na Umoja: A selection from Writings and Speeches 1952-1963.* Dar es Salaam: OUP.

Nyerere, Julius, K. 1968. *Freedon and Socialism, Uhuru na Ujamaa: A Selection from Writings and Speeches, 1965-1967.* Dar es Salaam: OUP.

Nyerere, Julius K. 1973. *Freedom and Development, Uhuru na Maendeleo: A Selection from Writings and Speeches, 1968-1973.* Dar es Salaam: OUP.

Nyerere, Julius K. 1994. "Ethics and the Economy". In *A Just Africa: Ethics and the Economy* edited by Viggo Mortensen. Geneva: Lutheran World Federation.

Nyerere, Julius K. n.d. *Africa Today and Tomorrow.* Dar es Salaam: The Mwalimu Nyerere Foundation.

Nyerere, Julius K. 1995. *Our Leadership and the Destiny of Tanzania.* Harare, Zimbabwe: Africa Publishing Group.

Nyerere, Julius K. 2011. *Freedom and Liberation: A selection of Speeches, 1974-1999.* Dar es Salaam: Oxford University Press.

Nyerere, Julius K. 2011. *Freedom, Non-Alignment and South South Cooperation, A selection of Speeches 1974-1999.* Dar es Salaam: Oxford University Press.

Piketty, Thomas. 2016. *Chronicles of our Troubled Times.* London: Penguin Books.

Piketty, Thomas. 2015. *The Economics of Inequality.* Cambridge, Mass: Belknap Press, Harvard University Press.

Piketty, Thomas. 2014. *Capital in the Twenty First Century.* Cambridge, Mass: Belknap Press, Harvard University Press.

Savage, Mike. 2015. *Social Class in the 21st Century.* London: Penguin Random House.

Schneider, Leander. 2014. *Government of Development: Peasants and Politicians in Postcolonial Tanzania.* Bloomington and Indianapolis: Indiana University Press.

Smith, William Edgett. 1971. *Mwalimu Julius K. Nyerere.* Translated by Paul Sozigwa. Nairobi: Transafrica.

Stiglitz, Joseph. 2015. *The Great Divide*. London: Penguin Random House.

Smith, William Edgett. 1972. *Nyerere of Tanzania: The First Decade 1961-1971*. Harare, Zimbabwe: African Publishing Group.

Therborn, Goram. 2013. *The Killing Fields of Inequality*. London: Polity Press.

Therborn, Goram. 2006. *Inequalities of the World: New Theoretical Frameworks, Multiple Empirical Approaches*. London: Verso.

Tutu, Desmond. 2013. *God is not a Christian: Speaking truth in times of crisis*. London: Rider/Random House.

CHAPTER 6. THE ROLE OF SOUTH AFRICAN CHURCHES IN THE REVITALISATION OF UBUNTU VALUES IN SOCIETY

John L.B. Eliastam and Wonke Buqa

INTRODUCTION

We attempt to answer the question whether Ubuntu is latently present in the theology and spirituality of African churches, and if so does this offer a resource to strengthen *ubuntu* in society? According to the Statistics SA 2016 Community Survey (STATSSA 2016), just over 78 percent of South Africa's population self-identifies as Christian. If this is the case, then the latent presence of Ubuntu in Christian spirituality and theology could be a significant resource for shaping social values. Hutchison (2012, 116) describes a number of reasons why religious institutions are ideally placed to mobilise social action and social change. Firstly, they are able to influence the political sphere at various levels. There are formal and informal structures within these organisations that can be used. They are a source of leadership, both from clergy and lay leaders. Finally, they play a role in shaping shared understandings of the situation and new shared meanings, thereby raising consciousness and motivating collective action. This suggests that African churches might be able to reinvigorate Ubuntu values in society.

The relationship between Christianity and traditional African values is not a new one. Christianity came to Africa enmeshed in western philosophy and values, as well as capitalism. This "incarnation" of Christianity is therefore already responsible, at least in some part, for an erosion of Ubuntu. Also, the proposal that Christianity might offer resources for the reinvigoration of Ubuntu in society presupposes an absence of its performance in broader society, and equally a performance of Ubuntu-like intersubjectivity within Christian lived religion.

THE PRESENCE AND ABSENCE OF UBUNTU

Ubuntu articulates the world-view that is reflected in the Zulu proverb *"umuntu ngumuntu ngabanye abantu"* (a person is a person through other persons). A person's humanity is realised and expressed within and through their relationships with other people.

Cornell and Van Marle argue that Ubuntu transcends major distinctions in Western philosophy because it is at the same time ontology, an epistemology, and an ethical value system. They write:

> *Ubuntu* is a philosophy on how human beings are intertwined in a world of ethical relations from the moment they are born. Fundamentally, this inscription is part of our finitude. We are born into a language, a kinship group, a tribe, a nation, and a family. We come into a world obligated to others, and those others are obligated to us. We are mutually obligated to support each other on our respective paths to becoming unique and singular persons (Cornell and Van Marle 2015, 2).

Ubuntu has been translated in a variety of ways: as "humanity" (Shutte 1993); "African humanness" (Broodryk 2002, 13); "humanism or humaneness" (Mnyaka & Motlhabi 2009, 63); or "the process of becoming an ethical human being" (Mkhize 2008, 35). Mkhize (2008, 43) further proposes that Ubuntu "incorporates ideas of social justice, righteousness, care, empathy for others and respect". Mnyaka and Motlhabi (2009, 74) write that Ubuntu, "is best realised in deeds of kindness, compassion, caring, sharing, solidarity and sacrifice".

For Tutu (1999, 34-35) the importance of Ubuntu is that, "'a person is a person through other people'. It is not 'I think therefore I am'. It says rather: 'I am human because I belong'. I participate, I share". The notion of Ubuntu points to the interconnectedness of human beings, with the implication that people should treat each other as though we are all members of an extended family (Gish 2004, 122).

Ackermann captures the implications of Ubuntu in the following statement,

> In this boundless human web I acquire my humanity as something which comes to me as a gift...shaped and nurtured in and through the humanity of others. I can only exercise my humanity by being in relationship with others and there is no growth, happiness or fulfillment for me apart from other human beings (Ackermann 1998, 19).

The erosion of Ubuntu in South African society has also been documented (see Cornell and van Marle 2005; Eliastam 2015; Enslin and Horsthemke 2004; Matolino and Kwindingwi 2013). Munyaka and Mothlabi (2009, 79) highlight the role of colonisation, apartheid and urbanisation in the erosion of Ubuntu: "African culture has been threatened, challenged, misused, and almost destroyed". The relevance of Ubuntu has been questioned in a society shaped by modernity, globalisation and urbanisation. Individualism, materialism and consumerism have had a corrosive effect on traditional cultural values, particularly among the youth. Cilliers (2010) surveys social realities in South Africa and argues that the country is experiencing a movement away from Ubuntu, where people are increasingly being treated like things. Biko (2013, 7) writes on the decline of ubuntu in South Africa, with an accompanying ethical collapse, and suggests that: "The increasingly common xenophobia attacks, the almost monthly service delivery strikes, the growing numbers of so-called wildcat strikes in the mining industry, the millions of instances of crime committed against all citizens, and the rampant corruption which prevents many government departments from successfully executing their mandates are leading indicators of societal decay".

PRACTICAL THEOLOGY AND LIVED RELIGION

What hope does Christian theology and spirituality offer for the revitalisation of Ubuntu? As practical theologians we try to understand how people live out their faith within their social contexts. We endeavour to describe and then critically reflect on praxis, with the goal of transforming praxis. Ganzevoort (2009, 1) has suggested that practical theology can be described as the "hermeneutics of lived religion". Where other theological disciplines focus on the texts that constitute religious traditions, or on the concepts and ideas that define the parameters of a religion, practical theology explores "the transcending patterns of action and meaning embedded in and contributing to the relation with the sacred" (Ganzevoort 2009, 3).

The notion of lived religion within practical theology (Streib 2008; Ganzevoort and Roeland 2014) refers to the religious practices of ordinary people in everyday life, thus moving beyond the sphere of institutionalised religious traditions. It is interested in the way people experience life and find meaning as individuals or groups, and in the religious practices within particular contexts and cultural settings. It is similar to what Ammerman (2007, 5) describes as "everyday religion", which elevates the experiences and perspectives of those who are not religious experts—even when these fall outside of the boundaries of organised religion. This emphasis on practical theology as lived religion results in a research focus that is broader than official church doctrines and laws. *Lived* religion may be contrasted, or even in tension with *learned* religion.

In a similar vein to this distinction between lived religion and learned religion, Michael Eze (2017b) makes a distinction between essentialist and performative notions of Ubuntu. Essentialist Ubuntu, like learned religion, looks to past traditions and dictates what should or must be in order to retain a pure version of Ubuntu—based on the way that the past is imagined. Performative Ubuntu is dynamic and involves confluence and dialogue with other cultures and discourses. It is Ubuntu as lived experience or way of life. Performative Ubuntu looks to the past to make sense of the present and shape the future. He argues that it is problematic, and potentially oppressive to try to find some ideal essence of Ubuntu. Instead he calls for a re-imagination of Ubuntu in a context of dialogue with other discourses.

Our question is whether such a re-imagination could take place in dialogue with Christian discourse.

LOOKING FOR UBUNTU IN AFRICAN CHURCHES

RESEARCH PROCESS

We conducted empirical *research* in which we asked people about the presence of Ubuntu in the theology and spirituality of African churches, and how this could be reinvigorated to strengthen Ubuntu in society. Twenty people were interviewed, including clergy, student ministers and lay people from both rural and urban contexts in the Eastern Cape Province and Gauteng. A combination of purposive sampling and snowball sampling was used, where leaders and lay people in a variety of African churches were approached, and then asked to suggest other participants.

Participants came from mainline churches, charismatic churches and African traditional churches, so their responses reflect diversity—and even fragmentation—rather than a unified voice that represents Christianity in South Africa. Semi-structured interviews were conducted in which participants were asked about their understanding of Ubuntu, their understanding of the relationship between Ubuntu and spirituality, and whether they saw signs of Ubuntu in the theology or spirituality of their churches that could be harnessed to strengthen Ubuntu in society.

When recording statements made by participants we have used pseudonyms to protect their identity, but also to preserve a sense of personhood for each of them.

DISCURSIVE THEMES THAT REFLECT UBUNTU

Within the multiple discourses that exist within and together constitute South African Christianity there are a number of discursive themes that have connotations of Ubuntu. These discourses draw on the Bible to give legitimacy to their normative role within Christianity.

The Imago Dei

Perhaps the most well-known discursive theme that is associated with Ubuntu is the theological notion that human beings are created in the image of God. This can be attributed to the work of Desmond Tutu, who developed a notion of Ubuntu that was "a theological concept in which human beings are called to be persons because we are made in the image of God" (Battle 1997, 64). In a preface to the reprint of

Biko's *I Write What I Like*, Tutu describes how, in line with this, the Black Consciousness movement "…sought to awaken in us the sense of our infinite value and worth in the sight of God because we were all created in God's image, so that our worth is intrinsic to who we are and not dependent on biological irrelevancies such as ethnicity, skin colour or race" (in Biko 2002, ix). Nolte-Schamm (2006, 377) points out that Ubuntu is now linked to the theological doctrine of imago Dei by many theologians. Many of the participants spoke of this notion as a theological foundation for Ubuntu. They affirmed that to be human is to be made in the image of God.

The doctrine of the Trinity
Three of the participants spoke of the doctrine of the Trinity as an expression of Ubuntu. Thami, a theology student, expressed this succinctly: The ontological nature of God as the trinity demonstrates Ubuntu. God dwells in harmonious relationship, you are in me, and I am in you and you are with me. You complete me, and you need me to complete you. God the Father, the Son and the Holy Spirit are interconnectedness that symbolises Ubuntu. God is family and that is symbolised by the doctrine of Trinity which teaches that people should embrace Ubuntu and live as families.

If the nature of God expresses such harmonious mutual love and interdependence, those that profess to follow God should reflect similar qualities in their relationships.

Specific laws in the Old Testament
There are a number of laws in the Old Testament that show an affinity to an Ubuntu world view. Siseko referred to passages like Deuteronomy 15, where debts were to be cancelled and slaves set free every seven years, and prescriptions in the law to not harvest the edges of fields so that the poor could glean from them. For Siseko, the year of jubilee, described in Leviticus chapter 25, epitomises Ubuntu. Every forty nine years the land would revert to its original owner, debts would be cancelled and slaves set free.

Siseko: We see Ubuntu practices and Ubuntu theology all over the Bible, but no one encourages us that such things are for us today. Even Jesus tells us that he is coming to fulfil the year of jubilee, but when we read that now we spiritualise it. We ignore the social and economic side.

The Body of Christ

The New Testament is replete with descriptions of the church as Christ's body. This metaphor invokes unity, especially unity in diversity. Aviwe stressed that this starts with accepting one another: If we are one body I can't reject you because you are different to me. We should not be scared of diversity whether in ethnicity, nationality or politics. We must all accept each other and in this way we show the world the power of God to change human hearts.

Mary explained: what it means for the church to be Christ's body includes the instructions to care for each other, to honour and respect each other, to respect differences. We are one body; we cannot say that we don't need each other.

The early church in the New Testament

The communalism of the early church described in the second chapter of the book of Acts is another discursive theme that reflects Ubuntu.

Michael: You just have to look at the early church in Acts to see Ubuntu. People sharing life in a genuine way, sharing their possessions, selling properties so that the poor in the church did not lack anything. I don't think you could see a better example of Ubuntu.

Mary describes her experience of similar practices: In the olden days people would bring sheep, vegetables, and cattle in the Church as part of support of the Church and *uMfundisi*. So in our days we can no longer operate in that way, there is money involved which also crippled Ubuntu values. *Isivuno* (harvest) project in the Church is based on Ubuntu, in that you share what you have with others.

The Bible encourages the same kind of connectedness that Ubuntu inspires. Setiloane (2000, 25) points out that both Ubuntu and the Christian way of life stress the importance of relationships between people and the way they live life together.

Loving one's neighbour

For many of those we spoke to the "Great Commandment" to love one's neighbour was one of the clearest expressions of Ubuntu in the Bible.

Mary: It's a simple thing. To love your neighbour. Jesus shows us by means of the good Samaritan that the neighbour is not our friend or family. It is that human being you find yourself next to.

Ackermann (1998, 20) points out that Jesus taught that our neighbour is the "radically other who is also the radically related". This neighbour has an irrefutable claim on us that requires us to love them as Christ loved the church. The love of God and the love of neighbour cannot be separated.

Care for the poor and marginalised

Care for the poor and concern for the vulnerable and marginalised are reflected in the teaching of Jesus and in the notion of Ubuntu. Setiloane (2000, 22) argues that the language of Ubuntu and the language of the Bible have a lot in common. He highlights care for the widow, orphan and the poor, and the biblical emphasis on the value of hospitality.

Most of the people we interviewed spoke of church programmes to care for the poor and vulnerable as a reflection of this. The church should stand in solidarity with the poor and the marginalised. However, Daniel made an interesting observation: It's almost like people have outsourced their responsibility to do this to a small group within the church that does the actual work. If they are paying some money, and they know that it funds such work, then they avoid the feeling of guilt that would be there if they do nothing.

The practice of mutual forgiveness

For many participants the many injunctions in the Bible to freely forgive those that wrong us reflect an Ubuntu mind set.

Mary: Christ is a good example based on the Biblical narrative of the women caught in act of adultery. That story is a good example of Ubuntu. Ubuntu says forgive as you have been forgiven, it should not be a repetition. Ubuntu is being killed by these people…saying forgiven… Jesus Christ is love and that love is based on forgiveness.

Acceptance

Participants spoke of biblical injunctions to accept people, to extend grace to them, and not to judge them.

Andile: Someone who demonstrates the qualities of Ubuntu is inclusive and does not categorise people. In certain instances some people may accommodate someone who is not loved by others. And you shall hear other people saying you know so and so has so much of Ubuntu.

142

As much as Andile's statement describes Ubuntu within his experience of Christian community, it also describes its absence. It is only present in "certain instances" and with "some people".

Andile: Our Churches at times are losing Ubuntu, they have a tendency to perpetuate violence, which is also against spiritual values. The Church has some prejudices against other people which I think she is not suppose to do so.... There are things church members calling them African and others non-African. For example, homosexuals, our Churches treat them as if they are second class citizens. By doing so, our churches deviate from Ubuntu practice.

DO CHURCHES OFFER HOPE FOR UBUNTU?

The discursive themes mentioned here do not represent an exhaustive list, but they reflect areas of congruence with Ubuntu described by the leaders and lay members of African churches with whom we spoke. There is no doubt that within Christianity there are theological and spiritual resources that resonate deeply with Ubuntu. The question we have to ask is whether these resources possess the vitality required to shape social values? Do they reflect an idealised, essentialised Christianity that is imagined, or are they evident in the performance of Christian spirituality? And, if so is it by a sufficient number of people to create momentum towards stronger Ubuntu values in society.

The harnessing of these resources to reinvigorate Ubuntu would require them to be expressions of actual lived religion rather than essentialist notions of what a Christian should believe and do. There are certainly individuals and faith communities where Ubuntu-like spirituality is present, but these stand against a number of other forces that seem to be pulling Christianity into a trajectory of un-Ubuntu. We will argue that the same social forces that have resulted in the erosion of Ubuntu have also significantly deprived Christian lived religion of its Ubuntu-like qualities. The ability of these discursive themes to reinvigorate Ubuntu has been diminished by the same social forces that have eroded the power of Ubuntu as a social value. Those we interviewed described this in various ways and we have tried to summarise the themes.

MODERNITY

The term modernity is used to describe and refer to the period that began with the so-called Age of Reason, the Enlightenment. It was a period in Europe that was characterised by the quest for epistemological certainty, the ascent of science, and the rise of capitalism. It gave rise to a largely secular culture, liberal democracy, individualism and rationalism among other things (Cahoone 1996). Nearly all of the participants spoke of the fact that the world has changed. Traditional social and religious values have been displaced. Science has challenged traditional notions of how the world works. Mungwini (2011, 774) argues that modernity has brought a new social ontology to Africa, with different values and new ways of thinking about the individual and the community. This alien philosophy of life obstructs the postcolonial yearning for traditional African values to become normative in society.

INDIVIDUALISM

While the Enlightenment placed the autonomous individual subject at the centre, thus contributing to the construction atomistic notions of society, much of the way in which the term individualism is used is derived from the work of Hofstede (1980). Hofstede defined *individualism* as an emphasis on personal autonomy and self-fulfillment, a concern for oneself and one's immediate family rather than the broader community, and personal accomplishment as the basis for one's identity. This in turn results in a focus on personal rights rather than civic duties. With individualism there is a focus on the individual as the basic unit of analysis. Oyserman, Coon and Kemmelemeir argue that Protestant Christianity and civic emancipation have contributed to the ubiquitous status of individualism in Western societies, resulting in a focus on individual choice, personal freedom (and self-actualization (Oyserman et al 2002). Ingelhart and Oyserman (2004) point out that economic development results in a shift away from collectivism towards individualism. For some scholars, individualism is so pervasive and so characteristic of modern society that they describe it as "individualised society" (Bauman 2001).

This shift towards individualism has accompanied both Protestantism and economic development in Africa, resulting in a greater focus on individual freedom and a diminished regard for social hierarchies and obligations. Praeg (2008, 378) notes the conflict between Western individualist and African communalist ontology that is evoked by Ubuntu. The individualism that accompanies capitalism and liberal democracy is diametrically opposed to the African communal understanding of anthropology, as well as to a Christian communal understanding of humanity (Vellem 2007, 176). Teboho reflects on this: The world has changed so much and that has affected the way we practice both Christianity and Ubuntu. It's a fast paced world of technology and social media, but these prevent real community. There is so much stress and pressure, and to deal with that I think everyone just looks after themselves. We want to know what's in it for me before we do something.

MATERIALISM AND PROSPERITY RELIGION

The proliferation of charismatic churches in Africa has contributed to the rise of a "prosperity gospel" that promises the faithful health, success, and material wealth (Jenkins 2006; Gifford 1998). In a context of economic hardship in Africa, churches hold out the offer of not only salvation but also success and affluence (Meyer 1998, 759).

This kind of theology often reflects belief in a system of cause and effect where both blessing and adversity are deserved by those who experience them. A telling remark was made by the affluent pastor of a poor church in a poor community in the Eastern Cape, he said, "Everything that I have is a result of God blessing my faithfulness. If God is not blessing others, they need to understand why and make their lives right with God".

Horsfield (2011) shows how new religious movements, such as the televangelist and megachurch prosperity movements, have adapted to culture and used new media technologies to spread all over the world. He writes:

> Positioning themselves within the opportunities and needs created by the global spread of capitalism, these local-based, media-extended religious movements offer packages of market-oriented, faith-colored solutions to dissatisfactions and opportunities created by such things as the rise of cultural pluralism, failures in post-colonial national rebuilding, and the economic and political uncertainties of globalization (Horsfield 2011, 3).

Baumann (1998) describes this as postmodern consumer religion. It is religion in which transcendence is consumerised, customised and commodified. While many churches and church movements would distance themselves from overt prosperity theology, its ideas have crept insidiously into much of the thinking of ordinary Christians. Varul (2008, 249) notes that Evangelical Christianity is offered more and more as a pathway to a "more contented, productive, successful, etc. personality, as a psychological self-help programme".

Daniel notes this trend: This prosperity Gospel is everywhere. And the pastors feed this thing, they are always pushing for tithes and offerings with the promise that God will make you prosper if you give more to the church. People think that Christianity is the way to have the best life possible. Church has become about being seen and having status. Many of our churches are for socialites more than for worship.

Zanele feels strongly about it: This prosperity thing turns everything upside down. People become selfish and focussed on themselves. If I even think that God exists to serve me, how am I going to think about other people, especially those less fortunate?

COMMODIFICATION

Berger (1967, 145) has shown that religions have had to become more like marketed consumer goods in order to compete with each other and other producers of meaning in a pluralistic and secularised world (see also Brouwer, Gifford and Rose 1996, 33 ff). For Finke and Stark (1992), contemporary religion can be understood as a marketplace that is characterised by competition, in which success is predicated on offering discernable value to consumers.

Religion has become a commodity that offers followers certain benefits in order to attract them and keep them loyal. The commoditisation of Christianity can be seen in the proliferation of new "church planting" franchises that seek to capture market share in new areas, based on the strength of their brand. While there are too many of these to list, an example of this is the Hillsong family of churches that started in Sydney, Australia. Most of the people we spoke to described communities where multiple tiny churches will meet in different classrooms at a single school, each trying to carve out a niche for themselves in fierce competition with the others.

146

CONSUMERISM

Slater has shown how consumption has become an identity marker for modern subjectivity:

> Many of our questions about the form we take as modern subjects, about how to understand the very relation we take as modern subjects, about how to understand the very relation between the everyday world and the public space, about our moral and social value, about our privacy and power of disposal over our lives, about who we are—many of these questions are taken up in relation to consumption and our social status as a rather new thing called 'a consumer'; we see ourselves as people who choose, who are inescapably 'free' and self-managing, who make decisions about who we are or want to be and use purchased goods, services and experiences to carry out these identity projects (Slater 1997, 5).

Slater (1997, 24f) shows how, in our materialistic, narcissistic and hedonistic culture, people are so concerned with "having" that "being" is marginalised and excluded in people's quest for freedom and consumer choice.

If consumption has become a marker of identity globally, our history in South Africa adds a further layer to this. Posel (2010) explores an emerging post-apartheid discourse in which freedom is constructed as a certain level of economic status and consumption. For Posel this conflation of freedom and consumption has its roots in the attempts by missionaries to "civilise" black people. Colonial rulers allowed natives a degree of upward social mobility if they adopted European dress and manners. Thus, a certain kind of consumption came to be a marker of social respectability.

Kgotso's words reflect this: It has become a status symbol to go to certain churches, whereas other churches are ignored because they are poor.

Teboho adds: People do this thing of church-hopping. They go where it will make them feel entertained and happy.

Vellem (2007) argues that as long as power and money are the dominant features of public life in South Africa, any kind of moral renewal is difficult.

DUALISM: THE SPIRITUAL AND THE SECULAR

There is an epistemological split that occurred within Christian discourse as a result of the wedge that the Enlightenment drove between faith and reason. Thami's comments illuminate the way this results in a dualistic spirituality: *Umuntu angakholwa and angabinabo ubuntu* (A person can have faith in God without Ubuntu). That is why you find a spiritual person in Church and when is out there in the community, there is no Ubuntu.... I have observed people who they speak, they are high spiritually. And if one comes being in need of food and the same people would deny food for that person.

Someone can be regarded as being spiritual, yet live without Ubuntu and show no care for other people. This raises the question of what it means for someone to be "spiritual" in this church context. Spirituality is reduced to an other-worldly pietism that is separate from the content of a person's life. Thami's observation can be extended to many sectors of the South African church, where highly affluent churchgoers embrace a spirituality that expresses anything but Ubuntu. The embodied aspect of Christian living has been lost and spiritualised.

Another example of this kind of dualism occurred in a conversation with two church leaders, one white and one black, about Ubuntu as a catalyst for forms of restitution or structural change that might lead to more just social and economic relations in South Africa. The white pastor remarked that, "The problem with talking about these things is that it breaks down our unity in Christ". He seemed to suggest that, even in the absence of relations characterised by unity in the 'real world', there was a kind of 'spiritual' unity that needed to be preserved.

The participants all agreed that this kind of thinking and living was common in too many churches. They also agreed that it should not be the case. Andile: Ubuntu and Spirituality should go together. ...Our spirituality always seeks the best for the people. I do not think there should be a separation between Ubuntu and Spirituality.

Du Toit (1998, 43) argues that "Spirituality is never authentic if it is divorced from life, one's own life and that of others". Spirituality is lived out in a specific community and embraces the whole of life.

OTHER INFLUENCES

Beyond these forces, which shape both Christian discourse and Ubuntu discourse, there are further complications when it comes to evaluating the ability of the spirituality or theology of African churches to promote Ubuntu values in society. At risk of superficial analysis, we would like to highlight some of these impediments.

Christianity is characterised by division and fragmentation rather than unity. While there is nothing inherently wrong with such a proliferation of diverse expressions of Christianity, there is not just a lack of unity across these divisions but also suspicion, conflict and animosity. This is hardly Ubuntu in action. Even within (or on the edges) of the boundaries that might constitute orthodox Christianity there are groups that regard the other as diabolical because of disagreement over some aspect of their theology or spirituality.

Then there is the impact that the so-called "Culture Wars" in the United States have had on Christianity in the global South through the proliferation of celebrity preachers on television. This has led, particularly among Christians who identify as Evangelicals, to a preoccupation with issues such as abortion, equal rights for LGBTQI people, opposition to evolution as an explanation for the origin of life, and opposition to cultural and religious pluralism. These have become as definitive of certain Christian agendas in South Africa as they are in the USA, usually to the exclusion of a focus on human rights, structural injustice and poverty Preoccupation with these issues has resulted in church communities that are characterised by ignorance, intolerance, and even prejudice more than they are by love and an open-armed invitation to the world.

Varul (2008, 250) argues that the threat of consumerism leads to those wishing to be faithful believers retreating into fundamentalism and literalism. There is a retreat into an essentialised faith. This in turn contributes to a retreat from the world into conservative pietism, and divisions where there is disagreement over doctrine or traditions.

CHRISTIANITY AND UBUNTU

It can therefore be seen that much of what has eroded the power of Ubuntu to shape social relations has also contributed to the shaping of new meanings in Christian discourse. This is by no means to generalise by suggesting that such trends can be discerned equally in all South African churches. There exists a wide range of discursive constructions of what it means to be a Christian. Not all reflect what we have described. For some, being a Christian involves a pietistic withdrawal from social and political issues. For others, a desire to express their spirituality in social action and altruism is evident. Unjust social structures are challenged, authentic community is built, and sacrificial acts of servanthood are evident.

Praeg (2008, 368) makes a helpful distinction between the *work of Ubuntu* and *discourse on Ubuntu*. He explains:

> While the former refers to everyday existence and gestures we recognise, in an everyday or commonsense understanding of the term, as manifesting *ubuntu*, the latter refers to the self-conscious reflection on what we have to understand about being African that would explain or make such actions understandable (Praeg 2008, 374).

The work of Ubuntu is seen in concrete acts that maintain or reflect cultural practices. Within discourse on Ubuntu multiple variants of Ubuntu discourse have been identified, each deployed in different ways and for different purposes. These include elite discourse (Matolino and Kwindingwi 2013), Ubuntu capitalism (McDonald 2010), Ubuntu philosophy (Shutte 1993), Ubuntu theology (Tutu 1999), Ubuntu ethics (Metz 2007). All of these have commonalities, but also differences where their meanings have been shaped as they intersect with other discourses.

Praeg (2008, 368) asserts that Ubuntu "is a function of the historical discourse on Africa, of the (post)colonial archive". In a similar fashion, the discursive themes within African churches that have been identified in this research are a function of an historical discourse on what it means to be a Christian, drawing on an archive of biblical traditions. As Weldes (2006, 179) has pointed out, discourses "are capital in the ubiquitous battle over meaning". Christian discourse and Ubuntu discourse have been similarly shaped through their intersection with the broader social discourses that we have discussed. They both exist in the same discursive space with the result that their meanings have been contested, appropriated, and reshaped.

What we have described as lived religion exists in the same kind of relationship with Christian discourse. There is even less cohesion between the multiple and often conflicting discourses that constitute Christianity than there is between the various Ubuntu discourses. However, as with Ubuntu, there are common strands and emphases. While there may be a robust social discourse on Ubuntu, the work of Ubuntu is only seen sporadically. Similarly, theological motifs and spiritual practices that are intrinsic to the discursive repertoire of Christians, the "work of Christianity" often betrays their absence. With both Christianity and Ubuntu there seems to be a growing disconnect between discourse and lived reality.

The result of this can be extraordinarily incongruous, such as the claim by Standard Bank, a predatory capitalist institution, that they embrace and live by the values of Ubuntu (McDonald 2010, 144). Or, churches that lock themselves in self-contained communities and encounter the "other" as a threatening label and not as a human being.

Mungwini (2011, 781) points out that the values of Ubuntu were reinforced by a specific metaphysics and social ontology that no longer carries the force it once had. Similarly, the degree to which Christianity is buttressed by political power and notions of authority and uniqueness has diminished. The hegemonic power of both of these discourses has been lost and the values they represent are now options in a sea of competing choices rather than foundational to life and community.

Verma (1991) argues that as a society makes a transition from being traditional to becoming modern the values of that society change—often significantly:

> The temporal locus of a value system is always the present .... The central reference point of a value system is the individual and the society of today. The past, that is tradition, is always in the court of life, seeking the lease of approval (Verma 1991, 532).

The inevitable question that seems to be posed to both Ubuntu and Christianity, in a context of consumerism and individualism, is "will they 'work' for me?". The people with whom we spoke during this research seemed sceptical about whether things could change.

Michael: Ubuntu theology is not difficult to find in the Bible, I think the problem is that it's too costly to follow. Imagine if affluent Christians in South Africa followed the example of the early church in Acts (pauses and shakes his head). I can't see it happening.

Teboho refers to the Apsotle Paul's example of Jesus as a model for self-emptying service and sacrifice in the book of Philippians: If people are not motivated to sacrifice and serve by the example of Jesus they are not going to do it because of *ubuntu*.

Mary: I have a gut feeling that it is impossible to revert, the only last thing which can reinvigorate Ubuntu is when people go back to do the will of God. Otherwise u*Thixo uzoliphelisa ihlabathi (God will bring the world into end)*. Without spirituality there cannot be Ubuntu. *Abantu* think that the value of life depends on having money. People think that life depends on money.

Andile: It will be so difficult to rejuvenateu Ubuntu in our communities, people were not as many as they are in these days, poverty is overwhelming now, population is too much, corruption has become normal, people suffering from anger, the space is limited, and violence is high. People do not trust each other, they poison one another, there is witchcraft, and spirit of togetherness is dying.

EMERGING INSIGHTS

While we have described what may seem to be a depressing picture of the increasing absence of Ubuntu-like spirituality in the lived religion of African churches we do not want to suggest that traditional Christian discourse or Ubuntu discourse no longer have value. Rather, their relationship with society has changed from being normative to being disruptive. However, given the congruence between ubuntu and the discursive themes within Christianity that are identified in this research, they offer a repertoire of actions that are both subversive and humanising in a dehumanising materialistic consumer culture.

Rather than look back on an idealised past that may or may not have existed in the way it is imagined, both can draw on their respective archives and inspire embodied action that disrupts the callous selfishness that is evident in so much of society. Embodied acts of Ubuntu and Christ-like living invert the values of a world that is increasingly without Ubuntu. They still hold out the possibility of the impossible: an embodied subjectivity that is more generous, compassionate, and more open to the "other".

Eze describes Ubuntu in a way that mirrors biblical descriptions of the body of Christ and reinforces the significance of both for our world.

A person is a person through another person means that our humanity flourishes through a dialogic process of relation and distance, of difference and uniqueness. Our capacities and human skills are distributed equally across different cultures. The idea of uniqueness and difference embody the subjective gifts (of humanity) which we bring to one another; an idealism in which we begin to see a different 'other' not as a threat but a complement to our humanity (Eze 2017, 101).

In a world where prejudice, racism and inequality eclipse individualism and materialism as social problems the performance of Ubuntu, and the performance of the discursive themes within Christianity that reflect it, offers hope for the disruption of these destructive discourses through embodied action that inverts their logic.

BIBLIOGRAPHY

Ackermann, Denise M. 1998. "Becoming Fully Human: An Ethic of Relationship in Difference and Otherness". *Journal of Theology for Southern Africa*, 102:17-18.

Ammerman, Nancy T, ed. 2006. *Everyday religion: Observing modern religious lives*. Oxford: Oxford University Press.

Bauman Zygmunt. 1998. *Globalization, The human consequences*. Cambridge, UK: Polity Press.

Bauman, Zygmunt. 2001. *The individualized society*. Cambridge: Polity Press.

Berger, Peter L. 1967. *The Sacred Canopy*. New York: Anchor Books.

Biko, Hlumelo. 2013. *The Great African Society: A Plan for a Nation Gone Astray*. Cape Town: Jonathan Ball Publishers.

Biko, Steve B. 2002. *I write what I like: A selection of his writings*, edited by Aeldred Stubbs. Chicago: University of Chicago Press.

Broodryk, Johann. 2002, *Ubuntu: Life Lessons from Africa*. Pretoria: Ubuntu School of Philosophy.

Brouwer, Steve, Paul Gifford and Susan D Rose. 1996. *Exporting the American Gospel: Global Christian Fundamentalism*. New York: Routledge

Cahoone, Lawrence E. 1996. *From Modernism to Postmodernism*. Oxford, Blackwell

Cilliers, Johan. 2010. "In search of meaning between *ubuntu* and into: perspectives on preaching in post-apartheid South Africa." *Preaching: Does it make a difference, Studia Homiletica,* 7: 77-87.

Cornell, Drucilla and Karin van Marle. 2005. "Exploring *Ubuntu.* Tentative Reflections". *African Human Rights Law Journal,* 5(2): 195-220.

Cornell, Drucilla and Karin Van Marle. 2015, "*Ubuntu* feminism: Tentative reflections". *Verbum et Ecclesia,* 36(2).

du Toit, Cornel W. 1998. "African Spirituality and the Poverty of Western Religious Experience." *Journal of Theology for Southern Africa* 100: 36-60.

Enslin, Penny and Kai Horsthemke. 2004. "Can *ubuntu* provide a model for citizenship education in African democracies?" *Comparative Education,* 40(4): 545-558.

Eze, Michael O. 2008. "What is African Communitarianism? Against Consensus as a regulative ideal." *South African Journal of Philosophy,* 27(4): 386-399.

Eze, Michael O. 2017. "I am Because You Are: Cosmopolitanism in the Age of Xenophobia." *Philosophical Papers,* 46(1): 85-109.

Eze, Michael O. 2017b. "The history and contemporary frame of Botho/Ubuntu: Philosophical and sociocultural complexities", paper presented at 2017 Mind and Life XXXII Conference: Botho/Ubuntu: A dialogue on Spirituality, Science and Humanity, Gaberone, Botswana, August 17-19.

Finke, Roger and Rodney Starke. 1992. *The churching of America 1776-1990: Winners and losers in our religious economy.* New Brunswick: Rutgers University Press.

Ganzevoort, Ruard R. 2009. "Forks in the road when tracing the sacred: Practical theology as hermeneutics of lived religion", Presidential address to the ninth conference of the IAPT, Catholic Theological Union, Chicago, July 30 – August 03.

Ganzevoort, Ruard R. and Roeland, Johan H. 2014, "Lived religion. The praxis of practical theology". *International Journal of Practical Theology,* 18(1): 91-101.

Gifford, Paul. 1998. *African Christianity: Its Public Role.* London: Hurst.

Gish, Steven D. 2004. *Desmond Tutu: A Biography.* Westport, CT: Greenwood Press.

Hofstede, Geert. 1980. *Culture's consequences: International differences in work-related values.* Beverly Hills CA: Sage.

Horsfield, Peter. 2011. "New religious "prosperity" movements and their social and economic implications". Paper presented to the Conference on media, communication, and democracy: global and national environments, RMIT University, Melbourne, Australia, September 1-2.

Hutchison, Elizabeth D. 2012. "Spirituality, Religion, and Progressive Social Movements: Resources and Motivation for Social Change." *Journal of Religion & Spirituality in Social Work: Social Thought*, 31(1-2): 105-127.

Jenkins, Philip. 2006. *The New Faces of Christianity: Believing the Bible in the Global South*. New York: Oxford University Press.

Matolino, Bernard and Wenceslaus Kwindingwi. 2013. "The End of Ubuntu." *South African Journal of Philosophy*, 32(2): 197–205.

McDonald, David A. 2010. "*Ubuntu* bashing: the marketisation of 'African values' in South Africa". *Review of African Political Economy*, 37: 139-152.

Metz, Thaddeus. 2007. "Towards an African moral theory." *The Journal of Political Philosophy*, 15(3): 321–341.

Meyer, Birgit. 1998. "'Make a Complete Break with the past'. Memory and Post-Colonial Modernity in Ghanaian Pentecostalist Discourse." *Journal of Religion in Africa*, 38(3): 316-349.

Mkhize, Nhlanhla. 2008. "Ubuntu and harmony: An African approach to morality and ethics". In *Persons in community: African ethics in a global culture*, edited by Ronald Nicolson, 35–44. Scottsville: University of KwaZulu-Natal Press.

Mnyaka, Mluleki and Mokgethi Motlhabi. 2009, "*Ubuntu* and its socio-moral significance". In *African ethics: An anthology of comparative and applied ethics*, edited by Munyaradzi F. Murove, 63–84. Scottsville: University of KwaZulu-Natal Press.

Mungwini, Pascah. 2011. "The Challenges of Revitalizing an Indigenous and Afrocentric Moral Theory in Postcolonial Education in Zimbabwe." *Educational Philosophy and Theory*, 43(7): 773-787.

Oyserman, Daphna, Markus Kemmelmeier and Heather Coon. 2002. "Cultural Psychology, A New Look." *Psychological Bulletin*, 128(1): 110-117.

Inglehart, Ronald and Daphna Oyserman. 2004. "Individualism, Autonomy, and self-expression: The human development syndrome". In *Comparing Cultures, Dimensions of Culture in a Comparative Perspective*, edited by Vinken, Henk, Joseph

155

Soeters, and Peter Ester, 74-96. Leiden, The Netherlands: Brill.

Posel, Deborah. 2010. "Races to consume: revisiting South Africa's history of race, consumption and the struggle for freedom." *Ethnic and Racial Studies*, 33(2): 157-175.

Praeg, Leonhard. 2008. "An Answer to the Question: What is [*ubuntu*]." *South African Journal of Philosophy*, 27(4): 367-385.

Setiloane, Gabriel M. 2000. *African theology: An introduction*. Lux Verbi, Cape Town.

Shutte, Augustine. 1993. *Philosophy for Africa*. Cape Town: University of Cape Town Press

Slater, Don. 1997. *Consumer Culture and Modernity*. Cambridge, UK: Polity Press.

STATSSA (Statistics South Africa). 2016. *Community Survey 2016 in brief*. Accessed 17 July 2017. http://www.statssa.gov.za/publications/03-01-06/03-01-062016.pdf

Streib, Heinz. 2008. *Lived Religion. Conceptual, Empirical and Practical-Theological Approaches. Essays in Honor of Hans-Günter Heimbrock*. Leiden: Brill.

Tutu, Desmond M. 1999. *No Future Without Forgiveness*. London: Rider.

Varul, Matthias Z. 2008. "After Heroism: Religion versus Consumerism. Preliminaries for an Investigation of Protestantism and Islam under Consumer Culture." *Islam and Christian–Muslim Relations*, 19(20): 237-255.

Vellem, Vuyani S. 2007. *The Symbol of Liberation in South African Public Life: A Black Theological Perspective*. PhD diss., University of Pretoria.

Verma, Roop R. 1991. "The Concept of Progress and Cultural Identity". In *Culture and Modernity*, edited by Eliot Deutsch, 526-34. Honolulu: University of Hawaii Press.

Weldes, Jutta. 2006. "High politics and low data: globalization discourses and popular culture". In *Interpretation and method: empirical research methods and the interpretive turn*, edited by Dvora Yanow and Peregrine Schwartz-Shea, 176–186. New York: M.E. Sharpe.

CHAPTER 7. WHEN WE KNOW, AND REFUSE TO KNOW: J N MAKUMBI'S KINTU AS 'AN INTELLECTUAL DISCUSSION'

Garnette Oluoch-Olunya

> ...the modern African intellectual elite ... have unquestioningly yielded to a narrow Eurocentric index of civilisation and humanity.
>
> —F. Nyamjoh (2015)
>
> ...nothing is ever complete...incompleteness [i]s the normal order of things.
>
> —F Nyamjoh (2015, 2)
>
> ...the self-managing, self-made individual of neoliberal and neo-Kantian Western thought is a complete delusion.
>
> —Jean-Pierre Warnier (2013)

INTRODUCTION

Jennifer Nansubuga Makumbi's powerful epic is predicated on, and weaves itself around the idea of Ubuntu. Whilst evoking myths of origins, which she cleverly interweaves into newer contexts in a story well told, Makumbi succeeds in destabilizing the notion of Ubuntu as the easy, natural, default mode around which African societies organized. She queries the presumed Afrcican belief that we all bound to respect others in a netwok of social relationships.

Locating her exploration of Buganda culture from the time of Kintu, the first man, she draws us through this traditional tale that is itself shaped by a world view that speaks to competing histories and experiences, of the arbitrary cruelties of monarchical rule of the *baKabaka,* and similarly, of colonialisms, both Arab and European, and their effects. At the heart of the story is a curse. In employing this trope to frame her narrative, another famous curse that of the biblical Ham, is invoked, in all its compelling power. It has, after all, led to the historical justification for the subjugation of black people. And yet critical readings of the Bible story prove it to be a power variously misread, and misappropriated, the 'curse' as sometimes cunning cover used to mask years of exploitation and oppression of such crafted (i.e., since Jewish antiquity) racialised distinctions as skin colour, the original story of Noah and Ham probably long-distorted with each retelling.[1]

Makumbi recasts the curse into a unifying trope, eschewing the overarching anxieties that surround who we are, and what we know by arming us with both African and western ways of knowing, as well as calling to question what Nyamjoh refers to as "the one-dimensionalism of resilient colonialism and the ambitions of completeness which it claims and inspires" (Nyamjoh 2015, 3). We know, counter-intuitively, that the consciousness required to be in ubuntu, in community, is an ideal; and that things are mutable, yet interconnected. Indeed, this is Miisi's quest, and struggle: he oscillates between mastery of western, and local knowledges, but it is his being in 'traditional' society, his discomfort with endogenous epistemologies that leads to a mental break. The safeguarding of Ubuntu by such intangible mechanisms as the 'curse' demonstrates the ways in which social justice was assured for all. Its fluidity, reach and severity, across realms, served as a stern warning and reminder of

---

1   The story is found in the Bible, in the Book of Genesis 9:20-27. It has been argued that Ham's transgression was that he spoke of Noah's disgrace—he was drunk, and naked—in the street, holding Noah up to public mockery. The actual 'crime' has been variously treated, with scholars citing Babylonia in the 1st millenia as a place where sexual modesty was guarded, making exposure of genitalia a serious matter. Others have suggested that Ham either sodomised, or castrated his father. Whatever the case, it was a vicious family feud with devastating consequences.

acceptable limits. My contention, and the tragedy, is that maybe we have lost vital aspects of the knowledge that made us social beings, and so cannot think in the way that is best for us.

***

KAMU KINTU

The novel opens violently, with the senseless killing of Kamu Kintu, by a mob. But as events unfold, it turns out that this death is not unconnected to an intricately woven family web that extends back generations to Kintu, the first Ganda. Kamu's name suggests the dimunitive, *ka,* and *kintu,* 'thing', hence 'small thing', maybe to deflect from the age-old family curse. He goes to his death in a trance, unbelieving: surely those raining blows on him could see "He was Kama Kintu, human. It was them, *bantu.* Humans?" (Makumbi 2014, ixvii). The incident starts innocuously enough, with no indication of the swiftness of its degeneration into anarchy. His fellow slum dwellers kill him in frustration at their own wretched condition. He has acquired, and disruptively flaunts cheap imitations of a stereo system, and a television: *Sonny* and *Pansonic.* In this area, people may be unaware of, or care little for the branded originals, Sony and Panasonic, these being well out of reach. More pertinently, they do not know where their next meal is coming from. But just as quickly as the temperatures rise and peak in this violent bloodletting, the people soon recover and are appalled at their loss of civility:

> The air in Bwaise had turned. Once Kamu died…, horror and disbelief arrived. *Is a human slayable just like that?* And the whole notion of taking a human life became so heavy that Bwaise stared incredulous as if some other place had done it. *How do you go to bed at night and sleep when you've killed a whole human, hmm? The world died a long time ago…everyone hates himself… people are not human anymore and all the buntu is gone* (Makumbi 2014, 171) (italics in text).

Retribution comes swiftly—10 deaths for 1— a private calling to account, boldly put on public display. Kamu's sister, Kusi, is the powerful army General Salamander who avenges her brother's death. And yet the timing of this death, almost as prelude to the family gathering, either suggests sacrifice, or serves as a sharp reminder to the validity of the curse. Whilst vengeance might be satisfying, it is only fleetingly so. Miisi is happy with his daughter's action, yet horrified that he finds satisfaction in such a barbaric act; that he is losing his humanity. He descends into an intermittent madness (Makumbi 2014, 420), reminiscent of the crisis that Ezeulu, Chief Priest of Ulu in Chinua Achebe's *Arrow of God* suffers. In beginning to try to understand what has happened to Ezeulu, and the magnitude of the forces at play, and which are ultimately of irreversible historical significance, Harry Garuba identifies what perhaps prompts the episodes. For him, it is that "two discursive orders, both claiming normativity, were established in the same social and geographical space" (Garuba 2014, 21). This constitutes not accommodative continuity with tradition, but a "fundamental dislocation" (Garuba 2014, 20-21). Casting beyond the postcolonial theoretical arguments for segue into hybridity or liminal existence in-between worlds, Garuba rightfully reads the pause as marking a deeper shift. He challenges the idea that this transition is natural, what Garuba calls normative, raising the added question of whether it is inevitable that change happen in just this way. He advances the argument that "probably nowhere else in the postcolonial world can subjects move between and inhabit two discursive and symbolic orders by simultaneous interpellation"—by which he means "the ability to operate under two different discursive orders and experience them as normative" (Garuba 2014, 22). Garuba contends that this influence of the West is deeply scarring, with an insidious transformative potential, and impact the full extent of which we have yet to fully understand. A much earlier Fanon had diagnosed the condition as a collective form of schizophrenia. Reflecting on the long shadow cast by the legacy of a sly colonial encounter in *Betrayal in the City*, Francis Imbuga identifies a similar rupture. He says, "when the madness of a nation [or clan] disturbs a solitary mind, it is not enough to say that the man is mad."

In *Kintu*, Miisi carries the weight of the clans 'madness'. How does he begin to comprehend, and accept the death of an 11th child, Kamu, as part of the fulfillment of the traditional curse, but also as part of the daily consequence of his living in a violence-prone slum neighbourhood? This is the kind of simultaneous interpellation Garuba refers to, above. Even more distressing, however, is the fact that he can withhold judgement of Kusi, and accept that she has avenged her brother's death by killing so many. We, of course, know that entire families were wiped out in Uganda in the period straddling

Obote's second term, Idi Amin and the AIDS epidemic, and it may be tempting to locate the violence in this context and thus explain Miisi's loss. That he cracks conversely demonstrates the compelling power of his Ubuntu. Yet in seeking this atonement, it is the tug of conscience that allows us to begin to explore the magnitude of the overarching moral loss of the Ganda, Uganda, and indeed, Africa. The symbolism of these deaths sits in the fractures of postcolony where Christian ritual jostles for space with the traditional. Makumbi has the slaying happen on 'Good Friday, the 9th of April 2004.' This date is significant, marking the denouément of the story; the Kintu family reunion is to take place from the 9th–12th, at the ancestral home in Kiyiika village, in Buddu. The enactment of this revenge killing, while dictated by the sequence of events, coincides with the most important ritual sacrifice on the Christian calendar, the crucifixion of Christ—and the thieves—and links directly to Miisi's doctoral studies in Cambridge, where he looked at 'The Centrality of Bloodletting to Religious Practice'. His work came out of a deep desire to understand human compulsion, what drove people to the extremities that he had already experienced from a young age. How do we rationalise the stories we tell ourselves about the things we do allow, like "religious murder being presented creatively as sacrifice or manipulatively as punishment?" (Makumbi 2014, 345). In looking for practical release from these social anxieties, Miisi draws parallels. In the Christian myth, the idea of human sacrifice is elevated, and celebrated as the perfect sacrifice. It is also the ultimate sacrifice, serving in lieu of all other human sacrifice, securing forgiveness for eternity.

Miisi *knows* the imperative of a blood sacrifice. He has lived in its vortex at home. His own father had sacrificed his eldest brother Baale, and kept him in the roof to ward off the curse, driving his mother to madness, arson (she set the entire family on fire, save him) and suicide (Makumbi 2014, 351). He has also studied it in the western academy, hoping to free himself with what he thinks is independent, untethered knowledge. He instead finds that all human activity is anchored in cultural specificity—is rooted in some local practice whose potential is realised only by way of a nurturing leadership. In the Old Testament, God himself provides Adam with a lamb, saving his son Isaac. In the New Testament, God offers His own son. Having scaled the heights of the western academy, Miisi recognizes the parallels with his own situation. He knows that Ntwire is merciless, and has been insatiable through the generations in his quest to avenge Kalema's death, killing along direct bloodline, and annihilating entire branches of the family. But what ancillary knowledges can he draw on now, as clan leader, to appease such an appetite? In what ways has he been prepared within his traditional and new culture to both perform the task, and to be receptive to its form? In the end, any possible interventions come too late for him. He loses all 11 sons. Kusi, his daughter, watches as the last to go, "Kamu's death snap[s] the last cable in his mind" (Makumbi 2014, 442). And still it is not enough for Ntwire. Although Muganda has warned that Ntwire will not go gently, hope lies in the expectation that he *will* go.

One of the market women, remarking afterwards the subsequent deaths of all involved in Kamu's killing, makes a curious statement: "that is what happens to a race that fails to raise its value on the market" (Makumbi 2014, xix).[2] If life at first appears cheap here, the price of atonement certainly suggests something of much greater value than the purely commercial. Ten heads fall with Kamu. Their deaths do not serve to cushion from, or expiate the curse. Rather, they merge into the daily humdrum, part of what in Nairobi we call 'normal' thuggery. That is the everyday way in which Kanani, one of the elders, hears about them on the news (Makumbi 2014, 376). A curious drama plays out on Kamu's domestic front as his partner abandons him in death, leaving him lying on the street. There is nothing tangible to attach her to him—no marriage certificate, no child, no extended family. She is bound by no legal or social obligation. She is, in a sense, free, but it is a spurious freedom. Even his death seems to offer no advantages, prompting her to hastily abandon their come-we-stay, in the process discarding the softer things that might have drawn them together—compassion, and humanity. And *she* remains unnamed, anonymous, a symbol of the disjointed and transient life of the slum dweller.

AFRICANEITY

The choice of epigraph used as portal to the text is an 1863 quotation from the military man and explorer John Hanning Speke. It is a privileging prism through which this African myth of origins is

---

2   This can also be read against the curse of Ham.

refracted, with Speke as the man who brought Uganda not only firmly under the European gaze, but who brought it fully into history with his 'discovery' of the source of the Nile. This last is suggestive of uncharted territory, waiting to be explored, conquered, civilised. Miisi recalls his school textbook that could not resist a small jibe in this caption, placed under a triumphant picture: "J H Speke Stood in this Exact Spot Somewhere Nearby".[3] This is the exact same spot, or indeed somewhere nearby, that Miisi's mother chooses as sanctuary for her son, allowing him moments of rest and recuperation, of return to sanity. Speke remains trapped in his time, harking back to readings of the Bible that have been used to justify European subjugation of Africa. These sentiments are insidious in nature, and in a Uganda that is today over 66% Christian, continue to cast a long shadow, drawing us back as surely as they did Makumbi. Descendants of Ham are to remain slave to Shem and Japheth, then *and* now. At its height, it is this idea that underwrote the system of Apartheid in South Africa, and racial discrimination based on colour bar in British East Africa. It is the extremities to which this idea was carried even as it, paradoxically, undermined other biblical principles that have led to the re-assertion of Ubuntu as a strategic intervention in the recovery of the qualities that define us as people, and make us human.

It is this trope that Makumbi appropriates, using this popular idea to interrogate an Africa that has lost agency, and one that is itself accursed. She goes deeper, elaborating through Ntwire, a *munnarwanda*, an inversion of the hamitic hypothesis partially advanced in the epigraph, that locks in a complex and layered intervention, not only eschewing the fallacy of a homogenous Africa, but challenging the pecking order in the classification of peoples. Her work has far reaching implications. Adamic Kintu is, for instance, located in oral tradition, but it is a tradition that intersects inevitably with these external influences. If we read Makumbi herself as a Ugandan writer, it is Uganda made in England, what she calls "an

---

3   This can be read as a humorous comment on the non-specificity of history. Speke was, of course, a missionary, propelled by eighteenth century European Enlightenment ideas of equality for all men, yet held hostage by its contradictions in colonial Africa.

artifact of the British".[4] As she sees it, this naming created an anonymous space belonging to no one even as the name brazenly suggested a country named for one group, the Ganda. In *Kintu*, she then appears to nationalize Ganda as local identity, a reading that has seen her accused of supporting Baganda hegemony—of being a royalist.[5] She is playfully provocative:

> Now we Ganda were known the world over for our hospitality because we treated those who settled amongst us well. However, we asked for one little thing in return for our hospitality; *one little thing*—that everyone who settled among us became Ganda. You see, it was important that we were all one people—same language, same life, same everything—so that people don't stumble on each other's differences (Makumbi 2014, 98)(my emphasis).

The 'one little thing' is, of course, everything.

***

It all begins when Kintu Kidda, the Ppookino (Governor) of Buddu Province welcomes a traveller, the Tutsi from Rwanda, Ntwire, and his newly born baby son Kalemanzira into his home. Kalema's mother has died in childbirth, and quite by chance, Kintu's wife is herself nursing. Kalema latches onto her breast, becoming her son and subsequently, a son in Kintu's home. As we are told, "as a rule, a child in Kintu's house was a child of the house" (Makumbi 2014, 27). Ordinarily, Ntwire had the option to be absorbed into the culture and become Ganda, but in this instance he stubbornly clings to primary identity, opting to remain Rwandese, and marginal, even as he desires the best for his son.[6] Nnalongo and Kintu choose to

---

4   In a conversation with Makumbi at Storymoja Literary Festival in Nairobi, 2015. In the text, the first time Isaac Newton hears Miisi speak English, he says 'African countries are a European imagination'. This alien concept can only be captured in its own tongue.

5   At Storymoja, as above. She spoke of the naming of Uganda for one group, the Ganda, leading to immediate loss of nationalist thrust: no one feels they own it. Even the Baganda identify specifically with Mmengo.

6   The traditional propensity to welcome and absorb others is a quality shared across many cultures. But the Hamites were supposed to be superior to the Bantu, and Ntwire in a sense bears this out in his

keep the truth of his birth from Kalema, as they do for the siblings born through Nnalongo's twin, Babirye's surrogacy. As Kintu asserts, "the children are mine" (Makumbi 2014, 18). When Kintu kills Kalemanzira accidentally, he retreats into despair. The incident is itself layered. Kintu catches Kalema drinking from his sacred gourd, a taboo. It is in trying to deflect this abomination that Kintu commits an even weightier one; what appears as an unremarkable slap to deflect the gourd kills Kalema. The seemingly small act— "I chastised him—a slap" (Makumbi 2014, 31)— has grave consequence; tradition dictates that he protects its instruments, and as he looks at the scattered shards of the gourd out of which Kalema has improperly sipped, and looks at Kalema lying dead beside them, he is paralysed by two things. The first is his role as custodian of tradition. He is instinctively primed to protect it, and this he does. But tradition itself seems to play a role in its own self-preservation, and this is where Kintu seems to have no control. The moment is itself surreal, with Kalema paying the ultimate price for what Kintu himself might have excused as a transgression, however grave. It is no ordinary slap, however. Makumi has it crashing into Kalema's jaw, after which "Kalema looked at his father, surprised, but his eyes kept rising *as if the slap had come from the sky*" (Makumbi 2014, 31).[7] But even more devastating is the realization that as Ppookino he has no authority over life; that the Ubuntu he has extended to Ntwire is not absolute, is not in his gift, and does not guarantee Kalema's young life. Indeed, Kintu may question his own being, and agency (maybe he *is* just a 'thing') given that life is elusive, and ephemeral, and death, a void; beyond reach. It is this knowledge that is unbearable, eliciting uncharacteristic behavior with dire consequences. Taiye Selasie captures the moment well in *Ghana Must Go*, when Fola loses her father:

> …knowing.
> That something has been removed.
> That a thing that had been in the world had just left it, …leaving behind it this empty space, openness. Incredible, unbearable, interminable

---

aloofness, and refusal to integrate; to satisfy the 'only' condition the Ganda set the foreigner.

7   My emphasis. Chinua Achebe might say it wears a hat.

openness appearing now around her, a gaping, inside her, a hole…Unappeasable…
The indifference of it (Selassie 2013, 105-106).

Confronted with the thinness of the line that separates life and death, Kintu grapples with this fragility, with the magnitude of the loss, and the indifference of death, even as Kalema, who cannot settle in the afterlife because he has not been properly interred, seamlessly negotiates his resting. Indeed, here, death appears indifferent only when it is at peace, which raises the question: What is humanity, after all, when confronted with its own mortality? In a prescient reading of Alex Kagame's work, D A Masolo captures the rationality through which Kintu can be best understood. In Masolo's reading of Kagame,

> humans, *Bantu*,… have a moral status that transcends any social or cultural differences … that despite differences in expressive cultures of the *Bantu*, there is a common and universal understanding of the unique status of *Muntu* within nature. No *Muntu*, in life or death, is, in thought or treatment, reducible to the category of lower beings, especially that of a thing, *Kintu*, or *Kitu*. …humans sustain themselves through processes of integration and functional interrelationships that are extended beyond the boundaries of change and transformation such as occur at death. [That] living relationships shift to imaginary inclusiveness by which the dead are reintegrated into social order (within their respective family and lineage systems) as historical markers of a moral continuum (Masolo forthcoming, 5).

This is the intricate relationship Makumbi carries in her story. Kintu's confusion in the novel comes out of knowledge of the logic that informs or underpins his actions and hence recognition of the magnitude and totality of his transgression, even though unintended. He has broken a cardinal rule of the mutual respect for right to life by taking it away, and his atonement must be commensurate with the breach. Ruminating on the incident, he is clear on the cause of his anxiety: "The problem was not that Kalema had died—that is what people do—the problem was that he had killed him" (Makumbi 2014, 42). He further failed in his social responsibility—to announce and therefore publicly mourn the death, as well as to restore trust and harmony in shared or community ritual. He acknowledges that "while

Kalema's death was a tragedy, not holding funeral rights for the boy was reckless" (Makumbi 2014, 49). Kintu complicates matters through negligence: "He should have announced the funeral as soon as he arrived; he should have gone up to Ntwire's house and told him, he could have sent one of the men ahead to break the news to the family…but it was now too late" (Makumbi 2014, 52). His cowardly abdication of duty is the root of all subsequent problems. In eschewing the tacit convention of mutual respect for personhood mediating human relationships, Kintu brings down a 'curse' on the family, indiscriminately visiting madness, alienation and death. The very notion of a curse, here framed by Kintu's own failure to act, is then played out in family lore, embraced by those who understand the rationality of tradition, and equally abjured by those who cling to a certain modernity. The seemingly powerless Ntwire does call the curse, even as Kintu stubbornly ignores the window he leaves open for renegotiation.

In *Kintu*, we begin to appreciate the scale of punishment that can result from a transgression of the rules mediating social conventions, and failure to seek atonement when in breach. In this story, tragedy results even when this breach is concealed from others; whether it is publicly staged, or enacted in private. And even those who do not believe in it still fall victim to its reach. This underscores the fact that the individual is given meaning through relationships with others, although it is also clear that Kintu himself bears a singular burden, an internal anguish. His silence locks him into contempt for moral decency, simultaneously jeopardising his authoritative role as custodian, especially of vulnerable outsider, a serious indictment on the values of Ubuntu. It matters little that Ntwire is the primary victim of this lapse; he is, however, not the only one, and that the tension seeps into other spaces is testament to the intimate and robust links Kalema shared with others. This tension immediately permeates into Kintu's relationship with his wife, who senses the slippage even without certain knowledge of it.

The Ppookino's choice of the reckless path of nondisclosure of Kalema's death is a lapse that is to cost him dearly. In a similar incident in Chinua Achebe's *Things Fall Apart* (1958), Achebe demonstrates the seriousness with which any killing of kin is taken.[8]

---

8   Interestingly, Miisi looks at Ikemefuna in relation to collective war sacrifice in his doctoral work.

By default, Okonkwo kills Ikemefuna, a boy in his custody who calls him 'father'—the boy runs to him for protection as the men appointed to the task try to kill him as decreed by the oracle, and afraid of being thought weak, Okonkwo strikes the fatal blow. The internal agony he goes through is keener than any externally imposed punishment. His action also alienates him further from his biological son, Nwoye, a relationship that is never restored. But Okonkwo also kills the old man Ezeudu's son accidentally, at Ezeudu's funeral. It is a community tragedy and he is quick to take his punishment; he is banished for 7 years. Okonkwo packs and leaves the same night with his family, and in concert, the men come and destroy his compound, cleansing it. The conditions of his banishment are understood by all, as is the certainty of his return, and restoration of harmony. Social justice is enacted swiftly, and meticulously, and yet it is restorative. The point here is that whilst Ezeudu is a kinsman, Ikemefuna is not, making death itself nuanced. Ikemefuna serves a specific purpose as sacrificial offering, as a spoil of war, awaiting the binding decree of the oracle. In life, Kalema is treated equitably, and the Ppookino's lapse might therefore be read, perhaps unfairly, as an application of a different standard for a non-Ganda. Kalema himself remains convincingly assimilated, even in death uncertain of his status as outsider, only expressing it as hearsay: "People say I am not your son" (Makumbi 2014, 41). And Kintu claims him even there.

Kwame Anthony Appiah in *The Ethics of Identity* (2005) helps us revisit this well-discussed question of agency, be it Okonkwo's or Kintu's, examining the extent to which we are responsible for our own choices and actions. He takes his cue from such enlightenment philosophers as Immanuel Kant, or more recently, the American philosopher John Rawls, and argues that it is not always the case that man is rational; that it is conditional. [The Enlightenment was about replacing traditional authorities with the authority of individual human reason, even as it struggled not to overturn traditional moral and religious beliefs]. Ubuntu presupposes the rational agency of man; what Appiah (2005) posits is the 'as if'—that we act 'as if' freedom is possible. Indeed, this is central to Kant's 'critical' philosophy--that we are suspended in the very arc of the possible. But even as Kintu acts within the realm of the possible, even as he responds within the logic of his society, an external logic is also called into play. Two things protect him, if only temporarily: his superior position as Governor where he holds counsel, and the fact that his relationship with the outsider, the *munnarwanda* Ntwire, doesn't *command* the same social obligations. Furthermore, Kalema has become his son. Nevertheless, Kintu continues to bear, in private, the burden that compels him to act, but as fear, rather than valour. It is by this same logic that Okonkwo could kill Ikemefuna—a 'son'—and escape banishment, the punishment for killing a kinsman. Indeed one is drawn to read the second killing in *Things Fall Apart*, that of Ezeudu's son, and Okonkwo's subsequent expulsion rightly as a tragedy, but one tinged with a measure of natural justice. It is the same Ezeudu that earlier draws Okonkwo aside and urges him not to take part in the killing of Ikemefuna: "that boy calls you father... Bear no hand in his death" (Achebe 1958, 114). But if Okonkwo carries an internal burden of guilt, and external expiation with a 7 year limit of statute, in *Kintu*, what at first appears as manageable gradually spirals out of control as the community is fractured by external factors. Even Ntwire, the aggrieved, can only guess at what Kintu's obstinate silences might mean as, clinging to hope, he questions and curses. He has no *locus standi* in this community, and must remain outside of the structures of justice, to which he calls nevertheless. Kintu, administrator of justice, fails to extend Ubuntu to the outsider in his household.

Words carry an immense power. The Bible has, for instance, helped to establish the solidness, the materiality of language, authoritatively calling to being, and giving substance. It is from this organic place of utterance that powerfully, hesitantly, Ntwire is at last drawn to speak, establishing the vortex that will draw in *bakintu* henceforth:

> ...Ntwire spoke up. It was as if he spoke his own language. His pain was harsh on the *b's*. Ns became *ny*, *ks* became *gs* and *ts* were muffled yet what was said was clear. He pointed his shepherd stick at Kintu.
>
> 'You see these feet', then he pointed at his feet. 'I am going to look for my child. If he's alive, I'll bring him home and apologise. But if I don't find him–to you, to your house and to those that will be born out of it—to live will be to suffer. You will endure so much that you will wish you were never born'. Ntwire's voice shook as he added, 'And for you Kintu, even death will not bring relief (Makumbi 2014, 56).

Ntwire hoped to stay the curse, hoped that Kintu might confirm that Kalema was still alive. But "No word came after him" (Makumbi 2014, 56).

Ntwire's tongue, made heavy by the slight to his humanity, settles back into the familiar patterns and accents of his homeland, invoking the certainties and affirmations of this humanity. Even in the state of not knowing, he reaches out—"I will bring him home and apologise"—but Kintu is unyielding.

In a speech to the Kenyan people in 2015, the US president Barack Obama captured the pause in this utterance with an old saying: "We have not inherited this land from our forebears, we have borrowed it from our children" (Obama 2015). It is in his stubborn silence that Kintu condemns his progeny to the misery promised in Ntwire's reluctant curse.

IN POSTCOLONIAL UGANDA: UNDERSTANDING MIISI PROPERLY

Uganda has a unique post independence history, hence neo-colonial trajectory. At the epicenter was the monarchy; successive Kabakas were largely known for their excesses. And it was quickly drawn into instability, first by Obote seeking to consolidate his position, and then by Idi Amin, whose expulsion of the Asians, and redistribution of resources locally led some scholars to read into these acts the routing of the colonial presence altogether, and denial of their impact. They pushed the fallacy that 'the imperialists were absent', and that Uganda's was a self-made problem (Saul 2004, 24). The political instabilities and civil wars of the Amin and Obote years in the 1970's and 1980's were indeed terrible, but they sit quite squarely on the colonial foundation. These years nevertheless saw old social hierarchies eroded, there was the collapse of moral and economic order—as well as unprecedented shifts in gender roles.[9] In the context of the subsequent quest for a moral centre after decades of bloodletting, Makumbi interweaves the riveting story of a family curse. In a country that lost its compass, and where "anything that gave them a chance to survive was moral" (Makumbi 2014, 343), it is a huge task.

---

9   Kusi is a case in point.

The moral question, which lies at the heart of these changes, is inextricably linked to the HIV epidemic, initially linked to sexual permissiveness, which ravaged Uganda just as Museveni came to power. Already in the grip of fear, the euphemism 'the dreaded' was whispered, so as to deflect the illness.[10] It was this fear that Museveni played on in his restructuring of the country. He championed "the need to return to traditional family values as a social prophylaxis against HIV ...creating a fear of AIDS in Uganda so that people would be too scared to be promiscuous" (Kuhanen 2015, 273). Museveni was not alone in reading HIV as a non-African problem: for him and the church (the Catholic Bishops), "HIV and AIDS represented a breakdown of sociocultural norms of Ugandan society and an encroachment of Western culture and lifestyles, most visible among the elite and youth" (Kuhanen 2015, 273). Indeed, "Sexual promiscuity appeared as an evil result of non-African, liberal and immoral un-Christian lifestyles, which provoked the youth and exposed them to HIV, threatening nation-building and national recovery" (Kuhanen 2015, 273). The church, now domesticated, is itself an import.

In the overwhelming devastation of the new epidemic, national expectation is itself not one of survival, but of death. Makumbi sensitively distinguishes the curse of Kintu, nevertheless. Suubi's story is arguably one of the most disturbing. Born into an indifferent world, she is suspected to have HIV and not expected to live, and is told so repeatedly. Alone, she defies impossible odds, on top of which she struggles with a stubborn dead twin, *and* stays sane. In her circumstances, one might argue that insanity would be a mercy. As twin spirit, however, she straddles the fine line between life and death, a reminder that death stalks life, always. It is through such characters that Makumbi skillfully allows herself to flow into forgotten areas of mythology and history, pressing into sensitive nerve centres, some taboo: incest, and rape, and its issue, suicide, Idi Amin, Islam, Christianity, the return of the Asians, colonialism, ethnicity, fourth termism, the bush war, child abduction, homo- and bi-sexuality, and as above, HIV. In the politics surrounding the treatment of HIV, Museveni demonstrates the tensions linking traditional cultural philosophy and western intellectual ways of seeing

---

10   See, for instance, Mary Okurut, *The Invisible Weevil.* (Kampala: Femrite Publications Ltd, 1994.

or understanding things, which *must* co-exist in our hybrid selves. In the privacy of their homes Ugandans did not talk about sex; now it was a national dialogue. For him, even the war against AIDS is pitched as ideological (Kuhanen 2015, 273).[11] With everything so overwhelmingly overdetermined, Makumbi is amazed that local anger at colonialism is not stronger. She even imagines "God poised with a can of aerosol *Africancide*" in the slums where, as she demonstrates, life appears cheap (Makumbi 2014, xvii). But it only appears so, as Kamu's death comes at a heavy price. His is a life that is interlinked most intricately through kinship, through bloodline, with the powerful Kusi, and their Cambridge educated father, Miisi. It is these links that Makumbi uses to unravel her central, unifying thread. We bear witness to the high price Miisi himself pays in neglecting his children. He pursues a further degree that does not help him save them.

Miisi, quintessential post-colonial, carries the curse of Kintu. It casts a dramatic shadow over his childhood, which ends in his mother's suicide. Taken in by British missionaries, they school, and eventually find him a sponsor in the UK. He is therefore exposed to the African desire for things western quite early, and eventually makes it west. Indeed, "Britain and America were the lands of humanity, the places Miisi longed to be" (Makumbi 2014, 342). He is in for a shock, however. First, his education sponsors, the O'Tooles, don't want to meet him. Coming from a place where money is valuable because it is scarce, Misii struggles to understand how anyone can spend so much on someone and not want to meet him (Makumbi 2014, 342). He conflates the value of money with personal and social value, and is painfully disappointed.[12] Keen to show them how well he used their money, Miisi doesn't yet understand the

11 See also Sylvia Tamale, ed. *African Sexualities: A Reader,* (Cape Town: Pambazuka Press, 2011). She is detailed and nuanced, and speaks of the re-medicalisation of African sexualities with this epidemic (FGM was first), and its western stereotyping as 'insatiable, alien, deviant'.
12 An idea advanced by Karl Marx, in Viviana Zelizer, A. *The Social Meaning of Money: Pin money, paychecks, poor relief and other currencies.* (US: Basic Books, 1994), 8. See also Georg Simmel, ed. David Frisby, *The Philosophy of Money.* 2nd edition, (London: Routledge, 1990 (1907)). I thank Professor Wambui Mwangi for enlightening discussions on Money.

ideology that money "is a single, interchangeable, absolutely *impersonal* instrument—the very essence of our modern, rationalizing civilisation"—and that money stands outside of relationships (Zelizer 1994, 1). If, as Gertrude Stein argues, "money is [just] money", and has no value outside of what we give it, then under capitalist ideology we have given it all value. Thus, money can be read, as Marx did, as a relationship between people masquerading as a relationship between things. Miisi may be in the west, but he is not of the west and so fails to make that fine distinction and hence, to understand the O'Toole's coldness. The first clause is clear, but the second makes no sense as he is yet to be exposed to the dehumanization that is intrinsic to capitalism as practiced in the west. It is these submerged values that inform relationships between people that Viviana Zelizer explores in *The Social Meaning of Money*, challenging the commodification of human relationships and the dehumanization wrought by the use of money under capitalist ideology.[13]

Next is the view of Africa. The horror stories linked with Africa were cast in Frankenstein mould, an admixture in which we are a monster hybrid, both European and African, and hideously so (Makumbi 2014, 333). In her elaboration, Makumbi demonstrates the circumstance that created the variant *Africanstein*,[14] called *Ekisode* in Luganda, and has Miisi ruminate on the dismemberment, and re-membering of Africa, with such ill-fitting European parts, they almost seem designed to break the Continent. And yet even the

---

13 Saul's is an erudite reading, and sensitive critique of Marxist analyses (as of early Mamdani) of the development of the State in Uganda. He uses as his springboard Frantz Fanon's insights regarding the postcolonial state, in which 'the national middleclass discovers its historic mission: that of intermediary…between the nation and a capitalism, rampant though camouflaged…'(17). Miisi has only seen the tip of the iceberg, although the Uganda to which he returns is too unstable and dependent on social capital to be as crudely capitalistic.

14 The British movie was itself first made under the title 'The *Curse* of Frankenstein'(1957). It was in its 1970 remake that it was retitled 'The Horror of Frankenstein.' Based on the novel by Mary Shelley (1797-1851), *Frankenstein*, also titled *The Modern Prometheus* is the story of Victor Frankenstein, a scientist who creates a life out of different body parts and is horrified at what he has made. In Greek mythology, Prometheus was creator/benefactor of mankind.

crudely grafted must be accommodated, and domesticated. Miisi himself

>...squirmed in the palpable inadequacy of the African—the violence, greed, selfishness and savagery. He in turn decided to concentrate on the things that made blacks more wholesome, human, natural, in antithesis to everyday manners, actions, tendencies and behavior of Europeans (Makumbi 2014, 343).

His anxieties were compounded by people's view of him on his return home. They saw him as alienated, as identifying more with western culture and so called him *muzungu*!

Western education has been an effective avenue for framing, and shaping African thought. Not allowing ourselves to think outside of its manichaen binary causes us to engage in the most conservative interpretation of African tradition. Makumbi challenges stereotypical notions of its role, particularly its purpose and function in post Idi Amin Uganda, where Makerere University once stood proudly as symbol of enlightenment in East Africa. It is now "the haunt of failures. Intellectuals stood out. A mournful and persecuted demeanour, a battered leather bag full of paper and worn away soles of shoes were the classic signs of an intellectual" (Makumbi 2014, 271). It is no wonder by the time Miisi returns to teach at Makerere with his Cambridge PhD in Anthropology, the students have given up on education: they just want the certificate. The spotlight is on both Makerere and Cambridge, once representative of the finest in education. At Makerere, the students' attitude is shaped by the anti-intellectualism of Idi Amin, who effectively destroyed the Academy. Miisi's degree in Anthropology is equally suspect, this being the discredited discipline that, anchored at Cambridge and Oxford, underwrote the colonial project by structuring hierarchically, and fixing the study of the native other.

In the village, they consequently "wore their intelligent face for Miisi, ready to sound intellectual" to indulge him (Makumbi 2014, 344). He

>...never talked about his research to the residents. What would he say? That he had spent four years exploring the possibility that bloodletting in society was buried deep in the human psyche where spiritual impulses lay? Understandably, the residents had nothing but contempt for Ugandans who got a chance to acquire

knowledge and chose to acquire the useless kind (Makumbi 2014, 345).

The villagers were pragmatic, wanting a real–medical–doctor, a healer. They are unable to reconcile Miisi's own quest to first understand and heal self by way of western education, notwithstanding that his focus was on the local. This is where Makumbi comes into her own, interweaving western modes of knowing with the traditional in 'simultaneous interpellation' (Garuba 2015, 22). Although Miisi's doctoral thesis topic may sound arcane, even irrelevant to the villagers, its substance comes out of their shared life. It is also crucial for his preparation, and understanding of the family tragedies and tensions, past, and present.

Miisi is the 'chosen one'. Makumbi selects this soundly educated man to lead the family through the traditional rites and obligations that will free them of the curse. The ancestors know where to engage him: in his subconscious. They visit often, and give clear instructions on how to work towards reuniting the family and breaking the curse. He thinks of these visitations as dreams, explaining them to himself within the scope of his experience; rationalising them as surely as he resists the inexplicable. As his sister observes, "Miisi was endowed with both cerebral knowledge and a non-cerebral way of knowing. But every time ours popped up, he squeezed and muted" (Makumbi 2014, 442). In Kiddu, he holds back, neither leading effectively, nor entering fully into the spirit of things. Already, so much he had thought was a dream is proving true as to make him afraid. He subsequently stays behind when the elders go to *o* Lwera to exhume the ancestors. His fate is already cast, however. We know Kamu is dead, and it is his late knowledge of this news that is the last straw. His fear makes him privilege only one way—the western way—of knowing (Makumbi 2014, 377). At the shrine, we are told "he felt a tinge of cynicism" (Makumbi 2014, 392), and indeed, he catches Muganda, the medium, who senses his reticence, looking at him with amusement. When he doesn't whisper into his stick in final release, the premonition that Isaac has over this too Anglicized elder— "tradition showed that reluctant mediums paid a heavy price" (Makumbi 2014, 384), and Kanani's skepticism of his dual role—for him "the seamless marriage of heathenness and intellectuality was unnatural" (Makumbi 2014, 378)—are borne out. In a sense, Miisi has already suffered the colloquial permanent head damage (PhD) that is complement to his intermittent inherited madness. He is both insider, and outsider, trapped in the interstices of the traditional and the western, as an actor/observer in both. Witnessing Suubi's possession by her twin spirit, the disciplined curiosity of his training kicks in at this "chance to observe the transpossession phenomenon", which he will analyse in due course (Makumbi 2014, 397). It is a curious phenomenon, and the one that might hold the answers to Miisi's deepest questions on sacrifice, and atonement. Her twin insists on being part of Suubi's life, while Suubi wants her to stay dead. They straddle two separate, but interlinked worlds. The clan is shocked that a twin can desire to destroy her other. But no one has taught Suubi to embrace the layered world that she inhabits, making hers a conflicted spirit. Her first aunt all but killed Babirye off, chastising the young Suubi, natural in her acceptance of her twin, for carrying on a relationship with her. Babirye had tried ever since to reenter Suubi's life, punishing her severely for attempting to separate what is in fact one soul. The twin motif is deeply complex, and Makumbi uses it to full effect, in situations of conflict, and conciliation. Isaac, for instance, believes he is 'visited' by Babirye and Nnakato of old, and although they are stillborn, they seal his relationship with Nnayiga; and between Baale and Kalema she demonstrates that twin souls are not necessarily born of one womb; that fellowship, that Ubuntu can be forged out of circumstance. We are not privy to Miisi's 'due course' analysis in the end. He struggles valiantly against traditional frames, thus denying them full agency.

It is to Muganda, symbolically named for the new nation, that we ultimately look for understanding. Like Miisi, he is a Cambridge man, now also medium. He embraces his role fully, slacks, polo shirt and designer watch notwithstanding, and equally at home in traditional dress. Reflecting on the role of dress, Miisi had himself earlier found comfort and identity in the 'traditional', now domesticated kanzu: "[He] was at one with himself. A *kanzu* made him feel authentic: African, Ganda, a muntu" (Makumbi 2014, 320).[15] The kanzu itself, of course, carries a history of earlier colonization by the Arabs, with western coat adding its own emblematic layer to the palimpsest of

---

15 Introduced by the Arabs in the first half of the 19th Century, it was first worn by Kabaka Suuna. It eventually trickled down, with the later addition of the uniquely Ugandan *Omulele* embroidery/trimming, and a coat, representing western influence. (*New Monitor* online)

influences that inform post/colonial modernity. It is an unstable place from which both Miisi, and Muganda, must select their armour. Charged with undoing the curse, Muganda's robing is layered with these multiple influences. And as matters come to a climax, he knots a traditional barkcloth over his kanzu, and dons other traditional paraphernalia to complete his regalia (Makumbi 2014, 394). He is keenly conscious of the nuanced nature of identities, which he bears with ceremonial gravitas, lending great dignity to the task. The ritual is prefaced by this invocation:

> I speak for Kintu's children—past, present and to come…. We've come together as children from a single spring to strip ourselves of a heritable curse. As we obtain peace of mind, we seek rest for our mother Nnakato, our father Kintu and brother Kalema. Ntwire shall let go of the child nursed on Nnakato's breast. Because Kalema found a home and family in Buganda, we shall sever all Ntwire's claims on the lad (Makumbi 2014, 394).

Makumbi ultimately challenges the ways we limit ourselves in our capacities to know, understand, and interact with the layered worlds we inhabit. She gives us a traditional world crafted around and predicated on Ntwire's revenge. In a relentless stream, it visits the promised cruelties on Kintu, and his progeny in a demonstration of Achebe's proverb that "if one finger brought oil, it soiled the others". Nevertheless, Makumbi insists on human agency. Misii may attempt to escape from the complications of interpersonal relations that are his heritage, but even in his embrace of the newness and distance of the west, he cannot escape from people. Repeated rejection as by the O'Tooles might have blunted his sensibilities, but he is not forgiven this lapse. He slides into madness for engaging with knowledge only partially, at one level. In Kiriikiya, madness is the familiar for this family, its genesis explained by the curse. Yet it is the depth of Misii's love for his son Kamu that precipitates the break. It is in similar vein that Suubi provokes Babirye's fury when she tries to kill her already dead twin. Isolated and rejected from childhood, she finds it difficult to suddenly embrace all these people, Babirye included. As she explains it to her newly-found cousin, Nnabaale: "Now this reunion is forcefully grafting and stitching all the pieces back together which is a good thing but in some cases, like mine, it does not work. I don't want the pieces back. I have lived without them for too long that I don't know how to live with them" (Makumbi 2014, 391). Ubuntu—relationships of personhood—provides the rationale in this epic, and for Suubi it is enough that she has to grapple with its reach into the next world. If it is crucial in living relationships, in death it is sacred. Suubi is conjoined to Babirye in life, and death, and must carry the bound Babirye with her always.[16]

The instructions accompanying the exhumation and reburying of Kintu and kin further serve to underscore the links between life and death, with the sanctity of death only secured by a life fulfilled in relationships, with both insider and outsider. It is the multiplicity of old failures that lead to this moment of atonement. Makumbi, seizing "the power to narrate" (Garuba 2015, 20) draws Miisi into the family vortex on this journey where nothing but the bloodline is certain, cutting across time and the liminal spaces between. She demonstrates what Garuba contends theoretically, bringing into play the "simultaneous interpellation as producing coeval subjects and coeval subjectivities that challenge the epistemic grounds of conventional dichotomous and binary conceptions of modernity and normalization" (Garuba 2015, 22). But where she has led us all along to think that Miisi is the carrier of clan destiny, his failure to imagine such an epistemic leap might be tragic were it not for the self-styled Great Aunt Bweeza (Magda). She has no such difficulty. She saw through the alienating trajectory of, and rejected religion, and aspects of western education early. She is also in constant struggle against the gender biases of her strongly patriarchal society even as she is ensconced firmly in tradition. From there, she is the constant, a clear-eyed gauge of both the traditional, and the present. She is sensitive to the nuances of the family and has prepared herself to be fully engaged, recognising that the reunion is only the beginning of the much longer process of release. In crafting this continuum of restoration, Makumbi diligently tugs at the same threads Suubi shuns, stitching back from frayed and tattered bits of patch, sometimes passing a painful needle through many folds to secure a seam. That she succeeds in fashioning this garment at all, in all its terrible beauty, is a tremendous accomplishment.

---

16 It is fashioned as jewelry. The cross of Christ, worn by Catholics, is such a symbol.

BIBLIOGRAPHY

Achebe, Chinua. 2006. *Things Fall Apart.* London: Penguin Books.

Appiah, Kwame Anthony. 2005. *The Ethics of Identity.* New Jersey: Princeton University Press.

Falola, Toyin. 2003. *The Power of African Cultures.* New York: University of Rochester Press.

Garuba, Harry. 2015. "Postcolonial Modernity and Normalisation: Reading Chinua Achebe's *Arrow of God* in the Present Tense", in *Chinua Achebe's Legacy: Illuminations from Africa,* edited by James Ogude, 16-29. Pretoria: AISA.

Kuhanen, Jan. 2015. "'No sex until marriage!': Moralism, politics and the realities of HIV prevention in Uganda, 1986-1996." *Journal of Eastern African Studies,* 9(2): 270-288.

Makumbi, J. N. 2014. *Kintu,* Nairobi: Kwani Trust.

Masolo, D A. Forthcoming. "Crafting Ideal Conditions: "Ubuntu" and the Challenges of Modern Society".

Nyamjoh, Francis B. 2015. "Amos Tutuola and the Elusiveness of Completeness." *Stichproben. Wiener Zeitschrift für kritische Afrikastudien,* 29 (15): 1-47.

Obama, Barack. 2015. "Remarks by President Obama to the Kenyan People." Safaricom Indoor Arena, Nairobi, Kenya, 26 July 2015. Available: http://www.Whitehouse.gov. Accessed: 3 April 2016.

Okurut, Mary. 1994. *The Invisible Weevil.* Kampala: Femrite Publications Ltd.

Saul, John S. 2004 [1976]. "The Unsteady State: Uganda, Obote & General Amin". In *The Politics of Transition in Africa: State, Democracy & Economic Development,* edited by Giles Mohan and Tunde Zack-Williams, 17-31. Sheffield: ROAPE/James Currey.

Selassie, Tayie. 2013. *Ghana Must Go.* London: Viking.

Simmel, Georg. 1990. *The Philosophy of Money.* 2nd edition edited by David Frisby. London: Routledge.

Tamale, Sylvia (ed.). 2011. *African Sexualities: A Reader.* Cape Town: Pambazuka Press.

Warnier, Jean-Pierre. 2013. "Quelle Sociologie du Politique? À l'école de Weber et Foucault en Afrique." *Pensar Global,* 1: 95-108.

Zelizer, Viviana, A. 1994. *The Social Meaning of Money: Pin money, paychecks, poor relief and other currencies.* US: Basic Books.

CHAPTER 8. ANTJIE KROG'S EXPLORATION OF UBUNTU

Jacomien Van Niekerk

INTRODUCTION

Antjie Krog is one of the voices currently contributing to the discourse on Ubuntu in South Africa, Her work is accessible yet thought-provoking. Krog bridges the divide between popular or general conceptions of Ubuntu and rigorous philosophical analyses. This chapter specifically traces Krog's exploration of Ubuntu in her non-fiction trilogy. However, the study could also potentially be broadened to include Krog's poetry (spanning four decades), her translation of other poets, her academic articles and pieces in newspapers, public lectures, among others. Krog has emerged as an increasingly visible public intellectual (Garman 2015) whose views are not only shaped by discourses around her but who also shapes those discourses. The latter can be seen in the contribution made to the Ubuntu discourse by Krog in coining the phrase "interconnectedness-towards-wholeness". As the debate rages on the existence and nature of Ubuntu, I believe much is to be learned from Krog's work. Though her exploration of Ubuntu is unsystematic, the overview I provide in this chapter highlights the important insights to be gleaned from Krog.

Krog first gained international recognition when she published her first non-fiction book in English, *Country of My Skull*, which was the result of her work as a journalist during the Truth and Reconciliation Commission (TRC) hearings which took place from 1996 to 1998. *Country of My Skull* has been translated into several languages, has received multiple awards, and has given Krog access to a global community of readers. Krog continues to write poetry in Afrikaans, and her poetry has been translated into English.[1] She has also donned the hat of an academic: she was appointed as Extraordinary Professor in the Faculty of Arts at the University of the Western Cape, and she spent nine months at the Wissenschaftskolleg in Berlin in 2007/2008 on a research fellowship and again in 2013.

Two further English works of 'literary non-fiction' have followed the first: *A Change of Tongue* (2003) and *Begging to Be Black* (2009). These three books have come to be regarded as a trilogy; I use the term 'transformation trilogy' in acknowledgement of the centrality of the theme of personal and collective transformation in all three texts. In this article the three texts will be read in conjunction with each other. I argue that several common themes run through all three texts, even though they differ from each other regarding form and content. Each text is characterized by a hybrid juxtaposition of genres (including history, journalism, autobiography and poetic techniques), a multiplicity of voices complementing that of the narrator, and chronological leaps. I believe the intensely creative, varied and ultimately inconclusive nature of the trilogy to be central to the interpretation of the three texts. However, in this article I won't be able to comment extensively on these textual features. My aim is to provide an overview of the ways in which Antjie Krog engages with the concept of Ubuntu in her trilogy.

Krog has been actively involved in the public discourse on Ubuntu, giving public lectures in which she explores the concept, and participating in academic conferences held around the subject. She has also published two academic articles (Krog 2008a and 2008b) that arguably entail a more 'academic', philosophical approach to the concept than in her trilogy. In this article, however, I concentrate mainly on the trilogy, since in these texts 'Krog, the academic'

---

1   Two anthologies exist to date of Krog's poetry in English: *Down to my last skin* (2000) and *Skinned* (2013). Her volumes *Verweerskrif* (2006) and *Mede-wete* (2014) were simultaneously published in English as *Body bereft* and *Synapse*.

intersects with 'Krog, the poet' and 'Krog, the prose writer'. In the trilogy, Krog contributes to the Ubuntu discourse in direct (academic) and indirect ('literary') ways. Antjie Krog has not been trained as a philosopher. Neither have I: I originally came to the trilogy as an Afrikaans literary scholar well acquainted with Krog's poetry. Consequently, Krog's incorporation of African philosophy should be read with the understanding that she is an amateur philosopher. I analyse the way in which Krog incorporates African philosophy and ponders the implications of an 'African world view' in her trilogy as part of a broader effort in her trilogy to understand and engage with post-1994 South Africa. Garman (2015) argues that Krog's power in the public sphere lies precisely in her utilisation of the literary or the aesthetic; this is an important insight to keep in mind even as I explore Krog's attempts at 'doing philosophy'.

UBUNTU AND 'INTERCONNECTEDNESS-TOWARDS-WHOLENESS'

During or closely following the nine months spent as a research fellow in Berlin in 2008, Krog published two academic articles on interconnectedness: "'...if it means he gets his humanity back...': The Worldview Underpinning the South African Truth and Reconciliation Commission" and "'This thing called reconciliation...': forgiveness as part of an interconnectedness-towards-wholeness". It is in these articles that she coins the term 'interconnectedness-towards-wholeness'. It is clear that Krog uses the term as a synonym for Ubuntu, for she frequently follows its use with the phrase "or ubuntu". However, Krog consistently prefers her own term, because she believes "the over-use and exploitation of the word ubuntu makes it nearly unusable" (Krog 2008b, 355).

She then goes on to place interconnectedness-towards-wholeness "firmly within the well defined and formulated broader African communitarianism as well as the more Southern African localized term of ubuntu". She continues:

> Interconnectedness-towards-wholeness [...] is more than just a theoretical knowledge that all things in the world are linked, it means both a mental and physical awareness that one can only 'become' who one is, or could be, through the fullness of that which is around one—both physical and metaphysical [...]

Wholeness is thus not a passive state of nirvana, but a process of becoming in which everybody and everything is moving towards its fullest self, building itself; one can only reach that fullest self [...] through and with others which include ancestors and universe (Krog 2008, 355).

This chapter will illustrate how Krog writes about 'becoming (whole)' "through and with others" in many varied ways in the trilogy. The term 'interconnectedness-towards-wholeness' is not used in the trilogy; instead, the word "interconnectedness" occurs frequently in *Begging to Be Black*, and throughout the trilogy Krog sometimes utilises the term Ubuntu. At other times she refers to an 'African world view' or completely refrains from naming the phenomenon she is describing.

All three texts of the transformation trilogy contain the word Ubuntu in their glossaries. The differing definitions of the term reflect the developing interpretation of the concept over the past two decades in the discourse on Ubuntu in South Africa. In *Country of My Skull* the definition of Ubuntu is "philosophy of humanism, emphasizing the link between the individual and the collective". In *A Change of Tongue* Ubuntu is defined as "spirit of fellowship and compassion in African society" and in *Begging to Be Black* as "world view based on the idiom *umuntu ngumuntu ngabantu*—a person is a person through other persons".[2]

In the texts of the trilogy themselves Krog refers to Ubuntu a number of times. Sometimes this is done by quoting her 'black' interlocutors, for example someone who states, "Whites [...] have no *ubuntu...* they choke on all their rights, but they have no human compassion" (Krog 2000, 59). Krog quotes the 'black' psychologist Nomfundo Walaza who defines Ubuntu as the ability to share with others that was to the detriment of 'black' people during colonisation (Krog 2000, 213). In writing about Desmond Tutu, she quotes Michael Battle's description of Tutu's "ubuntu theology" and she provides Battle's reference to John Mbiti's well-known aphorism "I am because we are, and since we are, therefore I am (Krog 2000,

---

2   Gade (2011) has shown that the proverb, "Umuntu ngumuntu ngabantu" has only become a veritable 'definition' of Ubuntu since 199?

143). The latter is similar to Krog's own formulation when she writes about Nelson Mandela and collectivism: "I am because I am with you" (Krog 2003, 259). The two aspects of Ubuntu that speak to Krog are the features of a communitarian society (which I will return to later) and the link between forgiveness and reconciliation and ubuntu.

In *A Change of Tongue*, Deborah Matshoba, a victim who testified at the TRC, states that "forgiveness is creating a culture of ubuntu, humaneness [...]" (Krog 2003, 157). After their conversation, Krog writes the following: "We make tea on the stove. Ubuntu. The most profound opposite of Apartheid. More than forgiveness or reconciliation. More than 'turn the other cheek'. It is what humanity has lost" (Krog 2003, 159). Years later, during her fellowship in Berlin, Krog attends a conference in Turkey where she presents an academic paper. She confronts her audience with the quote by Cynthia Ngewu (made famous by Krog's *Country of My Skull*) about what should happen to perpetrators of apartheid crimes: "We want to demonstrate a humanness [ubuntu] towards them, so that [it] in turn may restore their own humanity" (Krog 2009, 211). The international audience at the conference is fairly uncomprehending of the framework Krog is positing, leading her to conclude sadly that as Sandile Dikeni said, "The world will never learn anything from Africa" (2009, 212).

Krog's academic articles (2008a and 2008b) both centre on interconnectedness-towards-wholeness as something which makes a radical kind of forgiveness as well as restoration of the perpetrator possible. Krog is critical of "the usurpation of the TRC process by Christianity and human rights" which "obscures how [...] a radically new way [of dealing with injustice], imbedded in an indigenous view of the world, had been put on the table by black people at the end of the twentieth century" (2009, 206).

In addition, perhaps controversially, Krog attempts to explain the phenomenon of 'black' South African xenophobia (particularly following the attacks on foreigners in 2008) by way of Ubuntu. She sees the urban centres of South Africans consisting of an "influx of rural people from tight interconnected groups" who have lost their interconnectedness "with their community, with its spiritual presence of ancestors, nature, etc." (2009, 235-236). When confronted with uprooted people from other African countries, South Africans want to distance themselves from the failure they associate with the rest of

Africa. Krog concludes, "it is not a case of ubuntu is dead, as I originally thought, killed by black people; it is the opposite: ubuntu is so very much alive that people do not survive these brutalizing-into-being-an-individual surroundings" (2009, 236). This interpretation builds on an earlier reference by Krog to A.C. Jordan's reading of the works of Tiyo Soga.[3] In the nineteenth century Soga remarked that the arrival of Christianity destroyed "wholeness", because Christians suddenly did not want to welcome non-Christians into their homes. "[Soga] said that interconnectedness is what takes place between the community and the stranger [...] and it is the specific task of the intellectual to be an advocate for the stranger—to insist on responsibility for the stranger as constitutive of collectivity itself" (Krog 2009, 185-186).

It is clear that Krog is extremely aware of the discourse on Ubuntu in South Africa, and it is one of the concepts (like 'transformation' and 'truth') that she seeks to unpack and understand in her trilogy (and elsewhere). Specifically, she feels that she needs to understand Ubuntu as part of her larger desire to understand 'black' people in South Africa in her quest for belonging to that country.

It is notable that Krog never engages with 'ubuntu philosophers' who attempt to articulate or apply the concept of Ubuntu. Arguably this would have fallen outside the scope and nature of her trilogy, but Krog *does* engage with a selection of African philosophers as I show below. The unfortunate result is that Krog seems to assume that the meaning of Ubuntu is self-evident in the South African context (or that the definitions given in the glossaries of her texts are sufficient). While Krog can assume knowledge of Ubuntu on the part of her audience in the academic articles, the same is not necessarily true of her trilogy. Despite the problematic nature of Krog's endeavours, I wish to turn to her *procédé* in her trilogy because I believe that large parts of it *are* helpful for our understanding of Ubuntu.

3   Krog is, in turn, paraphrasing Mark Sanders (2002: 124-126, and elsewhere).

TRACING THE EDGES OF UBUNTU IN THE TRANSFORMATION TRILOGY

A series of conversations[4] that took place between Krog and the Australian philosopher Paul Patton in Berlin contribute to the more 'academic' slant of *Begging to Be Black* as compared to the other two texts in the trilogy. However, the questions that can be abstracted from these conversations occur, in my opinion, throughout the transformation trilogy. They centre on the legacy of colonialism in Africa and South Africa, the place of 'white' people in South Africa, and what constitutes truly ethical conduct in the post-colonial context of a South Africa governed by the 'black' majority. It is beyond the scope of this article to explore each of these questions, but I believe that Krog's engagement with Ubuntu stems from the latter issue. She repeatedly states in *Begging to Be Black* and elsewhere that after 1994 the "Western or European frameworks" that had guided her in the past have become "useless and redundant" (Krog 2009, 93). She believes that there is something intrinsically different about a 'black' or 'African' world view, and she endeavours throughout her trilogy to pinpoint what that different world view entails.

During the second conversation with Patton, which she titles "Petrus's story", the fictional character Petrus from J.M. Coetzee's *Disgrace* (to whom *Begging to Be Black* is dedicated) becomes emblematic of the misunderstood 'black' Other. Krog ascribes a monologue to Petrus in which he states, "I function within an ethic that is communal to the core. The benefit to the community, whether they are the living, the living-dead or the still-to-come, is what determines whether something is good or bad. [...] But I, Petrus, am being held captive within an ethic that is individual and Christian-based to the core [...]" (Krog 2009, 102). In this quote, Krog is captivated by the implications of a communitarian culture.

Communitarianism is described as follows by Es'kia Mphahlele in an essay on African humanism: "The African begins with the

---

4   The conversations are as follows: "Lines of Flight" (Krog 2009: 92-93), "Petrus's Story" (2009: 99-102), "Imagining Black" (2009: 122-123), "Been There Done That" (2009: 155-156), "Interconnected With Whom?" (2009: 184-186), a number of informal conversation on the way to and in Turkey (2009: 203-206, 208-212), "Xenophobia" (2009: 235-239), and "Formation of the Self" (2009: 266-269).

community and then determines what the individual's place and role should be in relation to the community. These are features of African humanism. It is a communal concept, and there are no individual heroes within the world it encompasses. Man finds fulfilment not as a separate individual but within family and community" (Mphahlele 2002, 147).

Krog's efforts to understand the "communal concept" of African humanism has not been the subject of existing studies. I therefore briefly examine the different ways in which she does this: firstly, by incorporating African orality in her trilogy: "Our oral poetry is our way of communicating with the divine forces, for poetry is a way of perceiving, a way of seeking to touch the Highest Reality beneath the surface of things" (Mphahlele 2002, 139). Secondly, I touch on Krog's analysis of cultural practices, and thirdly on her focus on three symbolic 'black' leaders: Desmond Tutu, Nelson Mandela and King Moshoeshoe I.

AFRICAN ORAL LITERATURE[5] IN THE TRILOGY

Quantitatively speaking, instances of African orality make up a small part of the transformation trilogy. Still, these parts of the trilogy belong to the various techniques through which Krog emphasises non-western phenomena as part of a broader argument in which she chooses 'Africa' over 'Europe'. It can also be argued that the examples of African orality are a way for Krog to explore African philosophy. The oral forms that feature in the trilogy are praise poetry, praise names, and folktales.

Praise poems (*izibongo* in Zulu and Xhosa) usually contain the lineage of the person being praised. In *Country of My Skull* Chief Anderson Joyi, a Xhosa chief of the Thembu group, appears in front of the TRC. Krog chooses to not provide his testimony in itself, but she records the genealogy with which the chief introduces his testimony. She interviews the chief afterwards and asks him why he chose to begin his testimony in this way. He answers: "Their names organise the flow of time [...] Their names put what has happened to me in perspective. Their names say I am a chief with many colours.

---

5   Krog has translated African oral literature as well as published poetry in the African languages into Afrikaans in an anthology titled *Met woorde soos met kerse* [*With words like with candles*] published in 2002.

Their names say we have the ability to endure the past... and the present" (2000, 181-182).

When one examines the genealogy, it becomes clear that only the last five generations mentioned by Chief Joyi reigned during and after colonialism; in other words, the pre-colonial period is more significant in a quantitative sense. This indeed places the chief's suffering under apartheid in some perspective, since it also suggests that his lineage will continue into the future. This significant passage possibly further suggests that Chief Joyi's lineage and testimony is emblematic of the other victims of apartheid: they, too, have a lineage and a context that might help them "to endure the past... and the present" (Krog 2000, 181-182). This is not done to undermine the testimonies recorded by Krog, but it does subtly open the possibility that 'black' people do not simply possess a narrative of victimhood under apartheid. Their life narrative involves being interconnected with the living and the dead, and that can be seen as empowering.

In *A Change of Tongue*, physical descriptions of Nelson Mandela echo a praise poem in Afrikaans that Krog wrote for Mandela in 1995 (Krog 1995a, 8-9), in which she transposed the prominent Southern African oral tradition of *izibongo* into Afrikaans (cf. Van Niekerk 2007). Krog also translated the praise poems by two Xhosa *iimbongi* with the help of Xhosa experts, and she replicates parts of the research she did on *iimbongi* (Krog 1994) in *A Change of Tongue* (2003, 206-207). Apart from composing a praise poem for Mandela, Krog allows herself to be so deeply influenced by this oral tradition that she composes a praise poem of sorts for her dead father at the end of *A Change of Tongue* (Krog 2003, 365).

In *Begging to Be Black* Krog analyses the different significant names that were given to King Moshoeshoe I. At birth his name was "*Lepoqo* (Dispute)" (2009, 22), and as he became older, the following names were given to him: "*Tlaputle* (Energetic-One)", "*Lekhema* (Hasty-One)" and then "*Letlama* (Together-Binder)": "the name given to him in his initiation praises" (Krog 2009, 23). Krog sees an important progression in these names, finally culminating in the praise name "Moshoeshoe" which was the result of a successful cattle raid. The *sh*-sounds in the praise poem that was created on the spot (*Ke'na Moshoeshoe Moshoashoaila oa ha Kali*) refer to "the fast, swishing, snappy, snipping way in which the raid had been carried out" (Krog 2009, 23).

A few pages later, Krog refers to other praise poems created for Moshoeshoe in which his ability to convince others to reform are at the forefront.[6] In other words, Krog supplements her extensive descriptions of Moshoeshoe's leadership and characteristics (which I will further explore below) with references to praise names and praise poems, similar to her incorporation of praise poems for Mandela.

Praise poems and praise names establish meaningful connections between the person they are centred on and the persons reciting them. The characteristics and achievements of the person being praised are recalled every time the praise poem is recited. The same applies to the connotations evoked every time a person's praise name is used. It is significant that *only* Moshoeshoe's final praise name survives in the public imagination.

In contrast to these examples of connectedness between humans, the folktale recorded in *A Change of Tongue* describes a deep connectedness between humans and nature. This well-known Fulani folktale involves a pair of twins, one of which was a boy and the other a snake. The human brother takes care of the various physical needs of his snake brother, and the snake brother educates the human brother on nature. One day, the human brother returns ill from the desert, unable to breathe. He suddenly coughs up seven wet, slimy lumps: a mist of sky, a word of giraffe, a burning moon, a weeping tree, a clump of water, a railroad track and a feathered wing. The human brother does not know what these things mean, but the snake brother says, "'I will teach you to become them, to see what they mean,' explained the snake-brother, 'and live with grace on the earth'" (Krog 2003, 321, abridged by me).

It is significant that Krog does not pedantically explain the folktale but rather engages it deeply yet subtly on a textual level by turning the 'seven lumps' into seven interludes. These seven interludes are central to the themes of transformation (Burger 2011, 33), of becoming (Polatinsky 2009, 86), the relationship between the

---

6   Krog quotes Daniel Kunene on the praises for Moshoeshoe: "the words *ho thapisa* mean 'to charm, to tame the wild nature of' [...] The word *charm*, with its meanings of attracting and winning over, sums up the technique Moshoeshoe used: no force or violence, but convincing people with gentle but firm domestication" (Krog 2009: 28).

self and the other and a moral way of living in South Africa, issues I believe to be key to the entire trilogy.

In summary, by placing examples of oral traditions in her trilogy, Krog is highlighting the fact that these forms are African and not western. She is educating her readers about literary forms that 'white' readers are generally unfamiliar with, thereby suggesting that there is something enriching about these indigenous traditions and the people who hold them. Moreover, the content of genealogies, praise poems and praise names illustrate, for Krog, a communitarian way of living, and the folktale she cites demonstrates the interconnectedness of all things in creation, something which I will show below is part of Krog's understanding of Ubuntu.

KROG'S ANALYSIS OF AFRICAN CULTURAL PRACTICES

In the very first chapter of *Country of My Skull*, Krog writes about the cattle raid that gave Moshoeshoe his name: "He who can steal as swiftly and silently as cutting someone's beard" (also see the section on praise names above). She asks a 'black' colleague, Mondli, "How can the deftness of stealing be a mark of honor? Why did Dingane ask Retief to steal back the cattle stolen by Sekonyela? Why would Mandela write in his biography about the cattle he and his cousin stole from his uncle? Do we understand the same thing when we talk about stealing?" (Krog 2000, 18).

Mondli answers that he was raised with the belief that stealing from 'white' people was not really stealing and that for Africans, stealing meant "taking cattle as a means of contesting power". However, 'white' people accused 'black' people of theft, "while at that very same minute you were stealing everything from us!" (Krog 2000, 18). This example is one of the instances where Krog explores moral issues in her trilogy. Are there universal principles about what is right and wrong, or can different cultures have different conceptions about this? Mondli's oblique reference to colonialism and apartheid already suggests that morality is not universally definable. Krog pursues this question with regard to different contexts in the three texts of the trilogy. The above quote about cattle raiding as ritual is one of several 'cultural practices' (for want of a better term) that are analysed by Krog in the trilogy, especially in *Begging to Be Black*.

191

Krog is struck by the way the missionaries (Eugène Casalis and Thomas Arbousset) that lived at Thaba Bosiu with King Moshoeshoe I insisted on interpreting morality in a singularly Christian context. However, in the Basotho they were confronted with a morality that depended completely on the social order, "a moral framework rooted in communal life which questions the idea of individual responsibility and conversion" (Krog 2009, 82-83).

An example of this communally-rooted morality can be found in the Basotho understanding of work. Krog writes about Moshoeshoe's request that the Basotho not be compensated for the work they did for the missionaries. Casalis and Arbousset interpreted this as exploitation, and were probably also irritated, according to Krog, by the fact that their own sacrifices seemed less impressive "if this very pagan community already had a notion of 'building' oneself through voluntary labour" (Krog 2009, 106).

Without being specific, Krog refers to "African philosophers" who define personhood within a "communitarian African world view": "Who you are, what and how you are, is built by you over the years of your life through caring interconnectedness" (Krog 2009, 106). Krog then proceeds to show that 'work' and 'personhood' were intricately linked for the Basotho. She draws partly on the work of the Comaroffs, whose research on the Tswana of the nineteenth century can be safely held as applicable to the neighbouring Basotho in the same time period. The Comaroffs explain the concept of *tiro,* work, as follows:

> [...] *tiro* was not an abstract quality, a commodity to be bought or sold. It could not exist as alienable labour power [...] Work, in short, was the positive, relational aspect of human social activity; of the making of self and others in the course of everyday life. Not only were social beings made and remade by *tiro,* but the product— namely, personhood—was inseparable from the process of production itself (Comaroff and Comaroff 2001, 274).

The above approach to work played out, among other things, as the phenomenon of communal farming among the Basotho. Whenever someone needed help with building a hut, planting or harvesting, he could call on the assistance of the community, and would in future assist his neighbours in a similar way. The missionaries were disdainful of this practice, since they saw no possibility for industry or trade in it (Krog 2009, 106-107). Krog repeatedly shows how unreceptive the missionaries were to practices or beliefs that deviated from their Christian-western framework. Eventually Krog avers that the interaction between the Basotho and the missionaries amounted to a clash of world views. Again drawing on the Comaroffs, Krog defines this clash between "two distinct world views" as rooted in the fact that "Western culture saw matter as neutral and man as the prime mover in his interaction with his surroundings, while the Basotho [spoke] openly of a world, 'connected and continuous', in which the inert has the ability to affect the lives of the living (Krog 2009, 113). She further states that the Basotho were not used to being confronted with a group of people who insisted that there was only one correct way to know and interpret the world, and who believed, "Those outside this 'true' way were inferior. They *could* enter the privileged way through conversion, but black people quickly realised that conversion made them 'like whites' but never equal to whites" (2009, 114).

This discovery that the world view of the Basotho was inclusive and therefore the direct opposite of that of the Christian missionaries, is an extremely important one for Krog. According to Mphahlele, this is one of the characteristics of what he calls African humanism: "our traditional humanism [...] is never exclusive, i.e. never shuts other people out [...]" (Mphahlele 2004, 285). In other parts of the trilogy Krog returns to this central aspect of the clash between colonialists and indigenous people, and between 'white' and 'black' people during and after apartheid. 'White' people continue to act from the assumption that their world view is the superior interpretation of 'reality', and this confrontation has an ethical dimension in that 'white' people see their practices and beliefs as morally correct and those of 'black' people as morally wrong.

SYMBOLIC LEADERS: TUTU, MANDELA, MOSHOESHOE

In *Country of My Skull*, Krog expresses her disappointment with Afrikaner leaders who refuse to take responsibility for apartheid and who fail to "[establish] a space within which we can confront ourselves and our past" (Krog 2000, 125). The absence of this kind of Afrikaner leader is juxtaposed with three symbolic 'black' leaders that Krog highlights in the three parts of the trilogy.

193

Desmond Tutu, the chairperson of the TRC, is portrayed by
Krog as a charismatic figure with great persuasive powers (Krog
2000, 22) and an influential rhetoric (2000, 61). Tutu comes to the
TRC with already-established notions about forgiveness and
reconciliation (2000, 23), which, according to academics, entails an
Africanisation of reconciliation: "The Church says: 'You must
forgive, because God has forgiven you for killing His Son'. Tutu says:
'You can only be human in a humane society. If you live with hatred
and revenge in your heart, you dehumanize not only yourself, but
your community'" (Krog 2000, 143). Krog also quotes Tutu's use of
the term "African *Weltanschauung*" in which he defines personhood as
something that depends on the community and involvement in the
life of the community (2000, 143).

In the course of *Country of My Skull*, Krog writes about Tutu in a
consistently emotional way. She finds the entire TRC process
"unthinkable" without Tutu, because "[i]t is he who finds the
language for what is happening" (Krog 2000, 201). Tutu is "[t]his
wonderful man in whose presence I always experience humanity at its
fullest—humanity as it was meant to be" (Krog 2000, 203). Not only
does Tutu *define* personhood and reconciliation within an African
world view, for Krog, he is the embodiment of a superior kind of
humanity. His inclusivity knows no bounds, as he weeps for both
F.W. de Klerk and Winnie Madikizela Mandela (Krog 2000, 210;
338). This inclusive approach to 'white' and 'black' perpetrators
enables Krog to feel a sense, however brief, of belonging to Africa
(Krog 2000, 338).

In *A Change of Tongue,* Krog identifies the western, individualistic
approach to leaders as problematic for Nelson Mandela's presidency.
Right through to the end of his term, according to a friend of
Mandela,[7] "[...] 'whites constantly sing the praises of Mandela, while
continuing to treat black people as they did before'" (Krog 2003:
259). This same friend explains to Krog that collectivism is not
empty rhetoric for Mandela, but a central part of him (Krog 2003:
257). The ANC could have chosen anyone to be its figurehead and
Mandela was to an extent an arbitrary choice. Krog quotes Mandela
as he emphasises that "[...] he is what he is because of others, black

---

7   Due to the fluid relationship between 'fact' and 'fiction' in Krog's
    trilogy, it is possible that this good friend of Mandela is an invention by
    Krog, a contraction of various conversations.

and white" (Krog 2003, 220) and "[...] 'I am the product of the people of South Africa'" (Krog 2003, 220).

Mandela's collectivism is properly underlined by Krog, who sees Mandela as transforming the Cartesian "I think therefore I am" into "I am because I am with you"—however, she has to add that what Mandela has accomplished far surpasses this simplistic opposition (Krog 2003, 259). Krog sees the essence of Mandela's autobiography as "The fact that you are interwoven with your community, and not your lonely singularity, finally determines your greatness" (Krog 2003, 275) and, "Mandela provides a totally new account of leadership within the nation [...]" (Krog 2003, 276).

Krog, however, struggles to relinquish her own individualistic perspective on Mandela. Like Tony Leon who compares Mandela with Gandhi and the Dalai Lama in Parliament (Krog 2003, 221), Krog writes about Mandela in an admiring, near-reverent way: "[...] he is teaching us a way of regarding the world, this miracle of a man, of being at grace with people, of being human in benign spaces, of preferring the skein of humanity to the fanatic purity of principle" (Krog 2003, 259).

The way Krog writes about Mandela is reminiscent of what Rob Nixon calls the "near-Messianic dimensions" of Mandela's reputation (1990, 43). During the 27 years of his imprisonment, Mandela was held up as a figure of salvation. Immediately on his release, Mandela started undermining this view by subordinating himself to the ANC (Nixon 1990, 43). However, Krog continues to portray Mandela as a saviour: not only of 'black' people, but also one who teaches 'white' people what true humanity is and teaches them about the superiority of collectivism to western individualism. This extraordinary "way of looking at the world" resides in "blackness" for Krog (2003, 259); nothing in her past could teach her this; she seems to find it only when sitting "opposite a black face" (Krog 2003, 259).

While holding up King Moshoeshoe I of Basotholand as an extraordinary leader like Tutu and Mandela, Krog does not withhold unattractive facts about Moshoeshoe in *Begging to Be Black*.[8] She asks how we can reconcile these facts (if they are indeed true) with an

---

8   There is a strong suggestion that Moshoeshoe murdered five boys when he himself was young, because they were disobedient (Krog 2009: 21-22) and that later in life he was responsible for the death of his first wife, Mamohato, (2009: 115-117).

otherwise remarkable human being. Krog partly leaves us with her own unresolved discomfort, but she also describes how, under the mentorship of Mohlomi, Moshoeshoe underwent a significant personal transformation and developed a comprehensive moral philosophy (2009, 23-24).

This philosophy is firstly illustrated by Krog by referring to the incident where a group of cannibals ate Moshoeshoe's own grandfather, Peete. Instead of condemning them to death, Moshoeshoe showed mercy to them and initiated them into his followers: "Through rituals, cattle and a safeguarded home, the cannibals could change their habits and earn their place back in the realm of humanity from which their behaviour of devouring fellow humans had expelled them" (2009, 26). This contra-intuitive behaviour of Moshoeshoe is appraised by Krog as follows: "he was not kind and caring out of weakness, but out of a strengthening belief that safety, care and trust unlocked powerful energies to the benefit of a community" (2009, 26).

Krog portrays the interaction of the missionaries Casalis and Arbousset with Moshoeshoe as emblematic of that of 'white' missionaries in Southern Africa, and, on a larger scale, of 'white' colonizers. Moshoeshoe was confronted with westerners who had admiration for him, but also saw him as inferior, and desired to appropriate him (Krog 2009, 19). Up until his death, Moshoeshoe remained the ultimate prize for the missionary who could convert him (Krog 2009, 21). Yet Moshoeshoe rejected the efforts at evangelising him; he believed that the Biblical morality taught by the missionaries was already familiar to the Basotho (Krog 2009, 78) and he openly questioned Christian morality. He did not believe in capital punishment (2009, 80) and failed to accept the justifications for war that the Christian missionaries tried to put forth (2009, 82).

Furthermore, Krog refers to several conversations and arguments between Moshoeshoe and the missionaries in which he tries to no avail to prove the equal value of Basotho beliefs and western beliefs. The image of Moshoeshoe that emerges in *Begging to Be Black* is that of a leader with a very thorough understanding of the philosophy that underlies the way of living of the Basotho. He is able to 'see through' the motivations and restricted world view of the missionaries and colonizers, but this only means that he has to endeavour to defend himself against their views for the rest of his life. Krog compares Nelson Mandela and Moshoeshoe and finds that both leaders were "exceptionalized" by westerners who in their "culture of individuality" could not conceive of a leader who is closely connected to his people (Krog 2009, 228).

THE ORIGINS OF UBUNTU

In *Begging to Be Black* Krog speculates that the interconnectedness she observes in 'black' people was inherited by them from the Khoisan, since the world view of the Khoisan is one which implies a cosmological dimension, "a human and non-human world that encapsulates plants, animals, a spiritual god and ancestors" (2009, 184). In the same way that the click sounds of the Khoisan survives in the Bantu languages, Krog argues, their world view significantly influenced the speakers of the Bantu languages. As attractive as this theory might seem, Michael Wessels (2012) has convincingly argued that there are in fact intrinsic differences between Khoisan spirituality and that of Bantu language speakers. He is also sceptical of the possible motivating factors guiding Krog's hypothesis (2012, 187) on which I cannot, in the interest of space, expand here.

A valid question that can be asked regarding Krog and Ubuntu, is the role of the spiritual for her. Based on her repeated criticism of Christianity, Krog does not appear to want to place her observations within a Christian framework. At the same time, she does appear to support an interpretation of Ubuntu in which spirituality is not absent. Notably, in *Begging to Be Black*, Krog is struck by an old man in Lesotho who explains his connectedness with all of the earth, and who speaks to "somebody or something that is near. Here. With us" (2009, 253)

I believe this issue of spirituality and Ubuntu requires further inquiry. Mphahlele easily states, that "African humanism [...] could never be a godless way of life. The African is a believer in the Supreme Being" (Mphahlele 2002, 151). Is Krog however correct in seeing this Supreme Being as reconcilable with the Christian God, as argued by Wessels (2012, 189)? Her references in *Begging to Be Black* include the work of the theologian Gerrit Brand on "African Christian Theology" (who quotes the theologian Manas Buthelezi) and works by Gabriel Setiloane, including the unpublished *How the Traditional World-View persists in the Christianity of the Sotho-Tswana* (Krog 2009, 291). What are the implications if Krog purports to be exploring an ethic which is rooted in an 'African worldview', but her ethics are revealed to be essentially Christian in nature?

KROG AND AFRICAN PHILOSOPHY

As stated earlier, Antjie Krog is not a philosopher. However, in her quest to understand 'blackness' or an 'African world view', Krog interacts with African philosophy in a limited way in her trilogy. She does not restrict herself to a specific trend, to use Oruka's terminology, but explores the work of a number of different African philosophers and pseudo-philosophers. Her own contribution also spans many different approaches to African philosophy. In all this, she has in part been influenced very specifically by the American philosopher Richard H. Bell as I shall demonstrate below.

Using Oruka's categories, the following brief remarks can be made. In her trilogy and her two academic articles, Krog briefly quotes or refers to: ethnophilosophers like John Mbiti, professional philosophers like Paulin Hountondji and Tsenay Serequeberhan, creative writer-philosophers like Wole Soyinka (Krog 2008a and 2008b) and philosophers who do linguistic analysis like Kwame Gyekye. One could even possibly argue that Krog does a kind of sage philosophy in the many conversations she has with 'black' people in the course of the trilogy, in an effort to understand certain phenomena and practices. With the help of certain interlocutors, Krog also attempts linguistic analysis. Though in the interest of space I cannot further expand on my contention regarding sage philosophy, this article does contain various examples of Krog's conversations with 'black' South Africans that at least partly illustrate my argument. I will only briefly go into Krog's linguistic analysis here before touching on the remaining aspects of her engagement with African philosophy.

In short, Krog's 'linguistic analysis' consists of an analysis of words in African languages for 'white' people. Krog herself does not speak an African language fluently, though she knows some Sesotho because of growing up on a farm in the Free State. In her translations of indigenous African poetry in *Met woorde soos met kerse* (2002),[9] Krog was aided by various 'black' and 'white' experts in the various South African languages. In the trilogy, Krog also relies on the

---

9   See note 7.

interpretations of mother tongue speakers of African languages as well as other experts (or purported experts).

The word for 'white' person in Sesotho is *lekgoa* (in the South African orthography) or *lekhoa* (the spelling used in Lesotho). The plural is *makgoa* or *makhoa*. In the related language Sepedi (or Northern Sotho) the spelling is *lekgowa* and *makgowa*. In *A Change of Tongue*, a group of 'black' children on Krog's childhood farm tell her that *makgoa* means 'baboons'. They provide the following justification for this: "Because baboons always look over their shoulders, because they look one way but walk the other way, because they do nothing—they just check out, check out, check out—the whole day" (Krog 2003, 85-86).[10] The domestic worker on the farm, Eveline, adds to this that in Northern Sotho *makgowa* means "those on whom we spit when we see them".

Although one does not want to doubt Krog's recollection of these childhood conversations, no Sesotho experts I consulted had ever heard of *lekgoa* meaning 'baboon'. Furthermore, the definition of the Northern Sotho form could not be confirmed by Sepedi experts, but seemed highly unlikely to them.

In *Begging to Be Black*, Krog further attempts to further investigate the word *lekhoa*. However, this is done in a wholly inaccurate and ineffective way. Firstly, she states that it is a class 7 Sesotho noun, and that nouns in this class are reserved for debased people, for instance the word for thief, *legodu* (Krog 2009, 59). This is incorrect as *lekgoa/lekhoa* falls in class 5, and the plural in class 6. Though it is true that South African Bantu languages have a so-called 'person class', classes 1 and 2 and 1a and 2a, many other words for people occur in other classes. It can be argued that both classes 5/6 and 9/10 have a higher frequency of loan words, for instance *lenyesemane* (Englishman) in class 5, and *tijhere* (teacher) in class 9. On this basis *lekhoa* falls in class 5 because it describes foreigners, but the fact that the word for 'thief' also falls in class 5, does not mean that further negative

---

10 West finds the reason for this definition very convincing: the fact that baboons look over their shoulders all day relates to the "surveillance and 'baasskap' assumed by the settler, always 'checking out,' which, in an ironic reversal is interpreted by the black farm labourers as inherent laziness, and in another twist, the reversal of the zoological terms reserved by the settler to mark the condition of the native" (2009: 81).

connotations can be given to class 5 nouns. After all, the class contains words like *lesea* (baby) and *lesole* (soldier).

Secondly, Krog reproduces the work of Tony Harding, author of *Lekgowa* (2009), who stated in a newspaper article (Harding 2007) and a related Wikipedia entry, that "[t]he word *khoa* as a noun refers to a kind of lice found on the hindquarters of domestic animals", and that "as a verb it could mean 'to fight' or 'to shout', or 'to lack decorum, to be rude, to cause embarrassment, to be disrespectful, to have no regard for other people'" (Krog 2009, 59). Again, Sesotho experts I consulted never heard of the definition of a kind of lice. The verb stem -*kgoa* does mean 'scream or shout', but dictionaries do not list the noun *lekgoa/lekhoa/lekgowa* as a deverbative of -*kgoa/-khoa/-kgowa*.

On the basis of Harding's faulty 'research', Krog concludes that *lekhoa* "indicates a disrespectful person, someone who is part of a class of people who lack respect for other human beings" (Krog 2009: 59). Using Said's term "the Other", Krog further speculates that the word *lekhoa* does not exactly 'other' 'white people', but rather "indicates a group that regards the rest of humanity as The Other" (Krog 2009: 59).

The only part of Krog's argument that can be said to have some validity is her use of a Sesotho idiom: "When a white person behaves humanely and contrary to the stereotype, it would be said that '*Ga se lekgoa, ke motho*' ('He/she is not white, he/she is a human being' (Krog 2009, 59). I believe Krog would have been wiser to use the research of scholars like Wim van Binsbergen (2001) who convincingly argue that the category of 'human', indicated by the root -*ntu*, is a closed-off category for 'black Africans and that it has been and still is virtually impossible for 'white' outsiders to belong to the -*ntu* category, i.e. to be a *muntu* (Nguni languages) or *motho* (Sotho languages). This avenue of inquiry links with the larger body of research into African personhood on which Krog touches.

Elsewhere in *A Change of Tongue*, Krog consults a certain professor of Xhosa, Prof. Mayekiso. He explains the importance of naming in traditional South African communities (Krog 2003, 184), and then proceeds to state that the speakers of African languages found creative ways of assessing 'white' people by means of language. "Xhosa and Zulu were the first black languages that named whites in South Africa. The first thing that struck them about whites was their blue eyes and their hair. Therefore some of the earliest names for whites are 'They-through-whose-eyes-the-wind-blows', 'They whose hair washes down from their heads' (Krog 2003, 184).

The list of names provided by the professor, reproduced in English translation,[11] takes up almost an entire page. Eventually, according to the professor, "the original inhabitants of Southern Africa started gauging the nature of white people" and gave them names like, "They-who-talk-to-others-as-if-they-are-bundles-of-washing", "A-language-spoken-with-a-sewn-mouth" [...] "They-who-just-speak-their-own-language" [...] "Latecomers-who-soil-the-water-as-they-grab-everything-for-themselves" (Krog 2003, 184).

Both Krog's analysis of the word *lekgoa/lekhoa* and the above list of names for 'white' people put forth the argument that 'black' people in South Africa, who had been negatively stereotyped for centuries by 'white' colonizers, had all the while been turning the tables on 'white' people. They captured the *true* nature of 'white' people in language in a way that should lead to intense self-examination on the part of 'white' people.

Despite its obvious shortcomings, the value of Krog's attempt at linguistic analysis lies in her efforts to understand aspects of languages she does not speak and to be humbled and show a willingness to learn from those languages. Throughout her trilogy, Krog in turn aims to 'turn the tables' on 'white' people by deliberately reversing colonial and racist assessments of 'black' people, by valorising 'blackness' and devalorising 'whiteness'. She exposes 'white' colonizers as supremely individualistic, greedy and opportunistic, and implies these features persist amongst 'white' South Africans today, who need to learn from 'black' people the superior values related to interconnectedness.

RICHARD BELL AND ANTJIE KROG

In *Begging to Be Black* Krog mentions in a diary entry that during her stay in Berlin she reads African philosophy for two hours every night (2009, 91). As mentioned above, two of the scholarly articles Krog produced in 2008 are relevant when writing about Krog and Ubuntu.

---

11 Some examples are in the original language as well as English translation, but the specific language is not identified. Other examples are only given in English.

201

In both articles, concepts like forgiveness and reconciliation play an important part in Krog's articulation of "interconnectedness-towards-wholeness". I believe this connection can be traced to a large extent to the book *Understanding African Philosophy: A Cross-cultural Approach* (2002) by Richard Bell.

Bell's book was a significant starting point of Krog's more academic exploration of African philosophy. The authors and works she quotes in her articles and in *Begging to Be Black* are often identical to Bell's bibliography— Hountondji (1996) and Serequeberhan (1994), or very similar, as in the case of Gyekye.

What is even more significant, though, is the similarity between Bell and Krog's approaches. Krog's quest for understanding has been referred to numerous times in this article. This intersects meaningfully with Bell's emphasis on "[u]nderstanding another culture" (the title of his introductory chapter). The target audience of Bell's book are privileged American students who must first be encouraged to care about the suffering of many Africans before they can attempt to engage with and understand African philosophy (cf. Presbey 2003). Both Krog and Bell in other words have a great yearning to truly understand Africa.

It appears to be thanks to Bell (2002, 66 and elsewhere) that Krog cites Kwame Gyekye when she places emphasis on the communitarian nature of African society (Krog 2009, 185). A further intersection between Bell and Krog is the way in which aspects like morality, justice, truth and forgiveness are seen as a natural extension of African humanism (Bell 2002, 40), and their interrogation of western individualism versus African communitarianism (Bell 2002, 67). Bell also explicitly writes about the South African context and finds a link between Ubuntu and restorative justice (2002, 89-90) in reference to the TRC (Bell 2002, 94). When writing on the TRC, Bell quotes several times from *Country of My Skull*.

Even though I aver that Krog owes a number of key insights, for instance into the TRC (to which she returns in *Begging to Be Black*), and especially around African philosophy, to Richard Bell, the fact is that Krog only read Bell *after* the publication of the first two texts of the trilogy. Therefore it is more apt to concentrate on the broad overlap that exists between the two writers, which, as I have already pointed out, centres on their shared desire to understand Africa, and their shared identification of ethics or morality as a key concept when engaging with African philosophy.

As this section shows, Krog does not attempt to make a contribution to African philosophy, but whether intentional or not, a "general ethnophilosophical desire" (Praeg 2000, 65 and elsewhere) underlies her trilogy. She is not only eager to probe the existence and nature of a uniquely African world view–she also desires for her readers to grasp the injustices done to Africa through colonisation and to recuperate the image they might have of Africa.

In *Begging to Be Black*, Antjie Krog says at one point in her conversations with the philosopher Paul Patton, "I am not necessarily interested in African philosophy versus Western philosophy, but rather in what kind of self I should grow into in order to live a caring, useful and informed life–a 'good life'–within my country in southern Africa" (2009, 95). This statement highlights the focus of Krog's efforts to understand an African world view, namely, her desire to transform herself, if necessary, in order to adapt to the 'black' majority in South Africa.

CONCLUSION

For centuries, as Krog demonstrates, 'black' people in South Africa were subjected to western frameworks and it was impressed on them that those perspectives were superior to their own. In an attempt to invert this, Krog explores Ubuntu (which she sees as a communitarian world view aimed at interconnectedness) with the goal of valorising African approaches. The variety of ways in which she does this—employing examples of African orality, engaging with symbolic 'black' leaders, analysing language and reading African philosophy—are part of the rich fabric of the transformation trilogy and cannot be separated from the many other threads and themes the trilogy contains. This chapter, however, concentrated mainly on the specific ways in which Krog has written a trilogy very firmly rooted in Africa.

In asking what the usefulness of Krog's nonfiction trilogy is for the study of Ubuntu, I believe that there are various possibilities that necessitate further research. Firstly, Mahmood Mamdani is possibly suggesting something akin to Ubuntu when he imagines a different sort of justice which can establish a "common political community between yesterday's colonizers and colonized"—"it needs to be seen more as the practical embodiment of empathy than as the settling of a historical score" (Mamdani 1998, 14). Krog's interest in the concept of Ubuntu definitely lies in part with this "practical embodiment of empathy" that can shape "interconnectedness-towards-wholeness".

Secondly, in *Begging to Be Black* Krog states that she does not want to live in a country that "only" protects the human rights of its citizens (2009, 248). The link between Ubuntu and human rights should be further explored in conjunction with contemporary theorising about the conceptualisation of human rights. Richard Bell, for instance, quotes at some length his research on Simone Weil, who in the early 1940s stated that there is mention in older Egyptian, Middle-Eastern and Eastern texts of "an earlier sense of morality that was not 'rights-based' and that had its roots in much more communitarian-based traditions" (Bell 2002, 67). Krog's ideas in her trilogy around reconciliation and restitution could be further studied in a global perspective shaped by "critical race studies" and communitarian theory: "While maintaining a principled support for individual rights (including voluntarism), it emphasizes social and cultural identity as comparable 'rights'" (Barkan 2000, 312).

Thirdly, this chapter could not truly explore the relationship between African spirituality and Ubuntu, a topic that requires further clarification. This includes a more rigorous study of spirituality in the transformation trilogy, including a spirituality that transcends human relationships and includes nature. For instance, in *A Change of Tongue* Krog writes about humans and cattle (2003, 88-89), and the seven interludes of this text suggest that 'becoming the other', for Krog, is not restricted to 'becoming black'.

In summary: Antjie Krog, as a 'white' creative writer and public intellectual in South Africa, has written an influential nonfiction trilogy in which the state of South African society after 1994 is probed and the focus is in particular on the coexistence of 'black' and 'white' people in the aftermath of apartheid. In examining the relationships between 'black' and 'white' and asking what the future holds, Krog deliberately refers to Ubuntu numerous times and in varied ways. She posits Ubuntu as the opposite of western individualism and states that the values of communitarianism and interconnectedness it entails are superior to those of western and Christian notions around personhood and ethics. Black leaders like Tutu, Mandela and Moshoeshoe all embody Ubuntu in her opinion. Growing out of her work on the TRC in *Country of My Skull*, Krog is captivated by the implications of Ubuntu for forgiveness and reconciliation in post-apartheid South Africa, a field of enquiry in which she has not been alone. However, this chapter placed her exploration of Ubuntu in a much broader post-colonial perspective.

Krog seems to be suggesting that the 'white' minority needs to learn to understand Ubuntu if it has a desire to understand the 'black' majority in South Africa. Krog does not pretend to be an expert on Ubuntu or to have the thoroughgoing understanding she is looking for, but her trilogy represents a worthy effort in exploring what Ubuntu means for 'black' people but also finally for all South Africans. Her contribution to the discourse on Ubuntu is of such a nature that it deserves serious attention by Ubuntu scholars.

BIBLIOGRAPHY

Barkan, Elazar. 2000. *The Guilt of Nations. Restitution and Negotiating Historical Injustices*. New York: W.W. Norton & Company.
Bell, Richard H. 2002. *Understanding African Philosophy: A Cross-cultural Approach to Classical and Contemporary Issues*. London: Routledge.
Burger, Willie. 2011. "'n Verandering van vorm as die vorm van verandering: Antjie Krog se 'n Ander tongval". *Stilet*, 23(1): 18-35.
Comaroff, John L. and Jean Comaroff. 2001. "On Personhood: an Anthropological Perspective from Africa". *Social Identities*, 7(2): 267-283.
Gade, Christian B.N. 2011. "The Historical Development of the Written Discourses on Ubuntu". *South African Journal of Philosophy*, 30(3): 303-329.
Garman, Anthea. 2015. *Antjie Krog and the post-apartheid public sphere: speaking poetry to power*. Scottsville: University of KwaZulu-Natal Press.
Gyekye, Kwame. 1987. *An Essay on African Philosophical Thought: The Akan Conceptual Scheme*. Cambridge: Cambridge University Press.
Harding, Tony. 2007. "As divisions blur, we will find new meanings for old words". *Sunday Times*, July 1, 2007.
Krog, Antjie. 1994. "Focus of the imbongi". *Die Suid-Afrikaan*, 49: 12–15.
Krog, Antjie. 1995. *Gedigte 1989-1995*. Groenkloof: Hond.

Krog, Antjie. 2000 [USA edition]. *Country of My Skull: guilt, sorrow, and the limits of forgiveness in the new South Africa*. New York: Three Rivers Press.

Krog, Antjie. 2003. *A Change of Tongue*. Johannesburg: Random House.

Krog, Antjie. 2008a. "'…if it means he gets his humanity back…': The Worldview Underpinning the South African Truth and Reconciliation Commission". *Journal of Multicultural Discourses*, 3(3): 204-220.

Krog, Antjie. 2008b. "'This thing called reconciliation…': forgiveness as part of an interconnectedness-towards-wholeness". *South African Journal of Philosophy*, 27(4): 353-366.

Krog, Antjie. 2009. *Begging to Be Black*. Johannesburg: Random House Struik.

Mamdani, Mahmood. 1998. When does a Settler become a Native? Reflections of the Colonial Roots of Citizenship in Equatorial and South Africa. Inaugural lecture: AC Jordan Professor of African Studies, 13 May 1998. Cape Town: University of Cape Town Department of Communication.

Mphahlele, Es'kia. 2002. *Es'kia: Education, African Humanism & Culture, Social Consciousness, Literary Appreciation*. Cape Town: Kwela.

Mphahlele, Es'kia. 2004. *Es'kia Continued: Literary Appreciation, Education, African Humanism & Culture, Social Consciousness*. Cape Town: Kwela.

Nixon, Rob. 1990. "Mandela, Messianism, and the Media". *Transition*, 51: 42-55.

Polatinsky, Ashley. 2009. "Living with grace on the earth: the poetic voice in Antjie Krog's A Change of tongue". *Literator*, 30(2): 69-88.

Praeg, Leonhard. 2000. *African Philosophy and the Quest for Autonomy*. Amsterdam: Rodopi.

Presbey, Gail. 2003. "Review of Understanding African Philosophy: A Cross-Cultural Approach to Classical and Contemporary Issues by Richard H. Bell". *Canadian Journal of African Studies/Revue Canadienne des Études Africaines*, 37(1): 138-140.

Sanders, Mark. 2002. *Complicities: The intellectual and Apartheid*. Durham: Duke University Press.

Templeton, Alan R. 1998. "Human Races: A Genetic and Evolutionary Perspective". *American Anthropologist*, 100(3): 632-650.

Van Binsbergen, Wim. 2001. "Ubuntu and the globalisation of Southern African thought and society". *Quest: An African Journal of Philosophy*, 15(1-2): 53-89.

Van Niekerk, Jacomien. 2007. "Biografie in die pryslied: Die bydrae van Antjie Krog naas twee Xhosa-pryssangers". *Tydskrif vir Letterkunde*, 44(2): 29-45.

Wessels, Michael. 2012. "The Khoisan Origins of the Interconnected World View in Antjie Krog's Begging to be Black". *Current Writing: Text and Reception in Southern Africa*, 24(2): 186-197.

West, Mary. 2009. *White women writing white: identity and representation in (post-) apartheid literatures of South Africa*. Claremont: New Africa Books [David Philip].

CHAPTER 9. RELIGIOUS AND INDIGENOUS FORMS OF RECONCILIATION: THE UGANDAN EXPERIENCE

Dominic Dipio

INTRODUCTION

This paper examines how the concept of Ubuntu is lived, particularly in the context of conflict and rupture of social relationships. There is a general appreciation that Ubuntu as humanness cuts across culture and race, although its practice and lived experience may vary in details, in different communities. Human beings cannot exist without conflicts, although, at times conflicts may become violent and lead to the destruction of normal social relationships. "Cognizant that social norms can be broken, traditional wisdom has put in place rituals to accompany the individual and community in the various stages and events of life so that individuals can be integrated into the community and their security and good health ensured." (Dipio 2008, 93). This paper explains and analyses the indigenous ritual logic of conflict resolution. Because 'togetherness' is still a key principle in African 'traditional' ethos, restorative justice mechanisms which are elaborately developed are often trusted above modern institutions of justice and redress. To appreciate this process of reconciliation and restoration, I will focus on northern Uganda, where the activities of a rebel group, engaged in active conflict with the Ugandan Government, had many casualties as a result of the conflict. Over twenty years of conflict between the rebel group, the Lord's

Resistance Army (LRA), and the Ugandan Government left untold suffering and trauma in its trails in northern Uganda. Although the negative effects of this war are diffused in the entire northern Uganda region, Acoli sub-region was the dramatic epicentre of activities. The atrocities committed were not always on 'strangers' but also family and community members. Furthermore, although some of the actors joined the rebels willingly, a large number were forcefully abducted, some of them, as mere children and indoctrinated by their leaders to commit crimes against the community. Some of them were so animalized that traces of humanism/Ubuntu were not visible in their actions. However, what remained indelible was the fact that these people were still members of the community; their actions caused suffering to the community and marred its image. In other words, the community, too, suffered the consequences of their crime, because of this sense of connectedness. The restoration of these members who have been estranged by crime is, therefore, as much in the interest of the community as it is in the intereste of those perpetrators who wish for reintegration. This is where indigenous ethos and institutionalized justice systems like the International Criminal Court (ICC) differ. The ICC has already indicted the top leaders of the LRA, who are to be tried for Crimes against Humanity. The Acoli modes of justice and reconciliation differ from the modern justice system, which seeks to isolate and try a few individuals away from the community. This is an anomaly in their ethics because people do not exist as individuals, but as part of community; and the consequences of individual actions affect whole communities. This explains the strong belief that it is the community's ritual of reconciliation that can heal and restore the rebels who have now returned home.

Ritual as a formal action is characterized by patterned behaviour, sequence of activities where "gestures, words, and objects" are employed; and it is usually performed in a designated place, with the objective(s) of achieving particular ends (Turner 1973, 1100). In ritual performance, the emphasis is given to the symbolic over the technical or functional. When competently performed, ritual, as part of a community's practice of the sacred, is believed to be effective in re-establishing social relations and order (Rothenbuhler 1998, ix). I find George Homans (1941) analysis of Malinowski and Radcliff-Brown's theories of ritual useful in appreciating the application of the ritual approach in re-establishing social order in situations like northern

Uganda. In their wide ranging research in this field of study, there are seven key elements present in all ritual performance:

1. **Anxiety**, which derives from someone's desire to accomplish something, but by himself, he is unable to achieve the desired result. In case of northern Uganda, it is the desire for peace and restoration of estranged relationship with members of the community who have committed the kind of atrocities that separates them from the community.
2. In a situation like this, the individuals desirous of restoration present themselves to the community so that the **ritual actions** they understand and believe in can be performed.
3. The individual's participation in the ritual, together with the community that is willing to receive him back, gives him confidence, although he may still feel a **secondary anxiety** that the ritual rites may not have been competently performed; or that the members may not have fully forgiven him and accepted him back to the community.
4. The above sense leads to the need for a **secondary ritual**, such as a purification rite, as a consequence of the secondary anxiety he experiences in the above instance.
5. The ritual participants, then, engage in actions or utter words that **rationalize the ritual** being performed. In the context of the Acoli conflict resolution ritual, such actions include the drinking of the bitter *oput* concoction and the pronouncement of words that express their remorse for the crime they have committed, and the determination not to do so again.
6. The importance of thick **symbolization** in ritual performance cannot be emphasized enough, for rituals are condensed with symbols. The symbolic may be expressed through words, objects and actions (postures). In this reconciliation ritual, the bitter drink the participants share, the kneeling posture with their hands held behind them, the sheep that are slaughtered in a particular way, and the meal the parties share in the end, are all part of the symbolization.
7. There must be a **function** for performing the ritual. This function remains in the frame of the symbolic because it does not produce the kind of visible results that magic does, for instance. This functionality is more psychological and spiritual: it restores confidence and dispels anxieties. Indeed, it gives members of the community agency and sense of freshness of a new beginning (1941, 171–172).

Ritual is communication that employs dramatic performance. Because of its community component, rituals create social cohesion, and this allows for co-existence of community members. In many African communities, this is still the preferred mode of conflict resolution and creating social cohesion (see Fernandez 1965, 917; Whitehouse and Lanman 2014). This is akin to what Rothenbuhler refers to as a certain sense of social compulsion that gets the participants to consciously participate in a ritual performance (1998, 10–11). The tension created by the paradox of compulsion and volition creates the anxiety that begins the series of actions. In order to understand the importance of the ritual approach to conflict resolution and the option for the restorative justice system, it is important to appreciate the world view of the communities we are focussing on.

INDIGENOUS WORLD VIEW ON TOGETHERNESS AND PEACE: ACOLI AND MA'DI

Like all human beings, peace and by implication, resolving conflicts is a cherished value of the Acoli and the Ma'di. Being together and living in good relationships with others is a key value of humanness, mutuality and the promotion of each other's dignity. Archbishop John Baptist Odama explains that for an Acoli, the most important thing is human life and human relationships; and an elder, Daniel Stephen Okello complements that "this recognition involves acknowledging and protecting the dignity of the other person in the spirit of togetherness" (Personal Interview 2014). In Acoli, there are words which describe this principle of togetherness: *bed kacel* (staying together, doing things together, helping one another), *bed a lwak* (togetherness, being with people), terms which the Ma'di cherish as *olu-alu*, are considered to be attributes of good human beings. In Okello's description:

> A good Acoli is one who is sympathetic and recognises the humanity of the other person; one who is not motivated by material gains but by the desire to create genuine relationship; one who is sincere and truthful; one who abhors theft; and one who adheres to traditional values (Personal Interview 2014).

The sense of togetherness and mutuality is so strong among the Acoli that although ranks and seniority exist, the reason people are held in high esteem is always related to their service to the community; such as those who defend the community from human and animal invasion (aggressions); persons of status such as hereditary chiefs, and others who earn recognition and respect by virtue of the services they render to the community. What maintains these ranks and positions is the good relationship that must exist between the holder of the title and the community. This is the principle of considering each other as equals in humanity, with due respect and recognition towards each other. To illustrate this point, Okello gives an example of the relationship between a "boss"—a Permanent Secretary—and his driver. The boss-servant relationship exists only in the office space. This relationship would change once the driver visits his boss in the family atmosphere, where he will be accorded the honourable respect and hospitality due to a visitor. In this spirit of togetherness and equality, one who holds a rank cannot look down upon those without ranks. It is this mutual respect that maintains those who hold positions of honour. It is for this reason that Okello refers to the boss-servant phenomenon as an artificial relationship—a performance.

The sense of connectedness and togetherness embraces everybody and even transcends the relationships among the living. The dead are also included in this chain of relationship of mutuality. The connectedness between the living and the spirit world is part of the cultural religious sense that ensures that the community remains together. Through ritual, the ancestors remain part of the life of the community as they are deeply involved in the affairs of the living. There is deep respect for the grandparents who have passed on, especially those who have been exemplary. These are constantly invoked in times of crisis. The ancestral spirits are believed to be closer to *Rubanga* (God), and therefore the community remains linked to them. Although the sense of this togetherness is deeply experienced with the immediate community that shares cultural values, this sense clearly transcends the family, ethnicity and race. People of different ethnicities and races have often responded to the needs of other human beings beyond their community. Thus, humaneness based on values has no ethnic limitations. Humans are attracted to other human beings especially in times of need. For instance, it has been a common practice in these communities for mothers to suckle the child of the one who does not have enough breast milk. Creating relationship, in this case, is valued above material possessions.

On the gender terrain, women are integral part of these communities. Okello explains that marginalization on the basis of gender does not exist in Acoli. Differences between men and women exist in the roles they play in the community, but not in the respect given to them and the value of these roles. Because of the patriarchal inclination of the communities, men who mistreat women were given heavy penalties in the logic of the community. The rampant violence reported against women today is not part of the cultural practices. These are acts of persons who live outside the value system of the indigenous community. The sacredness of women in many African cultures is so pronounced that the cleansing ritual for the one who kills a woman, whether this is accidental or deliberate, is detailed, complex and expensive to conduct. To this effect, the Ma'di say, *'izi abika okpwo'* (it is an up-hill task to carry out an expiatory ritual for the blood of a woman). Indeed, women play central roles even in the spiritual and ritual life of the community. The value of peaceful co-existence is not limited to the human family. In indigenous world view, harmony between human beings and the other elements in the universe is equally important.

RELATIONSHIP WITH ANIMAL WORLD: EXAMPLE OF THE MA'DI

In indigenous African cultures, human beings live in awareness of their connectedness and relationship with other creatures in the universe, and a fair balance has to be maintained for harmonious co-existence. In this section, I will synthesize one aspect of such a relationship to understand the importance of peace and harmony in the world view of African, even when it comes to the relationships with non-humans. The community appreciates that harmony can be destabilized between human beings and the animal world, for instance. And when this happens, rituals are performed to restore the harmony. Among the Ma'di and the Acoli, like many African communities, conflict resolution rituals are classified according to the types and gravity of the conflicts. Although principal conflict resolution rituals exist among and between human beings, the killing of some wild animals, by a hunter, attract an elaborate ritual, similar to that of a warrior in battle. The death of the following wild animals, which the Ma'di describes as "hot-blooded" (*ari aci*), like human beings cannot go without ritual: leopard (*odu*), lion (*ebi*), buffalo (*odru*) and elephant (*lea*).

The key person here is the hunter—a professional who combines as a warrior—who has a special relationship and knowledge of the animal world. He is in charge of the community's security from both wild animals and enemies. The hunter is therefore an elite member of traditional society, and because of the significant security role he plays, he is often "fortified" with the knowledge of the occult. To quote from Ayo Adentuntan's research on the narratives associated with the Yoruba's hunter,

> The hunter's special role derives in large part from his relationship with the mundane. To the Yoruba, the bush or forest is not just the habitat of flora and fauna, but also of spirits.... In other words, the bush or forest is the realm of the infinite where the giant rat may tie the hunter's dog, the *iroko* ... might tell the hunter in which direction to seek game, and porcupines could perform in a concert (2014, 2).

The relationship between the hunter and the wild animals in the forest is not just of enemies, but it embeds "mutual respect" and recognition of the other's "rights". The hunter and the animal have equal chances to get killed in their encounters. Thus, when any one of the above mentioned animals, especially a leopard, are killed[1] special rituals are required to re-establish harmony in the worlds of animals and human beings. As with Yoruba hunters, there are many salacious narratives of hunter-animal contests in the cultural memory of the Ma'di and in their folktales. Of all the wild animals, the leopard, its small size notwithstanding, is considered to be the most cunning, and killing it tests the exceptional skills of the hunter, and becomes a status symbol for masculinity. It was offered as gifts to the chief to be used as carpet and to line up the walls of royal houses, as dance costume won by warriors to show off their prowess. It was a highly celebrated conquest that is matched with an equally expensive ritual of appeasing the disorder created in the animal world and cleansing oneself of the animal's death. The Ma'di believed that performing this ritual was crucial to drive away the spirit of the animal that lingered around the killer and may cause him psychological and physical harm, commonly manifested in

---

1   Today, game and hunting of wild animals is illegal, and hunting as a traditional activity is on the ebb in many communities.

hallucinations and madness. The hunter's entry into the community with the dead animal was preceded by a cleansing ritual. A male crier who is part of the hunter's company performs his *cira* (a unique signature sound that marks a man's identity) to announce the approach of the hunters, so that all able bodied persons in the homestead stand in anticipation. A team of elders—male and female—go to meet the returning hunters on the way. The women carry a calabash of semi liquid mixture of fermented sour flour (*durakasa*) used for beer-brewing as they perform *ciliri* (celebratory sound made by women). The elder of the home—a male—goes with a leafy *melemele* tree twig (what the Acoli call *obokolwedo*) for sprinkling the light paste of the sour flour on the hunters. The leaves of this tree that is described by the Ma'di as "peaceful" is used to cleanse the hunters of the blood of the animal so that they do not bring "dirt" into the homestead that may negatively affect the family.

The triumphal entry of the hunters into the homestead is marked by a funeral dance, *jenyi*. This is the same dance performed when a great warrior dies. Meanwhile, the dead animal is laid near the *gubo* and the main hunter lay besides it in mock death. The *gubo* is an important space where conflicts were settled. The *gubo* (*abila* in Acoli) that represents the ancestral spirit is physically presented as a defunct grinding stone (*oni endre*) with a deep depression in the centre. This stone is placed in the compound, usually near the granary, as a presence of the *ba buga* (living-dead: ancestral spirits) in the homestead, who continued to be involved in the significant events in the community, as interested parties. The *gubo*, therefore, is the "altar" where family issues are presented and settled, ordinarily. It is on this stone that the hunters sharpen their spears and pray for protection before they left for the forest. The stone's physical appearance makes it suited for *lejo ti drojo* or *lejo ti aku jo* (literally meaning, covering all problems); so that once a problem has been settled, it should not be "re-awaken" or stirred to cause misunderstandings again.

The funeral dance (*rabika*) in this ritual is understood as an honourable send off for the animal, and an expression of remorse for spilling "hot blood", and that it was not wanton but a life-and death encounter in self-defence. This is the most the community can do to appease the animal family—staging a heroic funeral dance in order to free themselves from the burden of killing. Part of the ritual is that the night after the funeral dance the hunter has sexual intercourse with the wife (if he was married). This is in celebration of the life that was about to be lost in the contest with the animal, as well as a desire to propagate brave warriors like the one who has survived the wild animal. Both husband and wife perform acts that imitate the action of an animal the following morning. Early in the morning, they run to the stream and drink water from the source, lapping it with the tongue as a leopard would. This symbolic act indicates mastery over the fearsome wild animal that has been killed. During these ritual days, the hunter lives in mortification of the body and denial of many pleasures, such as eating food without salt for three or four days, depending on the gender of the animal killed. It is only when the ritual cycle is complete that peace is restored in the psyche of the hunter and the community (see Dipio 2008, 97–100). I have made reference to how indigenous communities took care to live in balance and harmony even with non-human members of the universe to underscore the importance of restoring peace and harmony among human beings, once peace has been broken. There is no limit to the human capacity to ensure that this happens. To fully appreciate the indigenous approach of restorative justice, it is important to understand the concepts of mercy and forgiveness in the context of justice. Exalted as these virtues may be, they are part of the human experience.

CONCEPTS OF MERCY AND FORGIVENESS IN THE EXERCISE OF JUSTICE

MERCY

One of the most remembered lines in William Shakespeare's *The Merchant of Venice* is on mercy. It explains the attributes of mercy as a "gift" that comes as a blessing, undeserved by the receiver; although it benefits both the giver and the recipient: "It blesseth him that gives and him that takes." In the order of things, it is the one who has power who can show/give mercy. Hence in temporal and mundane affairs, kings/judges are the one's associated with clemency. It is in this regard that God is described as infinitely merciful. Mercy is more of God's nature as mercilessness is part of human nature. Prophets Isaiah and Jeremiah explain this unique attribute couched-in-compassion justice of God. God's mercy/compassion surpasses that of a Mother for her child (Isaiah, 49:15); and although from time to time, God rebukes his beloved children, his compassion never leaves them as they are forever his darlings in whom he delights (Jeremiah 31:20). This compares with human orientation toward brutality in the ways they deal with those with whom they are in conflict. In such cases, their indiscriminate ruthlessness engulfs the innocent children, the aged, and women without mercy (Isaiah 13:18; Isaiah 47:6; Jeremiah 6:23). Thus, in showing mercy, human beings practice what is easily God's nature. Compassion and mercifulness towards someone deserving punishment is the noble face of power. Shakespeare has a sense of this in *The Merchant of Venice*:

> But mercy is above this sceptred sway,
> It is enthroned in the hearts of kings,
> It is an attribute to God himself;
> And earthly power doth then show likest God's,
> When mercy seasons justice (*The Merchant of Venice*, Act 4 scene 1).

Justice is, evidently, one of the most important (religious) values. In Christianity, for instance, it is required that we treat each other justly. However, God's justice is intertwined with his compassion/mercy and love for humankind. This is manifested in letting his Begotten Son, Jesus, to die a painful death on the Cross as a penalty for the sins of humankind (Romans 3:23 – 24). Jesus is the open door for Christians to obtain God's mercy, at all times. Mercy is spoken of in the context of retributive justice. Yet when it comes to nobility of action, bare justice is inferior to justice. Justice that is couched in mercy elevates human action to the level of nobility, and saves another person. There is something gratuitous in the act of Mercy. It is freely given to the one who stands condemned before the law. It does not have to be earned or deserved by the recipient. It is desirable that our pursuit of justice is tempered by mercy because we share the same humanity and we could, ourselves, be in the same position as the one needing our clemency. It is for this reason that mercy comes as a free gift. This aspect of gift is what mercy shares with forgiveness. However, the judge/king who gives mercy to a condemned person may not be the direct victim of the offence, as it is in the case of everyday relationship where one forgives a neighbour who has offended him. Mercy comes as a gift in retributive justice system, because although one feels the moral sense to be merciful, it is not obligatory to do so. Mercy in this sense is intimately linked to justice (Card 1972, 191). It is an act that benefits another person who does not deserve it. The benevolence of the dispenser may not follow any logical paradigms. As Jason Beckett (2007) explains it, mercy is an unconstrained decision that leads to beneficial result for another person.

> Mercy is a holistic understanding–an empathy–which contains more than the total of its atomized équivalents, however composed and (re)constructed. In this sense mercy does not decriminalise action, it simply removes it from the sphere of normative évaluation, it 'a-normativises' and so 'a-criminalises' (2007, 218).

As a category that belongs to the transcendental virtues, mercy giving, as a disposition, does not follow any rules. It happens as a result of the giver's benevolence. "Mercy happens, nothing more" (Beckett 2007, 233). It is part of the expansive and incredible human capacity for benevolence and kindness even when they are not required to do so. Although mercy is exalted, it still belongs to the range of human action and capacity. It is among the noble actions that human beings are capable of; although it remains predominantly associated with the logic of God-action, which is difficult for human beings to comprehend.

FORGIVENESS

Forgiveness is a condition for enjoying one's quotidian life. Inspirational speakers and authors like Frederic Luskin (2002) and Jack Kornfield (2011) emphasize the important point that it first benefits the giver even before it does the recipient. One who releases forgiveness lives a healthier life and avoids being trapped in a negative condition. Forgiveness that liberates the giver has to be given without further humiliating the one who has offended, and particularly the one who seeks forgiveness; for the process of seeking genuine forgiveness is, itself, the path of humility and self-humiliation. This explains how forgiveness blesses both, but especially the one who gives because s/he transcends the trap which presents itself as a (transient) pleasure of 'having power over' and of seeing the one who has offended suffer. But this pleasure is more like a bubble that soon bursts because its corrosive effects do not only damage the one who withholds forgiveness; but the same person may be in need of forgiveness from someone else. The immediate value of forgiveness, therefore, is for the person dispensing it; for such a person sets himself free from the burden of the other person's offence against him. Indeed, the one who has offended may even be oblivious of the pain he has caused. This is all the more reason why the offended person must forgive for himself. One can understand Jesus' teaching and command to forgive always; not just "seven times", but "seventy times seven" (Matthew 18:21–22), as an advice of self-preservation, above all else. More than an ideal, this is a practical teaching for 'healthy' living, and for the sake of the person hurting for not having forgiven another.

Forgiveness is not about forgetting, condoning or excusing an offense someone has committed against you; and it does not necessarily mean reconciling with the other party, although it is a pre-condition for reconciliation. It is, indeed, desirable that forgiveness leads to reconciliation, and 'repair' of relationship between conflicting parties. Frederic Luskin (2002, vi–viii) explains that forgiveness is more about the health and happiness of the giver than that of the receiver. It helps one move forward with his life. It points to a future that offers a possibility of a happier relationship with self and the other. It is about healing the person who has been hurt and restoring his peace than it is about the one who has hurt. It is the one who has been hurt who 'does' something, to let go the feeling of resentment towards the other person. This positive action ends up empowering the giver who comes to realize the importance of not allowing his pain define him. This emphasis on the giver, however, is not to ignore the importance of the other party—the offender—in the process of forgiveness. One person gets hurt as a result of another's action. But the offender may also suffer the negative consequences of his action and may need the forgiveness of the offended party. He may need to be released from the 'burden' of his offense. In the eyes of the law, suffering from the consequences of a crime is legitimate. A person may still be prosecuted for an offence even if he is forgiven by the offended person. Forgiveness belongs to the 'greater good' category of virtues like love and peace. According Luskin, forgiveness goes with a sense of gratitude about the importance of being alive and ensuring a high quality to life in the future. One realizes the importance of giving up negativity in order to regain the peace we often miss for being unforgiving. Gratitude is experienced by both parties. For the one who gives, it is realization that life is so much larger than the pain he feels from an offense. His is sharing in the magnanimity of God who forgives us when we turn to him. For the recipient of forgiveness, the gratitude springs from getting a chance to live more qualitatively his 'new lease' of life. The expected outcome is a positive one for both parties. This is reflected in Jack Kornfield's (2011) teaching on the process of forgiveness, which included the resolve, on the part of the parties, not to let such a situation ever happen again. Awareness of all that had happened in the past—the pain, the grief, and the loss—presents forgiveness as a deliberate choice an individual or conflicting parties make to take the step forward to let go and forgive. In such a process, it becomes clear that it is no longer a question of forgetting, condoning or excusing the wrong committed. Rather, it is a decision made to move on without ever looking back, in spite of the pain experienced in the past. Seen in this respect, forgiveness becomes a matter of survival. Although it appears to be an option to forgive or not to forgive, in reality, it is as an imperative for healthy living. It is worth observing that forgiveness is not given only when it is sought since its corrosive effects reside in the one who 'hold' something against the neighbour. In Christianity, a typical example is the last 'act' of Jesus before he died. He forgave those who have killed him, before they even asked for forgiveness, because "they do not know what they are doing" (Luke 23:34).

Glen Pettigrove (2007), drawing from Christian teaching on forgiveness explains that forgiveness has to do with "releasing", "letting go" and "gifting" someone liable to penalty for an offense committed. I quote his description of forgiveness at length:

> These nuances reflect two aspects of forgiving. First, forgiving involves foregoing the pursuit of a legitimate complaint that one has against another. We might call this the negative aspect of forgiving in so far as the forgiver refrains from acting in a particular way toward the wrong doer. The positive aspect of forgiving is highlighted by the imagery of the gift. Forgiveness is a gift that is offered by the one wronged, rather than something earned or deserved by the wrongdoer. That which is given is ordinarily described as love: the one who forgives loves.... Thus, Christian forgiveness involves a foregoing and a giving whose aim is reconciliation between the wrong doer and the wronged (2007, 431).

Reconciliation and the re-establishment of loving relationship become the active and tangible gifts (fruits) of forgiveness. On the other hand, the bitterness, anger, and malice (Ephesians 4:3–32) that resides in the unforgiving heart principally hurts the person himself. The importance of forgiveness is underlined in Christian teaching, both as a teaching and unavoidable emergency for the one who wants to live a more positive life. In different ways, Jesus teaches his disciples that one cannot say a worthy prayer to God if he has not forgiven his 'neighbour'. When he taught his followers the prayer beloved by God, the "Our Father", which is really a "Family" prayer, he makes it clear that the worthiness of the prayer resides in one having forgiven the other, before any form of communication, including sharing a meal (Matthew 6:6–13). In another instance, Jesus teaches that when you are headed to the altar of God, to offer him sacrifice, and you remember that you have resentment against your neighbour, you must abandon your gift offering, and pursue the one you have offended or resent for having offended you, and ask for his forgiveness before you can offer your gift to God (Matthew 5:23). In Jesus' teaching, good relationship with neighbour is the starting point of good relationship with God. No sacrifice and other acts of devotions count when one has resentment towards another human being. Kornfield explains that forgiveness is the courage to say, "this suffering stops with me…. I will not pass it on to my children … to unending generations" (Kornfield 2011). Indeed, as Pettigrove (2007, 433) explains, understanding the value of forgiveness for the giver does not even require the mention of God forgiving us only if we forgive our neighbour, because it is good for our physical, quotidian living. In it is embedded the principle of the Golden Rule: being sensitive to the needs of the other; and doing unto the other what you would wish done unto you. In accordance with this principle of reciprocity, you should forgive someone just as you would wish to be forgiven when you wrong another. Free yourself from judging and condemning others by paying attention to the "plank" in your own eyes rather than focusing on the "spec" in the eye of the other (Luke 6:31). This extreme Christian teaching is about loving/forgiving one's enemy. If we apply this principle to forgiving members of the same community/family who stand in need of forgiveness and reconciliation, perhaps the ritual approach of reconciliation employed in indigenous justice system becomes easier to understand. The crime/offence once forgiven is to be removed forever. When we wonder about the human capacity to forgive horrendous wrongs, it is important to realize that we naturally recoil from evil and we are shocked by it because we are oriented towards the good. This is clearly articulated by D. Tutu and M. Tutu (2014) in their *Book of Forgiving*:

> Our nature is goodness. Yes, we do much that is bad, but our nature is good…. When someone does something ghastly, it makes the news because it is the exception to the rule. We like surrounded by so much love, kindness and trust that we forget it is remarkable. Forgiveness is the way we return what has been taken from us and restore the love and kindness and trust has been lost. With each act of forgiveness, whether small or great, we move towards wholeness. Forgiveness is nothing less than how we bring peace to ourselves and our world (2014, 6).

Both mercy and forgiveness are transcendental actions that belong to the category of virtues that lead to greater good and that are largely associated with a God-disposition. In religious spirituality it is God who is credited for being all-forgiving and most merciful (Twambley 1976). Indeed, in the synoptic Gospels, the Jews were offended by Jesus when he openly forgave the sins of a sick man brought to him. They said, "He is blaspheming; who can forgive sins but God alone?" (Mark, 2:7). When we practice these higher and paradoxical virtues, our actions can be described as godly. However, while mercy remains a virtue that cannot be rationalized, forgiveness can be rationalized as part of our quotidian experience. It directly influences one's quality of life. Having explained the concepts of mercy and forgiveness as qualities that define noble human actions, in the next section, I will discuss how forgiveness is an integral part of indigenous ritual of conflict resolution and restoration of harmony to society, once this has been de-stabilized. Forgiveness is forward-looking, and offers a chance for communities and individuals to live qualitatively. The ritual of Ma'di conflict resolution, around the *gubo* (symbol of ancestral spirit) emphasizes this irrevocability of resolution of conflicts:

> In its physical form, the *gubo* is an old, time tested stone, a symbol of age, experience and wisdom that is believed to resolve all problems. If a seed is placed under a stone, it will not germinate but suffocate. This is what it means to solve a problem around the

gubo. As the *gubo* is a stone that can never be used for grinding, the rituals performed here are supposed to be successful so that the problems do not re-emerge. In the *vura* or family gathering, the *vura dri* or eldest member will proclaim, 'The *gubo* has now covered the problem and it is over! The one who re-awakens it will be visited by terrible consequences!' (Dipio 2008, 98–99)

The following section describes and analyses the *matoput* conflict resolution mechanism preferred by members of the Acoli community in dealing with hundreds of the victims and perpetrators of the LRA war, and how the principles of this approach are related to the values of Ubuntu.

CONFLICT MANAGEMENT AND RESOLUTION AMONG THE ACOLI

When a person has behaved like an 'animal' or lives outside the principles of humanness, that individual is still part of the community. The concept of a death sentence and permanent separation from community does not exist in many African world views. In the past, where people were captured or abducted as war booties, in accordance with the respect for life, these persons were gradually fully integrated into the community. If the person abducted was a girl, she would grow up to be married into the family. When she attains the position of motherhood, so venerated in African societies, she enjoyed the privileges, rights and responsibilities accorded to all mothers in Acoli culture. In situations where relationships were severed due to conflict among different ethnicities (outsiders) or clans, the ritual of *matoput* would be performed to restore the broken relations, to express total forgiveness and to heal the painful memory of the past. Depending on the nature of the crime, different items, including a human being, may be required for compensation. For instance, the death of a son in such a conflict would be compensated for by a female from the opponent community. In the logic of the Acoli community, human compensation must, in case of the death of a man, always a female. The reason for this is that as a reproductive agent, a woman would generate lives to reinforce the community that has been robbed of a son. This is an added value because the woman comes from 'outside'. As a mother, grandmother, and later an ancestor she is fully integrated into the everyday and ritual life of the community.

In conflict resolution, community elders would seek to understand the root cause of the misbehaviour. There could be several reasons for the unbecoming behaviour of a member that leads to crime. Perhaps such a person is under a curse? Has he inherited some negative traits from his ancestors that the community may not be aware of? Or is it because the community value system has broken down? For each of these questions, ways are sought to redeem the individual, so that no one 'gets written off' from the community. Besides, all the above questions point to how the individual is connected to the community and the good or bad he does are also linked to the community. The common African saying, "It takes a whole village to bring up a child" makes sense here. Once the root cause is identified, usually the problem gets resolved and normalcy returns to the life of the person who begins to 'live again'. If the individual moves totally away from the values of the community, in most cases, such a person may leave the community on his own because he would feel uncomfortable within it. Thus, no one gets excommunicated on the basis of the crimes they have committed.[2] There is plenty of room for correction, forgiveness and integration into community, and unfailing hope that relationships can be restored. In the words of Archbishop John Baptist Odama, one of the key interviewees for this research:

> In our community, there are no prisons or walls to separate 'good' people from 'bad' ones. If anything, it is the community which is one's prison. But being in this 'prison' is to help the person reform. This process which is deeply respectful of the person's humanity, in turn, motivates the individual to recover and renounce criminal ways. Remorse in this 'prison' is felt once and for all. Once this is done, no reminder and record is kept of the previous crime. The

---

2   In some African communities certain crimes such as the spilling of a kinsman's blood attract automatic, temporary expulsion from the community even if this is accidental. We see this in Chinua Achebe's *Things Fall Apart*, when Okonkwo's gun accidentally explodes and kills a kinsman but even this is more of a re-location into another related community—the land of the maternal uncles. Among the Ma'di too, the clan of one's mother is a haven for one to seek any form of asylum. The maternal uncle, in this culture is perceived as all accommodating. After a grace period, the repentant 'criminal' may return if he so wishes.

individual recovers holistically in psychological, social, moral and spiritual aspects (Personal Interview 2014).

The Acoli consider the returned LRA members as part of their community who need to be reconciled and integrated into the community through the indigenous mechanism which they appreciate as wholesome, than the ICC. Similar to the post-war Sierra Leonean situation Sara Terry portrays in her documentary film, *Fabul Tok* (2011), the community prefers to draw from its repository of indigenous knowledge on the justice system. In this cultural context, "there is no bad bush to throw a bad child" (Terry 2011). In the spirit of co-responsibility the community shares in the weaknesses and strengths of its members. Evidently, this is a fairly long and concerted process of reconciliation and healing that involves the individual person and the entire community to work out a healing process. The final stage of this ritual process is what the Acoli refer to as the *matoput* ritual of reconciliation.[3]

TRADITIONAL RITUALS OF RECONCILIATION

The Acoli community prefer that the government give blanket amnesty to all the former rebels who would like to return to the community. This amnesty would then be mediated by the traditional justice and reconciliation ritual of *matoput* that involves the drinking of a bitter herbal concoction by the participants. The underlying point in this ritual is that human beings are not meant to be apart from each other. They are human because of their togetherness and connectedness. Therefore, if anything happens to break their connectedness, every effort must be made to restore the relationship. Relationship is central to personhood and human-hood. In Acoli, the words *roco kwo* (repair life), *roco wat* (repair relationship) shows how well developed the process of reconciliation and conflict resolution are developed in their hierarchies.

---

3   Among the Ma'di, a neighbouring ethnic group to the Acoli, this ritual is generally referred to as *tolu koka* (catching of the axe). Violent conflicts with neighbours that involves the use of weapon (spear) is referred to as *ajusi anyuka* (the folding of the spear blade). The Acoli and Ma'di conflict resolution rituals are very similar in their structure and patters. At time the same ritual items are used.

Ordinarily a simple ritual common among the Acoli and the Ma'di, used for receiving persons who have been away from the community for a long time, involves stepping on a fresh egg. The concern about restoring harmony and peace is so important that anyone who has been away from the community, and has been involved in activities/professions that involves violence, such as being in the army (where killing an enemy is often inevitable) would be subjected to this ritual of cleansing. A forked twig of *opobo* tree is cut and placed at the junction of the path leading to the homestead, and an egg is placed between the forked points of the twig. The person who has been out of the community for a while steps on the egg before he enters the homestead. The *opobo* (*inzu* in Ma'di) tree is characterised by the slippery sap underneath its bark. This is itself symbolic, just like the egg. The whole point of this ritual is that, in the many years of absence from the community, someone may have engaged in anti-community behaviours that will affect not only the person, but the family and the community if the returnee is not cleansed and reconciled first. The person must step on the egg barefoot so that his flesh gets into contact with the egg and he feels the sense of crushing the egg under his feet. The psychological effect of this is the realisation that the crime one has committed out there caused death, and may bring unhappiness and misfortune to the community. No one is supposed to be indifferent to the death of another human being. Hence, the egg becomes the 'victim' that is sacrificed to cleanse and absolve the person from the sins committed, whether they were intentional or accidental. The egg is considered innocent and pure, and therefore a kind of detergent. The *opobo* twig which is slippery serves the same purpose of cleansing: that no 'dirt' may sticks onto the person; it should slip away.

Another important symbol used in reconciliation ritual is the *labir/layibi*. This is the stick that is used for lifting the lid of a granary—the traditional food store in African homesteads. It is a symbol of total welcoming. The person who has returned home can now partake of the foods and drinks provided by the family. The handing of the *labir* to him shows that now he is part of the family and he is welcome to eats from the same source. Just like in the bible story of the Prodigal Son (Luke 15:11–32), in case he has been starving out there, now he is welcome to help himself with whatever foods the family has. Sharing foods stands for the fullness of humanity and togetherness. This is the equivalent of sharing of Holy

Communion among Christians. This is the point at which the person is given a seat, offered a drink, food or water to bathe: an indicator that one is now family.

Even when one is integrated into the community, the process of reconciliation through talks continues. A trusted member of the extended family will accompany the individual throughout this extended period of healing and reconciliation. The family is a trustful environment in which those who have been estranged from the community are humanized and integrated. The trusted relative listens to the person without condemnation. This relationship of trust and love disarms the confessant and restores his confidence to speak the truth freely. If the person is not yet ready to speak, he will request for more time and even days to 'rest'. It is only when he is ready to speak that the trustworthy person gives him empathic hearing, followed by gentle advice and instructions. The returnee, in this case, is treated as a patient, delicately attended to so that the process does not abort. The returnees desire to feel welcomed as members of the community who are fully forgiven. In the case of welcoming a large number of returnees, as in the case of the LRA, a temporary centre would be constructed with competent resource persons who can attend to their psycho-social needs for at least three months, as they are prepared to undergo the *matoput* ritual and be integrated into their families. In the three months transition period, family members would pay regulated visits to the returnees at the transitory centre. This process gradually prepares both parties for the re-entry of the estranged member into the family.

THE *MATOPUT* RITUAL PROCESS

The *matoput* process is a long and complex one. It is administered in redressing serious cases of conflict such as when two clans have had a fight that has resulted into death, or when atrocious killings have been done like in the case of the LRA. The *oput* is a shrub like plant that is found clustered together, as if in bundles. One of the dominant features of this plant is the bitterness of the root, which is dug out, cleaned, crushed into pulp to prepare a calabash of a bitter drink from. The content of this calabash is drunk by the participants in the process of the reconciliation ritual. In this ritual process, the conflicting clans are brought face to face with a third party (mediator/group of elders), to help the people restore their relationship. It involves truth telling before the mediators (chiefs/elders). There is no room for lies here, because the process is deeply spiritual and religious, involving the pronouncements of curses and blessings. The ancestors and their memories are invoked: the spirit of the virtuous ancestors who are remembered for their righteousness and good neighbourliness are invoked. They become symbolically among the ritual participants.

It is the representatives of the communities that are involved in the ritual although the offence may have been committed by an individual. This, again, underlines how the individual exists in connection to the community. The reconciliation is, therefore, ultimately between the two communities. For the process to begin, the offender first confesses and admits his guilt to his community, so that it is the entire community that takes responsibility for the crime of its member, and apologizes to the offended community. Then the culturally acceptable rate of compensation for the nature of crime is discussed. Was it accidental, in self-defence, or intentional? All these attract different rates. Archbishop Odama explains that the crucial principle in fixing the rate of compensation is guided by the desire for restoration of relationship. So that if the rate is too high and hinders reconciliation, it will be reduced to ensure that the process of reconciliation is not jeopardized.

Once the compensation is done, the two sides (communities) bring forth animals, usually sheep, from each side. The heads of the two animals are place facing the side of the opponents. The animals are then cut unconventionally in the middle and the opposing sides exchange their halves: each side takes the half of the other. The symbol is "sharing of each other". These are different clans who now become "parts of each other" in order to make a whole. This phase is followed by the drinking of the *oput*—the bitter concoction in the calabash—placed in their midst. The content of the calabash is drunk by both sides: the perpetrator and the victim. The two parties line up in opposing sides, and step forward in pairs, one from either side. They kneel before the bitter calabash with their hands held behind them as if they were prisoners. This is a symbolic gesture of being totally disarmed, and showing unwillingness to harm the other. In this kneeling position, the pairs bend and drink together from the same calabash. Their heads touch in the process and this enhances the sense of togetherness and progressive friendship being reconstructed or renewed. They perform this act of drinking as they utter words of contrition, *abalo* (I have sinned); as the other party responds, "what we have done to each other is bitter indeed". The *oput* is not a pleasant drink. It is bitter. This is the tactile symbol of the bitter fruits of violence and their regret for it. The content of the calabash must be finished.

This process is followed by the cooking of the ritual animals and celebrating their pact of unity. Remember the halves of the animals are mixed together as the two parties cook the meals that they share together. If the group is big, other animals, beside the ritual ones will be slaughtered to enhance the celebration. The celebration is punctuated by solemn, ritual speeches and utterances of words by elders on both sides. That such a thing should never be repeated is the emphasis of the talks. Everybody gets to know that the relationship between clan A and B has been restored; and no more bloodshed and conflict is expected between them.

The ritual is principally the same even where the conflict is between different ethnic groups. There are slight variations such as identifying a neutral location, usually a border point between the ethnicities. Furthermore, the ritual of bending the blade of the spear (*ajusi anyuka* in Ma'di) is added to the process. In this case, each of the two sides will provide a spear, and a representation on either side will bend the blade downward, rendering it ineffective for battle. They then exchange the inutile spears with each other. The symbol states: "I am handing over my weapon—my security—to you. I do not need my defence before you, for you have become my defence— my brother—as I have become yours. We shall, therefore, not raise spears against each other." The ritual is endorsed by solemn words as explained above. The ritual becomes binding and irrevocable. A ritual of this nature happened between the Acoli and the Ma'di/Lugbara from West Nile in the 1980s, following the violence in the Idi Amin and Milton Obote regimes of the 1970s and the 1980s. During this era, the hitherto friendly Nilotic communities became hostile and suspicious of each other and whole communities from the West Nile region had to flee the country to avoid vengeful extermination when Idi Amin, from an ethnic group in the West Nile, was overthrown by the combined forces of Ugandan and Tanzanian soldiers in 1979. The opportunity came for the two communities to reconcile after 1986, when President Museveni took over power. During this reconciliation, the two communities recalled their previous sense of togetherness, and expressed the determination to remain friendly to each other. Blessings and curses were pronounced on the occasion and both communities make it their responsibility to keep the peace. Hence, during the LRA conflict with the Ugandan Government, people from the West Nile, formally, refused to participate in the fight against the LRA, for fear of spilling each other's blood in the battle. Rituals, indeed, play significant role to stabilize, create a sense of solidarity and promote peaceful-coexistence in community (Whitehouse and Lanman 2014). Indeed, as Rothenbuhler explains, "Everyone who performs a ritual accepts the idea, at least, implicitly, that his or her patterned behaviour is symbolically meaningful and effective. That is, participants in ritual are doing something symbolically; they are using symbols to act social purposes" (1998, 26).

The belief in the force of indigenous rituals in contemporary times where the participants are practising Christians point to what Gauri Viswanathan says how conversion to a new faith operates in a convert. There is a continuous interaction between the 'new' and the 'old' in the convert; and he precisely sees the power of conversion in the "blurring between the objects to which the convert assimilates— and those he (or she) challenges with a free crossover between assent and dissent" (Viswanathan 2011, 519 –520). Although conversion involves a "sudden turning from", just like it was with St. Paul on the road to Damascus, it is often too much to expect and imagine that the convert will totally renounce using his previous experience and knowledge, especially in times of crisis. Conversion is never a straight jacket, but rather a continuous negotiation between the two faiths; of assimilating the new and critiquing traditional culture on one hand, or using the frame of the new to renew the old culture, making both cultures reside in the convert (Viswanathan 2011, 520). This appears to be the context of the indigenous performance among these communities which are predominantly converted to Christianity. Most converts seek to indigenize Christianity into traditional cultures so that it is compatible with local culture. This is an aspect of the syncretic project that African converts to Christianity have variously engaged in. The emergence of independent Christian churches in the colonial history of Africa reflects this. Among the Ma'di, for instance, it is now the norm for the local clergy to use the leaves of *mememele* to bless the congregation in Catholic ritual of the Mass. This is a plant the community uses widely in their indigenous rituals prayers and

231

word rituals; and it makes so much sense to them than the *aspergillum* (sprinkler).

ESTABLISHMENT OF THE PEACE WEEK IN GULU ARCHDIOCESE

The Peace Week was initiated in 2006, under the leadership Archbishop John Baptist Odama, as a practical community effort at solving the layers of ethnic conflicts that plagues the northern Uganda region during and after the reigns of Idi Amin and Milton Obote II in 1970s and 1980s respectively. Although there were no open wars between and among the thirteen ethnicities in the region, tensions were evident among them. GANAL is an acronym for Gulu Archdiocese, Nebi, Arua and Lira Dioceses of northern Uganda. This acronym, also, stands for the major objective the Archdiocese set for itself to: "Grow All New, Alive in Love" (GANAL). The region, under its religious leaders, realised that the war of the 1970s and 1980s had disconnected and fractured them; yet they belong to the same archdiocese although they come from different ethnicities and language groups. The church, thus, thought of rebuilding the unity of the region, the Archdiocese and healing the wounds of violence they had experienced. The Peace Week brings the diverse peoples together and creates an occasion for them to talk to each other, to pray, to recreate and eat together.

This event that started in 2006 is carried out annually; and revolves from parish to parish within the archdiocese. In its nearly ten years, it has born many good fruits. People of all walks of life are attracted to the Peace Week celebrations. Annually, a theme is identified and keynote speakers invited to facilitate the discussions. The groundbreaking, first Peace Week that took place in the Adjumani Parish focused on addressing the key questions: "What happened that led to the wave of mistrust and conflicts among us that broke our peace and mutuality"? "And how can we now work together to rebuild the broken trust?" Since then, the people in the region have come to value the Peace Week because it has freed them from the *fantasies* of conflict and stereotypes. They are now beginning to interact freely and enjoy the diversities in each other's cultures. The amazing outcome of the annual Week of Peace is explained by Archbishop Odama thus:

We have now gone one step further. Now families in the host diocese happily provide accommodation for visiting ethnicities in their homes and villages. They come together to the Parish where the seminars take place. Feeling at home in each other's home is a great development from where we started. Sleeping together, under the same roof, and eating from the same bowl is a sign of trust. Formerly this was difficult because there was thick mistrust among the people.[4] (Personal Interview 2014)

The Peace Week has become a grand regional activity, largely sponsored by the people who work for its continuity. They value it because it expresses their shared desire for peace, love and togetherness. It is a celebration of their realisation that they cannot be complete, happy and prosperous when they have poor neighbourly relationship. The realisation that we are happier when we are connected to other people outside our ethnicities shows that human beings are not just attracted to members of their ethnic group. Indeed, life is richer in diversity.

The annual theme for the Peace Week is now determined by the holistic needs of the region. This is how the programme of Tree Planting has been integrated into the Peace Week celebration. The northern part of Uganda, largely considered as marginalised, uses the occasion of getting together to address issues related to their development as well. This is how tree-planting, as part of human relationship with the environment has come about, following the realisation that human beings cannot prosper if they disrespect the environment (see Bukenya 2013). Each diocese brings reports of their tree-planting activity to this occasion and a trophy is given to the one that has planted most trees. The result of this activity is remarkable in some dioceses.

This initiative of Peace Week is still restricted in northern Uganda. It is the dream of the Archbishop of Gulu that this tremendous success can be replicated and rolled out in other parts of Uganda that are certainly in need of building trans-ethnic peace and good neighbourliness. This is an actual need, because although it is often swept under the carpet, ethnic and regional tensions do exist in Uganda and they are often activated at moments of tension. The

---

4   To re-iterate the archbishop's words, Okello informed me that he would appreciate it greatly, if his children could marry across ethnicities.

divide between the Greater North (largely Nilotic ethnicities and poorly developed) and the South (largely Bantu ethnicities and better developed) is one of such divides. As the celebrations of the Peace Week indicate, there is no room for tribalism in genuine humanness. Because of the attractiveness of humanness (see Tutu and Tutu 2014), it is easy for 'tribal' rings to be burst and transcended by a more inclusive perspective of humanity as our race. Today ethnic barriers are fast loosening. Indeed stereotypes and suspicions are easily broken when human beings interact. Both Archbishop Odama and Okello recommend this as a needed programme for Uganda to help break the kind of negative ethnic stereotypes in which some people are still trapped. I quote the Archbishop at length, on the imperative to build a universal culture of humanism that transcends sectarianism:

> Our nation needs to promote the sense of connectedness among its 65 ethnic groups which are all equal to each other. We must go beyond these boundaries to be truly human. The more we come together as a people, the more we shall grow in our humanness, the more we shall develop, and the more we shall become richer.... Living in connectedness makes us more peaceful. Experiencing the world as a member of the human family enriches us; and our humanity is impoverished when it wears a sectarian lens.... I belong to the human family. I feel this in the warm receptions I get whenever I travel to different parts of the world. The people I interact with, all over the world, show me that my dimension is universal human-hood although I am Ugandan by nationality. In this sense, my dimension is Ubuntu, because I feel connected to other human beings, regardless of our various forms of identifications. To have this sense at a global level is still a challenge for many. This kind of universal ethnicity where one would feel at home in every corner of the world is still to be constructed around the world. There is a hope for this to succeed because unity and harmony are among the strongest desires of human beings (Personal Interview 2014).

CONCLUSION

Indigenous form of conflict resolution and reconciliation is similar to and yet distinct from the Christian ritual of reconciliation/penance. Both focus on restoring the broken relationship between the community and the individual, and between the individual and God, respectively. Community participation is very strong in indigenous reconciliation. Although the Catholic ritual had aspects of community participation in the Early Church, today, the sacrament of reconciliation is a private and individual affair between the priest and the penitent (Hanna 1911). This is a major difference. Furthermore, in Catholicism, a sinner may be excommunicated from the community for certain categories of sin. In indigenous practice, excommunication, imprisonment and permanent separation from the community do not exist. Temporary separation from community occurs when a crime leads to one taking refuge in exile. This may be self-imposed or embedded in the logic of the community's cultural beliefs. One who operates outside the moral code of the community feels a sense of loss and deprivation. The temporary withdrawal of the community's love "might reform the offenders because of their wish for re-integration" (Kresse 2007, 169). In due course, the community gets equally involved in ensuring that the persons re-integrate and humanize its estranged members.

The system of retributive justice employed by the International Criminal Court (ICC) isolates and prosecutes criminals away from their social and cultural contexts. This, in the logic of indigenous system, is destructive and a reason for continued estrangement of the community members. Locking up a criminal in jail for a couple of years does not lead to restoration of relationship, which is a principal value in the *matoput* ritual. Furthermore, truth and contrition are difficult to establish in the process, since it is mostly about the accused defending himself against an accuser. Large sums of money are spent in the process of acquiring the best lawyers for the case; and the art of logical argument is often what makes one win a case (see Terry 2011). Although this win-lose paradigm has its own merits, it does not build social relationships and renew a community's sense of solidarity as the ritual approach does. The graphic ritual drama that involves the entire community aims at transforming the whole person and communities in their physical, psychological, social and spiritual dimensions. The participants transcend the world of the living to include the spirit world of the ancestors who are cherished members of the community. In this atmosphere, the confessant who seeks to be re-integrated into the community experiences solidarity with his community that is welcoming him back.

The contemporary post-colonial experiences of many African communities tend to be more critical, especially in the face of challenges. There is a more positive disposition towards looking back to the cultural logics when communities are not satisfied by the solutions provided by modern conventional systems. This shows how cultures continually interact and revise each other in the everyday experiences of life without one totally dominating the other. Peter Van Der Veer (2011) explains how the post-colonial subject is inevitably engaged in global conversations. We are in different stages of the experience of modernity, which is itself, a "process that is of long duration, in principle always unfinished and riddled with contradictions. The notion that an already finished, modular modernity is shipped from Europe to the rest of the world is contrary to historical evidence" (Van Der Veer 2011, 535). There are evident continuities and discontinuities as we live our conversational identities as people exposed to various cultures. For these 'global conversations' to be authentic, it cannot be one-sided, where the West speaks and the rest of world listens and follows.

In some instances, there are bold cultural steps taken by Africans to "reclaim" traditional values that were officially dismissed because they were considered backward and 'satanic'. The monologic approach of evangelization early Christian missionaries used, that left no room to open up to other versions of the 'truth' is now rightly criticised by post colonial writers like William Baldrige (2011). This is what he refers to as "colonizing in the name of Christ", when Christians confuse their confession of faith with absolute knowledge of God—a disposition which invites challenge from those whose versions of knowledge are shut out. He considers this as not only hubris on the part of the preachers, but a challenge to blasphemy; for "Who can claim absolute knowledge of reality but God alone?" (Baldrige 2011, 528). This observation about the relationship between the missionaries and the Native Americans can be applied to other spheres of knowledge and practice such as the justice system discussed in this chapter. We have a lot to learn from each other. Obviously, the models from the West cannot be applicable to all local situations; and clearly the colonial project has not succeeded in eradicating many indigenous practices that are the bedrock of the people's psyche and identity. The everyday is often characterised by negotiating, assimilating and challenging knowledge that come from diverse sources. It is a positive move that Africa is becoming more confident in putting forward its ethos such as Ubuntu to the global stream of knowledge. Our humanity is enriched by opening up to other people's way of seeing and experiencing the world, so that we can dialogue with them.

BIBLIOGRAPHY

Adeduntan, Ayo. 2014. *What the Forest old me: Yoruba, Hunter, Culture and narrative Performance*. Pretoria: Unisa Press.

Beckett, A.J. 2007. "Mercy, Particularity, and the Map from the Void". *Archives for Philosophy of Law and social Philosophy*, 93 (2): 217–235.

Baldrige, William. 2011. "Reclaiming our Histories'. In *The Post-Colonial Studies Reader*, Second Edition, edited by B. Ashcroft, G. Griffiths & H. Tiffin. London: Routledge.

Bukenya, Austin. 2013. *A Hole in the Sky*. Oxford: Oxford University Press.

Card, Claudia. 1972. "On Mercy". *The Philosophical Review*, 81 (2): 182–207.

Cohen, Raymond. 2001. "Language and Conflict Resolution: The Limits of English". *International Studies Review*, 3 (1): 25–51.

Dipio, D. 2008. "Symbolic Action and Performance in the Conflict Resolution Rituals of the Ma'di of Uganda". In *Performing Community*, edited by D. Dipio, L. Johannessen and S. Sillars. Oslo: Novus.

Graham, Fabian. (n.d.) "Ritual and Symbolism". Retrieved January 6, 2015: https://sites.google.com/site/4fabian/ritual-and-symbolism.

Hanna, Edward. 1911. "The Sacrament of Penance". In *The Catholic Encyclopedia*. New York: Robert Appleton Company.

Homans, G. C. 1941. "Anxiety and Ritual: The Theories of Malinowski and Radcliffe-Brown". *American Anthropologist, New Series*, 43 (2): 164–172.

Kornfield, Jack. 2011, "Forgive for you". Retrieved January 6, 2015: http://greatergood.berkeley.edu/gg_live/science_meaningful_life_videos/speaker/jack_kornfield/forgive_for_you/

Kornfield, Jack. 2011. "What Forgiveness Means". Retrieved May 8, 2015: http://greatergood.berkeley.edu/gg_live/science_meaningful_life_videos/speaker/jack_kornfield/what_forgiveness_means/

Kresse, Kai. 2007. *Philosophizing in Mombasa: Knowledge, Islam and Intellectual Practice on the Swahili Coast*. Edinburgh: Edinburgh University Press.

Luskin, Fred. 2011. "The Choice to Forgive". Retrieved May 8, 2015: http://greatergood.berkeley.edu/gg_live/science_meaningfu l_life_videos/speaker/fred_luskin/the_choice_to_forgive/

Luskin, Fred. 2011. "Forgiveness Requires Gratitude". Retrieved May 8, 2015: http://greatergood.berkeley.edu/gg_live/science _meaningful_life_videos/speaker/fred_luskin/forgiveness_r equires_gratitude/

Pettigrove, Glen. 2007. "Forgiveness and Interpretation". *The Journal of Religious Ethics*, 35 (3): 429–452.

Pettigrove, Glen. 2007. "Understanding, Excusing, Forgiving". *Philosophy and Phenomenological Research*, 74 (1): 156–175.

Rothenbuhler, Walter E. 1998. *Ritual Communication: From everyday Conversation to Mediated Ceremony*. London: Sage Publications.

Terry, Sara. 2011. *Fambul Tok*. New York: DVD Video.

Turner, Victor. 1982. *From Ritual to Theatre: The Human Seriousness of Play*. New York: Art Journal Publications.

Turner, Victor. 1973. "Symbols in African Ritual". *Science, New Series*, 179, (4078): 1100 – 1105.

Tutu, Desmond and Mpho Tutu. 2014. *The Book of Forgiving*. New York: Harper Collins Publishers.

Twambley, P. 1976. "Mercy and Forgiveness". *Analysis*. 36 (2): 84–90.

Van Der Veer, Peter. 2011. "Global Conversations". In *The Post-Colonial Studies Reader*, Second Edition., edited by B. Ashcroft, G. Griffiths and H. Tiffin. London: Routledge.

Viswanathan, Gauri. 2011. "Conversion, 'Tradition' and National Consolidation". In *The Post-Colonial Studies Reader*, Second Edition, edited by B. Ashcroft, G. Griffiths and H. Tiffin. London: Routledge.

Whitehouse, Harvey and Jonathan A. Lanman. 2014. "The Ties That Bind Us: Ritual, Fusion, and Identification". *Current Anthropology*, 55 (6): 674–695.

CHAPTER 10. REVISITING CURRENT NURSING ETHICS: CAN UBUNTU FOSTER AN ENVIRONMENT FOR ETHICS OF CARE?

Fhumulani M. Mulaudzi, Ramadimetja S. Mogale & Mogomme A. Masoga

INTRODUCTION

The nursing profession remains one of the noblest and respected professions which emphasise caring and support (Oosthuizen 2012, 50). The International Council of Nurses' code of ethics, which is informed by international declarations on human rights aims to promote nursing as a caring profession that upholds human rights, including such critical issues as the right to life and dignity. In South Africa, the issue of human rights is dealt with in Chapter 2 on the Bill of Rights in the Constitution of the Republic of South Africa Act No 106 of 1996. On the right to health, subsection 11 states that "everyone has the right to life". The main goal of nursing training is to socialise student nurses and inculcate the virtues of humanity such as respect for autonomy, compassion, trust, honesty and social justice. The training of nurses emphasises the basis of humanity as a foundation of the duty to care. Team players such as nurse educators, nurse managers and professional nurses in the ward are expected to be positive role models who instil professionalism and the caring ethic in student nurses. It should be noted that the nursing ethics emanated from western philosophy and medical science which emphasise human rights and duties and individual autonomy (Haegert 2000, 496). Cobbah (1987, 310) argues that Human Rights is a western concept which negates the African way of living as well as the socialisation of African people. Western science has for the most part determined what counts as 'legitimate'. Nurses are expected to adopt the morals and ethics of caring from ways of knowing which, for many of African nurses, differ from their own, consequently, alienating them from the communities they serve (Offor 2009, 299). In this case it is argued that the cultural beliefs and indigenous practices of both nurses and the communities they serve are often overlooked.

Cobbah (1987, 312) asserts that Africans have not attempted to articulate in an African sense, the meaning of human dignity or perhaps human rights that flows from an African perspective in such a way that they can be useful to the rest of the international human rights community. However African scholars such as Wiredu (1992), Mbigi (1997), Mbiti (1970) and Makgoba (1997) introduced the African Philosophy of Ubuntu which informs the African methods of ethics that resonate with the African way of living. Ubuntu is a Nguni word (from Xhosa, Zulu, Ndebele and Swazi people of South Africa) that emanates from an African proverb "Umuntu ngu muntu nga bantu" (a person is a person through other persons). The proverb emphasises that a person can only exist or become a person because of the existence of other persons (Mulaudzi, Libster & Phiri 2009, 47).

A BRIEF THEORETICAL GROUNDING OF UBUNTU PHILOSOPHY

In this section we map out the theoretical grounding of Ubuntu philosophy in relation to health and life; wherein life is seen as the core of human life and development (Shutte 2001, 127). Human life is central to African world view hence the emphasis by the African society's on the preservation and promotion of health and life. The two are seen as gifts from God (Manda 2012, 134) and ancestors. God and ancestors (Modimo le badimo) in African culture are the two main "Beings" who reside in the spirit world and responsible for our living and welfare (Manda 2012, 140). The spiritual duo is the custodian of health and life. Ancestors are the guardians of the morality of the group, i.e. community in family or tribe or nation (Daryl Forde). They discharge this responsibility with excellence and effect because they are Badimo, Va-dimu, Wa-zinu (Swahili) literally "the people of Modimo (Divinity) and transmitters of Modimo's essence, energy, Vital Force" (Sawyerr 1970; Setiloane 1976). Masoga (2012) in his research on Umuntu–humanity and ancestors looked at the work of Setiloane where it was noted that to an outsider the most abrasive and challenging element in African Theology is its teaching on the ancestors. Researchers and writers have given African Theology and its teaching on the ancestors some new names to explain it to foreigners, e.g. "The Living Dead" (Mbiti 1970) but in vain. Actually the concept of Ancestors relates to the African understanding of *Umuntu-Motho*, i.e. its estimate of the human person (man). This understanding is embedded in the view that the human person is incorruptible and continues to exist after corporal death. The belief that the human person shares in Divinity is much more pronounced and practically acknowledged in African Theology than in Western Theology. Western Theology appears to be somewhat averse to this belief as reminiscent of *Humanism*, which is regarded as a heresy of the last century in the West. Africans declare simply that *Motho ke Modimo*—a human person is something sacred or even divine, i.e. it participates in Divinity, without necessarily claiming equality with it.

Setiloane (1986) declares that African Theology from African Traditional Religion, views the human being *umuntu-motho* as dynamic. A human being is *"force vitale"* (Tempels); and as such possesses *Seriti-Isithunzi*, a magnetic energy, which makes it a relating entity in "vital participation" (Mulango 1990, 122) with similar entities, which may be human or not. It is against this background that the link between health and life is of importance in humanity as it is about the 'vital force' *serithi-isithunzi* derived from the all-pervasive and original Source of Being. This accounts for human indestructibility and therefore, continuation in 'vital participation' for the continued sustenance of the physically living as well as for ethical—moral purposes. It is for this reason that healthcare providers—in our case nurses—are obliged to ensure righteousness when taking care of patients as humans and other beings in nature, animate as well as inanimate.

Not only are nurses obliged to take care of the patients but also patients' families and their communities because according to Setiloane (1986) a human person's worth inheres and is rooted in belonging: *I belong therefore I am* (Mbiti 1970). Being is belonging, and nothing is that does not belong. In the end all belong to *Mong* (Sotho) Tsoci (Nupe) the Owner. The belonging is dynamic as a being interacts with other beings in and with the cosmos. "For the Bantu (as with other Africans) beings maintain intimate relationships with one another" (Mulago 1990, 122). The living strengthen their dead by appeasing them to keep them happy (inkonzo-Nguni, Tirelo-Tswana). The departed in turn exert a real vital influence on the living and on their destiny. The visible world is one with the invisible; there is no break between. Therefore at any one time any community is more than the sum total of the physical elements that compose it. Community, therefore, is a cauldron, an interlocking circuit in which the members, not only human, exist in interdependence on one another.

UBUNTU AFRICAN ETHICS AND THE CASE FOR NURSING ETHICS

The discussion on Ubuntu African ethics and nursing ethics places emphasis on the fact that human beings exist based on their relationship with other human beings. Interrelatedness, which goes along with the African philosophy of Ubuntu, promotes cohesiveness and solidarity and negates individualism (Haegert 2000, 495). Chuwa (2014, 34) posits that the Ubuntu philosophy poses tensions between individual rights and universal rights. Both Haegert and Chuwa argue that individuals are viewed as patients with autonomy. However autonomy in an African context emphasises a community-based mindset in which the welfare of a group is greater than the welfare of a single individual in a group. This can be equated to the ethical theory of utilitarianism which places emphasis on taking decisions in a way that benefits the majority of individuals (Mulaudzi, Mokoena & Troskie 2009).

Furthermore, according to Chuwa (2014, 34), the core of such decision making processes promote the spirit of communitarianism where the needs and the rights of a community take precedence over personal rights. Personal rights from an African perspective are perceived as subservient as they are defined by the rights of other (community) and they thrive in a relational setting (Chuwa 2014, 36). This is because Africans judge ones 'personhood' according to their ethical behaviour and morality towards others (Le Grange 2012).

As stated earlier the intention of this paper is to propose the infusion of the philosophy of Ubuntu as a critical aspect in the training of nurses in order to optimise nursing education in South Africa. As a philosophical underpinning Ubuntu philosophy will advocate a nursing practice that can reclaim and revisit indigenous ways of caring in our healthcare sector. The reclaiming will therefore involve relational caring, which is based on Ubuntu. The relational caring that is embedded within Ubuntu does not only underscore communal ethic over and against individualism but it upholds both individuality as 'personhood' and communalism together. It is for this reason that we envisage nursing care and practices that are underpinned by Ubuntu principles as they will definitely promote collective intelligence and wisdom that are relational in nature.

UBUNTU RELATED NURSING CARE

Ubuntu is the basis of the morals that binds all Africans together. Ubuntu tends to approach cultural protocols, values and behaviours as an integral part of caring for another. Ubuntu philosophy emphasizes values such as respect, caring, compassion, kindness, warmth, understanding, sharing, humanness, reaching out, wisdom, a sense of belonging and an obligation to another. Ubuntu is a concrete manifestation of the interconnectedness of human beings—it is the embodiment of African culture and lifestyle. Ubuntu should be seen as the potential of being human that articulates a basic respect and compassion for others (Anderson 2003, 25). Ubuntu is a seminal factor in the formation of perceptions that influence social conduct in a society (Anderson 2003, 25). Ubuntu contextually implies a human character that is associated with mutuality, respect, reciprocity and connectedness (Manala 2002, 1038).

Shutte (2001, 15) expounds that the term Ubuntu stands for something of colossal power and value; hence it is imperative to describe and define Ubuntu comprehensively and deeply as much as possible. Ubuntu is known for its liberative, emancipative values that are based on 'collectivity', caring conduct and lifestyle found among the people of Africa. The values of Ubuntu are solidarity, interdependence, group belonging and group-centeredness (Manala 2002, 1039). Ubuntu/vhuthu is a concept that is derived from proverbial expressions found in several languages in Africa. However, it is not only a linguistic concept but it also has a normative connotation that embodies how we ought to relate to one another—what our moral obligation is towards the other (Le Grange

243

2012, 331). Ubuntu beseeches for the essence of humaneness that is worth; and this essence of humanity needs to be cultivated and nurtured (Letseka 2014, 547) among the newly nursing cadres. The cultivation and nurturing of this essence will result in the emergence of humane knowledge (Letseka 2014, 547) which will direct the new nursing cadres to act humanely towards the patients. Additionally, from humane knowledge an appreciative understanding of each other as people emanates (Letseka 2014, 547).

CULTIVATING UBUNTU IN NURSING PRACTICE

Cultivating Ubuntu involves the 'coming into presence' (Biesta 2006, 9) of self in a changing social and biophysical world. The sense of wholeness and interconnectedness of self with the social and natural, by implication means that caring for others also involves a duty to care for nature. Ubuntu connects three ecologies, namely; self, social and nature. These are inextricably bound with one another (Guattari 2001). Cultivating Ubuntu, by definition, therefore involves healing of self, the social and nature.

The training of our nursing students should be aimed at the betterment of patients. Caring and compassion should underscore nursing training and practice as founded on Ubuntu (Haegert 2000; Manala 2002). Such training and practice will recognise the scientific, literary and philosophical elements that are familiar to the African context (Offor 2009, 305). Notwithstanding the fact that nursing is a holistic active provision of service to those who are ill (Shutte 2001, 145), the stated elements will reach the home of those emotions and impulses which are the determining factors in the development of human character (Manala 2002, 1037).

The training and education of nurses matters deeply, since by its very nature this training is grounded in human connection. Such training seeks a meaningful discourse where a genuine understanding can occur in order to establish relationships and commitments that recognize human connection (Kunyk & Austin 2012, 382). Human connection is crucial in nursing practice. However, it becomes insufficient when not linked to Ubuntu especially in healthcare environments. It is here where there is a need for continuous support that enables individual nursing cadres to excel in their performance without losing sight of communalism as one of the branches of Ubuntu.

However, the training of nurses in South Africa is still based on imported theories which lack contextual components of African philosophy with a gap on students' own culture (Metz 2010, 374). This explains the gap that exists between philosophical and cultural relevancy within the current curricula on the training of these new cadres. In their scientific work, Adejumo and Lekalakala–Mokgele (2009) support this, aptly indicating the progress made on areas of knowledge development by South African nursing scholars from 1986 to 2006. A closer look at this work points to a lack of an African perspective; as none of the designated areas of knowledge are on "decolonizing nursing scholarship". It is possible to adopt a decolonial nursing perspective in the current nursing curriculum. This can be done by weaving through ontology and epistemologies that embody indigenous knowledge systems (Manala 2002, 1038) and by incorporating Ubuntu into the current basic education and training programme. There should be a shift in policies and programs that will reflect the needs and wishes of the people we are serving. Of importance, we need to decolonize our minds through radical change and transformation of our curricula. Our curricula should be informed by the ways of knowing rooted in our own cultures. We need to move from rhetoric and start implementing the models of care that resonate with the real lives of our patients.

PRINCIPLE ETHICS VIS-À-VIS UBUNTU

Nursing care and practices that are underpinned by Ubuntu principles promote collective wisdom and collective intelligence that is relational in nature. These principles foster personal commitment that enhances accountability and responsibility towards others, a spirit of collaboration, connectedness, sharing and flexibility (Chuwa 2014, 34). Accordingly, the philosophical underpinnings of Ubuntu emphasize personal traits of respect, caring, compassion, kindness, warmth, understanding, sharing, humanness, reaching out, wisdom and neighbourliness (Mulaudzi, Libster & Phiri 2009, 49). To this extent, it is correct to say that Ubuntu and nursing can complement each other (Mulaudzi, Libster & Phiri 2009, 48). Despite this eminent complementary relationship between nursing and Ubuntu, the current nursing care practices are based on principle ethics that negate the relational aspect of care as reflected in indigenous African culture (Haegert 2000, 497). Principle ethics entail both general and specific rules of behaviour described and prescribed by the code of conduct (Beauchamp and Childress 2009; Resnik 2012, 2). The general rules of behaviour assert duties, obligations, rights and responsibilities (Resnik 2012, 3). The abovementioned rules emphasize principles such as non-maleficence, beneficence and fidelity and justice (Beauchamp & Childress 2009; Nortvedt, Hem & Skirbekk 2011, 194).

Equivalently, the ethics in Ubuntu advocate connectedness and mutual respect that is enshrined within the values of caring, compassion, unity, tolerance, respect, closeness, generosity, authenticity, empathy, hospitality, conscience, conformity, sharing and communitarianism (Mulaudzi, Libster & Phiri 2009, 47). According to Chuwa (2014, 33) Ubuntu as an ethic has three main components. The first component is the caring ethics that provide an in-depth understanding of the existing tension between individual and universal rights. The second component is the individual's human relationship which is judged by one's morality of considering the wellbeing of his/her fellow man (Chuwa 2014, 36). The other component is reciprocity of care wherein every individual has an irreplaceable part to play within the community and society (Chuwa 2014, 39). As ethists, Nortvedt et al. (2011, 196) confirmed, the three components beseech for relational moral ontology that demand that healthcare professionals act according to both Ubuntu ethics and principle ethics.

The major concern in principle ethics is morality, where the motive is a duty towards the community (Chuwa 2014, 36). Such a motive challenges self-interest and individualism (Resnik 2012, 3). Conversely, individualism emphasizes uniqueness; differences and independence (Gumbo 2014, 68). Additionally, individualism is characterized by competitive tasks wherein an individual is seen as a distinct entity from his/her community (Gumbo 2014, 76). In as much as individualism is viewed by many as the enemy to Ubuntu (Gumbo 2014, 77), it should be noted that those who support this character (individualism) tend to prioritize themselves, thus contradicting communalistic way of life. Such individuals emphasize the aspect of Ubuntu which speaks about personhood only while underrating communal life. Therefore, we argue that by definition individualism is not an enemy of Ubuntu per se but individual people create individuality. Ultimately such individualistic character breeds self-centredness, competitiveness, jealousy and greed. The latter erodes the moral fibre of the nursing profession and the African way of life (Gumbo 2014, 69).

Similar to education and training, the organisational structures and systems where nurses ultimately work promote the 'personhood' component of Ubuntu. Teamwork is afterall not only essential for total quality patient care. Above all, it is one key tenet underpinning Ubuntu. As a result, it is important to turn the existing patient care teams in our hospitals into Ubuntu centred working teams. As such teams tend to explore moral experiences and interactions of team members in healthcare environments (Kunyk & Austin 2012, 382). Ubuntu centred teams in our hospitals will create nursing cadres that will be cognizant of the fact that their performance is not only based on themselves as individuals but and with efforts of others as demands by Ubuntu nursing care.

VIRTUE ETHICS AND UBUNTU

According to Resnik (2012, 4) virtue ethics are defined as the traits that individuals progressively develop through practice and imitation. These inculcated practices provide the standards and norms by which a person guides his/her day to day behaviour. In addition, virtue ethics determine the attitudes towards political, economic, social issues that one comes into contact on daily basis (Waghid, & Smeyers 2012, 15). Importantly, they support principle ethics regarding autonomy, justice, beneficence, mutual respect, engagement, embodiment, and environment. In our case, the virtues describe what kind of nurses we should strive to be. As nurses, we argue that nursing care practices should merge both principles— based and virtue ethics in order to provide care holistically. None of the two must supersede the other. The fusion can be possible if we embrace the indigenous ways of caring in our healthcare sector and training of the young nurses (Hall, du Toit & Louw 2013). This would therefore require us to incorporate relational caring, based on Ubuntu (Gumbo 2014, 68). Above all, there is an indication for a commitment to holistic caring in nursing.

RECOMMENDATION: A HOLISTIC MODEL OF CARE UNDERPINNED BY THE UBUNTU AFRICAN ETHICS

The questions related to nursing ethics are as follows: Can a single model assist in instilling the caring ethics in the nursing profession?

Can principle based ethics continue to be applicable in different contexts without contextualisation? Similarly, can Ubuntu be applied without taking cognisance of the principle based approach? What do differing systems hold in common and where do they diverge?

The holistic model of care based on Ubuntu may be used as a point of departure to revive the sacrosanct values of our profession. A holistic model of care underpinned by Ubuntu epistemologies is desired within the nursing profession. It requires us to embody and practice collective wisdom with the inclusion of African philosophical principles. The African philosophical principles may assist us to move from the known (Ubuntu) to the unknown (western philosophy), for improved patient-centred care and better health outcomes. The idea is that one of us is not as smart as all of us. Through mutual respect, trust, self-denial and avoidance of *I for We*, the holistic model of care can be achieved. The training of nursing must aim at producing accountable, virtuous nurses who are prepared to serve the public with pride whilst having Ubuntu. In his work *Elders decry the loss of Ubuntu*, Gumbo (2014: 68) postulates that the values that define Ubuntu are: togetherness, brotherhood, equality, caring, sharing, sympathy, empathy, compassion, respect, tolerance, humanness, harmony, redistribution, obedience, happiness, wisdom, communalism, communitarianism, kinship, group solidarity, conformity, human dignity, humanistic orientation and collective unity. The said values provide the branches of a holistic approach to clinical nursing practice, management and research with nursing education as the root of Ubuntu.

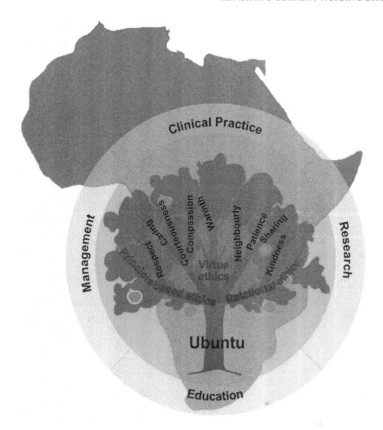

Figure 1

The holistic model of care includes among others tenets such as mutual respect, reciprocity, receptivity, being empathetic, responsibility for the others, reconciliatory role modelling, dialogue and communication. The type of care in reference here recognizes and integrates the principles and modalities of body-mind-emotions-spirit in clinical practice on daily basis as put forth by Mariano (in Dossey 2012, 59). The nurse in holistic model of care is seen as an instrument of care that requires reciprocal relationships with the individual patients, community where the patients come from and with colleagues (Dossey 2012, 34). The above stated relationships are philosophical standpoints that define a nurse's contextual social bonds that facilitate collectivity and inter-subjectivity within

249

communalism (Gumbo 2014, 68). Through the holistic model of care, we will be able to provide Ubuntu related nursing with virtues as in Figure 1.

CONCLUSION

From an academic point of view Ubuntu is challenging as it highlights valuable aspects of African ways of life, principles and ideas that are often overlooked or ignored (van Hensbroek 2001, 5). Our understanding and knowledge of nursing ethics and care should be deeply rooted in African culture and practices. In our ways of producing and constructing knowledge, we long for nursing ethics and nursing care that will resonate with the philosophy of Ubuntu.

Our deepest moral obligation is to become more fully human. And this means entering more and more deeply into community with others. This means living Ubuntu which is guided by collective wisdom. As nurses it is demanded of us to think of how "we" can excel or what "we" will benefit as opposed to how can "I" excel? What will "I" benefit? This will improve our service provision and access to healthcare.

BIBLIOGRAPHY

Adejumo, Oluyinka and Eucebious Lekalakala-Mokgele. 2009. "A 2-Decade Appraisal of African Nursing Scholarship: 1986–2006". *Journal of Nursing Scholarship*, 41(1): 64-69.

Anderson, A. M. 2003. "Restorative justice, the African Philosophy of Ubuntu and the diversion of criminal prosecution". Accessed from: http://www.ncjrs.gov/App/publications/abstract.aspx?ID= 202433.

Beauchamp, Tom L. and James F. Childress. 2009. *Principles of biomedical ethics*, Sixth Edition. New York, Oxford University Press.

Biesta, Gert. 2006. *Beyond learning: democratic education for a human future*. London, Paradigm Publishers.

Constitution of the Republic of South Africa No. 108 of 1996. Retrieved from http://www.acts.co.zawhtdhtml.html.

Cobbah, Josiah A.M.1987. "African values and human rights debate: an African perspective". *Human Rights Quarterly*, 9 (3): 309-331.

Chuwa, Leonard T. 2014. *African Indegenous Ethics, Advancing Global Bioethics*. New York: Springer.

Dossey, Barbara M. 2012. *Holistic nursing: a handbook for practice*, Sixth Edition. Burlington, Jones & Bartlett Learning.

Gumbo, Mishack T. 2014. "Elders decry the loss of Ubuntu". *Mediterranean Journal of Social Sciences*, 5 (10): 67- 77.

Guattari, Felix. 2001. *The three ecologies*. Translated by Ian Pindar and Paul Sutton. London: The Athlone Press.

Haegert, Sandy. 2000. "An African ethic for nursing". *Nursing Ethics*, 7(6): 492-501.

Hall, D. du Toit, L. 2013. "Feminist ethics of care and Ubuntu". *Obstetrics & Gynaecology Forum*, 23: 29-33.

Le Grange, Lesley. 2012. "Ubuntu, ukama, environment and moral education". *Journal of Moral Education*, 41 (3): 329–340.

Letseka, Moeketsi. 2014. "Ubuntu and justice as fairness". *Mediterranean Journal of Social Sciences*, 5(9): 544.

Kunyk, Diane and Wendy Austin. 2012. "Nursing under the influence: A relational ethics perspective". *Nursing ethics*, 19(3): 380-389.

Manda, Domoka L. 2012. "Confidentiality in African healthcare ethics: a problematic concept?" *Journal of Gleanings from Academic Outliers*, 1 (1): 131-149.

Manala, Matsobane J. 2002. "Education for reconstruction: a post-apartheid response to the education crisis in South Africa". *Hervormde Theological Studies*, 58(3): 1032-1055.

Makgoba, Malegapuru W. 1997. *The Makgoba Affair: A Reflection on Transformation*. Johannesburg: Florida Hills.

Masoga, Mogomme A. 2012. "A critical dialogue with Gabriel Molehe Setiloane: The unfinished business of the African divinity question". *Studia Hisofiriae Ecclesiasficae*, 323-344.

Mariano, Carla. 2012. *Holistic nursing: scope and standards of practice in Holistic nursing: a handbook for practice*, Sixth Edition. Burlington: Jones & Bartlett Learning.

Mbigi, Lovemore. 1997. *The African Dream in Management*. Randburg: Knowledge Resources Ltd.

Mbiti, John S. 1970. *The concept of God in Africa*. London

Metz, Thaddeus. 2007. "Ubuntu as a moral theory: reply to four critics". *South African Journal of Philosophy*, 26(4): 369-387.

Mulago, Vincent. 1990. "Traditional African Religion and Christianity". In. *African Traditional Religions in Contemporary Society*, edited by Jacob, K. Olupona. New York : Paragon House.

Mulaudzi, Fhumulani M., Martha M. Libster and S. Phiri. 2009. "Suggestions for creating a welcoming nursing community: Ubuntu, cultural Diplomacy, and mentoring". *International Journal of Human Caring*, 13(2): 45-51.

Mulaudzi, Fhumulani, Rosemare Troskie and Joyce Mokoena. 2000. *Basic ethics in nursing*. Sandown: Heinemann.

Nortvedt, Per, Marit H. Hem and Helge Skirbekk. 2011. "The ethics of care: role obligations and moderate partiality in health care". *Nursing Ethics*, 18(2): 192-200.

Offor, Francis. 2009. "The imperative of sustainable development in Africa: Anyiam-Osigwe's sage philosophy as an applied example". *Journal of Sustainable Development in Africa*, 10 (4): 299-311.

Oosthuizen, M.J. 2012. "The portrayal of nursing in South African newspapers: a qualitative content analysis". *African Journal of Nursing and Midwifery*14 (1): 49–62.

Resnik, David B. 2012. "Ethical virtues in scientific research". *Accountability in Research: Policies and Quality Assurance*. 19(6): 329-343.

Sawyerr, Harry. 1979. *God, Ancestor or Creator*. London.

Setiloane, Gabriel M. 1976. *The image of God among the Sotho-Tswana*. Rotterdam: Cape Town.

Setiloane, Gabriel M. 1986. *African Theology: An introduction*. Johannesburg.

Shorter, Aylward. 1975. *African Christian Theology*. London.

Shutte, Augustine. 2001. *Ubuntu: an ethic for the new South Africa*. Cape Town: Cluster Publications.

van Hensbroek, P. Boele. 2001. "Philosophies of African Renaissance in African intellectual history". *QUEST An African Journal of Philosophy*, XV N (1-2): 127-138.

Waghid, Yusef and Paul Smeyers. 2012. "Reconsidering Ubuntu: on the educational potential of a particular ethic of care". *Educational Philosophy and Theory*, 44(S2): 7-20, doi: 10.1111/j.1469-5812.2011.00792.x.

EPILOGUE: REFLECTIONS ON PERSONHOOD THROUGH THE EYES OF A.C. JORDAN'S *THE WRATH OF ANCESTORS*

James Ogude

INTRODUCTION

When I started interrogating the idea of personhood, especially in Africa, it became clear to me that African literature, particularly foundational narratives, have always been concerned with contestations around the idea of personhood—what it means to come into being; how Africans are located in their world and indeed the totality of the universe within which Africans find themselves. A major pre-occupation has been with how Africans define themselves in their world and what forms of ontological outlook inform this world. The concern was particularly more urgent among those foundational writers of African literature who located their craft between the difficult periods of colonial occupation and its immediate aftermath. They had to wrestle with what it meant to be human against the onslaught on their personal dignity both as individuals and as a race. Indeed, a cursory glance at Sol Plaatje's *Native Life in South Africa* (1940/1980), Chinua Achebe's *Things Fall Apart* (1958), Flora Nwapa's *Efuru* (1966), Ngugi wa Thiong'o's *Weep not, Child* (1964), Grace Ogot's *The Promised Land* (1966), Ferdinand

Oyono's *Houseboy* (1966), Es'kia Mphalele's *Down Second Avenue* (1959), and Peter Abrahams's *Mine Boy* (1946)—to name but a few— shows that the thematic thrust of these narratives was restoration— returning the black people's humanity to themselves. This is to say that the framing of the black people's lives by the colonialists worked to deny the humanity of blacks. The two theorists that have been so central to the restoration project; of awakening a black consciousness in the minds and soul of blacks are Frantz Fanon (1965) and Steve Biko (1978). Separated by almost two decades, the two theorists would insist that the greatest project confronting the black race today is the violence inflicted on the psyche of the colonised black subjects—a psyche of inferiority. It is for this reason that Fanon (1965, 32 – 33) would insist that, "the terms the settler uses when he mentions the native are zoological terms. He speaks of the yellow man's reptilian motions, of the stink of the native quarter, of breeding swarms, of foulness, of spawn, of gesticulations. When the settler seeks to describe the native fully in exact terms he constantly refers to the bestiary".

It is not, therefore, surprising that anti-colonial literature's thematic thrust always swivelled around identities. Much of this contestation was often described as a contestation around culture; hence a preponderance of the so-called themes of cultural conflict in foundational narratives. On critical reflection, it has become evident that much of this contest was really a contest around personhood— what it means to be human and what goes into that process of becoming a person. It was really about what defines a humane person and those processes through which what we call persons come into being. That is why, for many Africans, the interpellation of Africans into colonial modernity as colonial subjects was really the anti-thesis of being human and an erosion of personhood. The cry of anguish by Toundi, the protagonist in Ferdinand Oyono's *Houseboy* (1966, 4), 'Brother, what are we? What are we blackmen who are called French?', speaks to the erosion of the black peoples' humanity under colonialism. The irony is that Toundi leaves his home to join Fr Gilbert at the church mission on the eve of his circumcision, an initiation ritual into his community, thereby staging a rejection of his people's culture. His dehumanization before he dies is both physical and psychical. Beaten and left to die allegedly for meddling in the sexual affairs of the colonial officials, we read: 'He was already rotten before he died' (95). The rot is more than physical because it is a metaphor for utter humiliation—total debasement of this ironic figure at the height of colonialism in French West Africa. The delusionary description of himself when he is hailed into white modernity here is apt: 'The dog of the king is the king of dogs'. Although Toundi's cry of disillusionment is directed at the hollowness of assimilation in the context of French colonialism, it is also a sharp critique of the European idea of personhood, embedded as it were on the idea of a free and intentional subject, autonomous and independent of the trappings of communal networks. It turns a mocking gaze at colonial modernity rooted in the rise and triumph of instrumental reason, celebrated in Europe as the ultimate signifiers of personhood. The twin warheads of reason and autonomy undermined the African idea of connectedness of human beings—a relational quality that not only connects people to people, but equally to the totality of the environment and the universe—the living and the dead (ancestors), land and a supreme being, among others.

My point is that African literature in its broadest sense has tended to engage with these issues, and that is the contestation around personhood and identity in Africa. Their starting point was that we are dealing with an injured continent and an injured people and therefore the questions they sought to ask were always going to be political and philosophically insurrectionist—seeking to explain, but also searching for a radical rupture.

In this concluding note, deliberately called 'epilogue', I want to focus on A. C. Jordan's novel, *The Wrath of the Ancestors*, largely because of the complex manner in which I believe it engages with competing ideas of personhood at a particular moment in Africa's history without being neither sentimental nor idealistic. It is a pragmatic approach, which was partly defined by the historical contingencies of his time, but also a deep understanding of his people's history and culture. A. C. Jordan, like the rest of the foundational writers in Africa, is grappling with precisely these issues and doing so at a turning point in African society. Many such moments exist in South Africa's journey and indeed in the history of the colonised in Africa generally. These are moments worthy of deep reflection, not only to identify the way African philosophy and knowledge systems have grappled with them, but also to register how they have adapted in these instances.

Originally published in Xhosa in 1940 by Lovedale Press, it stands out as the first real novel in Xhosa. It was later translated into

English by A. C. Jordan himself, with the help of his sister, Pricilla P. Jordan. As many critics have noted, it is a historical narrative of epical proportions. Although often cast as a historical narrative, the novel is also profoundly human in its thematic concerns. It is a story about tradition as much as it is a story about a community in transition—a society in the cusp for change. At the risk of oversimplifying the plot, it is a story of a young Mpondomise prince who reluctantly leaves the University College of Fort Hare before completing a semester and goes back to the land of his ancestors to take his place as king of the Mpondomise. His ideas prove to be too far ahead of those of the people he has to lead, and his reign ends tragically and prematurely. On the surface of it, the text reads like a story about a clash of cultures—the clash between the so-called traditional and modern values—a familiar thematic thread that runs across a number of foundational narratives in Africa. Indeed, Jordan is adept at giving us a sharp juxtaposition between church-people and those holding traditional beliefs; school people as opposed to red ochre people; boarding school activities and the *inkundla* or assembly at the royal palace. While drawing attention to these historical and social tensions besetting a society in transition, Jordan does not pass judgement, but instead allows the readers to assess for themselves the impact of what is presented as a confrontation between two human and historical civilisations. The text is fundamentally about how societies can manage or mismanage historical change to the detriment of their own existence as individuals and as a community.

My interest though is in how this text, which speaks to two streams of human history, works to unsettle fixed ideas of personhood, while equally addressing itself to the enduring value of the everyday, especially the spiritual and ritualistic practices of the community. They draw on these symbolic structures in order to shape their daily lives, social and political institutions. In this novel, Jordan draws attention to two streams of personhood in tension, while pointing to a possibility of compromise, of a third space within which personhood could be formulated as a constant negotiation between competing versions of human history.

Firstly, Jordan presents us with a compelling story of a community whose history and social relations has been defined by interdependence and a social hierarchy that emphasises this connectedness and the social, political and moral obligations of those who live in it. And although they are by no means equal, the social obligations that bind these people together would seem to supersede individual autonomy. And so when the young prince is called upon to abandon his university studies to return home in keeping with the wishes of his late father, he is torn between obeying his own personal strivings and ambitions and the burden that his community has placed on him. It is both a moral and political obligation all rolled into one. This is what the Bishop tells him when he goes to discuss his impending decision to stop his studies and follow his father's will to lead his people:

My son, though I am a white man, I have lived among Africans for a long time and I have a deep respect for some of their customs. I know that among your people the wishes of the dead—especially of a parent—are sacred (Jordan 1980, 38).

Signalled here is a relational quality that not only points to the young Prince's obligation to his people, but also more importantly to the ancestors, his late father's wishes. One could argue that in taking the bold step to reclaim his crown in keeping with the wishes of his late father, the princess was re-establishing some harmony in the disconnected relationship between the living and the dead. When he decides that he will choose and pick what he can honour (e.g. marrying outside his father's wish), he is creating disequilibrium.

Jordan is at pains to draw a very strong communal ethos at work in this society; an ethos that is nevertheless rooted in intricate and complex symbolic structures; myth and magic; ancestral reverence and the whole ecological system. In this community, the symbolic structure and its associated mythology is embodied in the snake that the Queen mother detests and finally kills. *Majola*, the mole snake is perceived as the watchful eye over babies. We read that *Majola* is,

The snake that visits babies when they are born. It never harms the baby or members of the family and the only friendly way to drive it away is for mother to squirt it with her own breast milk. It visits the baby to prepare it for a successful and safe adult life. It comes as a friend and protector.

This narrative subverts the conventional notion of a snake as merely venomous and introduces a broader African interpretation that understands the serpent as a friend and a member of a dynamic ecology. What we have here is a critical inversion of the symbolic value associated with the snake in European or Judo-Christian thought in which the snake is seen as venomous or treacherous respectively. Instead what is captured is a complex understanding of personhood which transcends the limited understanding of Ubuntu as a relationship between people, but rather points to the fact that people derive their sense of self and community not only out of natural, individual or material qualities but out of deep bonds that connect them with other human beings and the environment (especially land, animals and plants). Self and the world are intrinsically tied in an intricate network of reciprocal relations and obligations that create the desired moral order and equilibrium between environment, the individual, the family and society (or the extended family which, ultimately, includes all humanity). Our personhood therefore is dependent not only on our relations to other persons but to the entities that sustain us and indeed make us. We are as much *Majola* as we are the King and that is what Ubuntu teaches us, and through Jordan we can appreciate the complexity of a concept that is ever caught between opening a pathway to a more humane world and being usurped for commercial gain and political rhetoric.

The second thing that Jordan draws our attention to is that although the young Prince returns to assume his place in a society which expects him to exercise his responsibilities in a context over-determined by specific socially derived obligations, the young King has changed. He is now a new product of a modernist project that he has been hailed into through his education. His newly acquired sense of agency is at odds with the agency rooted in the connectedness of people and interdependence that has given him his current status and authority. He can accept the dying-wish of his father that he returns to reclaim his crown, but he cannot accept his wish that "*he should marry the princess royal of the Bhaca!*" (141). He wants to exercise individual autonomy and to shape the direction his community must move, but they will not allow him to forge a new idea of personhood outside the norms established by the community.

One of the first tensions within the text, especially when the young chief has taken up the leadership of his people, is how to reconcile a modernist idea of progress and development and the beliefs of his people that he has reduced to superstition and witchcraft. This is reflected in King Zwelinzima's insistence, for example, that goats of his people should be destroyed so that the diviners may be thrown out of work. This would seem to be the beginning of alienation of the King from his people. He is impatient with the ways of his people yet he has readily accepted authority vested in him by tradition which he seeks to dismantle in haste. Sulenkama, the Great Chief of the House of Majola, cautions him to tread carefully: "We have to realize that the belief in witchcraft and diviners is very deeply rooted in the minds of our people. Now while we want to abolish these beliefs, we must on no account hurry the people. It's sympathy they need. And if you don't give them sympathy, it's sure to lead to a serious clash" (177-8). Similarly, the wife, while enjoying her role as the Queen Mother, insists on accompanying her husband to the Bhunga (royal assembly) in spite of the open disapproval of her husband's people. In spite of the protestations from the people in the royal palace, she kills *nkwakhwa*, the royal snake never referred to by name, but as '*Majola*'. In the face of it, she is unrepentant and abrupt.

It is quite clear, although not put in so many ways, that Jordan neither fully approves of the traditional norms rooted in communal interdependence nor a reckless embrace of individualism which seeks to assert autonomy without due respect to those rituals and symbolic structures that continue to inform the lives of so many people.

But Jordan is also sceptical of total subservience to communitarian ethos or is it communal tyranny? The community's grammar of speaking is framed in nationalistic language, often evoking purity of the community and harking back to a past that is elusive; and a language of exclusivity rather than inclusivity (best captured in the rupture and dissent that ensues during the meeting called to discuss the action of the mother queen). We witness self-interest couched in the lexicon of communal interest (e.g. Dingidawo's selfish motives and scheming against his nephew), and indeed unyielding patriarchal practices which continue to hold sway under the guise of respect for tradition and some unchanging rituals of staging power and authority.

Communal tyranny, as opposed to communal consensus that often defined communal deliberation, now threatens and destroys the genuine human desire of the young Prince—Zwelinzima—to exercise a voluntary choice to marry a woman that he desires regardless of her station. In killing the royal snake, the Queen Mother was possibly acting from a mother's natural instinct to protect her baby. A self-interested and blind response, based purely on communal history and ritual, condemns her without any attempt to understand the motive behind her actions. She is driven to a state of schizophrenia and commits suicide with the crown prince. The tyranny of communal ethos also drives the King to a state of delirium and he too commits suicide. Is 'the wrath of the ancestors' against those who deviate from the ways of the community or is Jordan pointing to a fundamental irony in the title, which is that any form of dogma, whether philosophical or political, is disastrous and detrimental to a humane idea of personhood or even the inevitability of confronting our interconnectedness? The King and his people are one but his change results in a new but difficult relationship and conversation between the King and his subjects—a conversation they are all trying to find the grammar with which to articulate but each fail in their respective ways to develop.

Evidently, pragmatic approach to understanding personhood should be a process of deliberate and careful negotiation between those values rooted in communal ethos and those that seek to reach out for individuality and associated elements of freedom to choose and act as free agents of change. Either of the extremes is likely to lead to disequilibrium and total disregard for what is human. For those who would disregard the everyday practices of the people, the letter from Nomvuyo to his friends is a relevant pointer to the pragmatism advanced in the text:

> My dear friends, the work you still have to do among the Mpondomise is enormous. Looking back on what I saw during my stay with you, I should advise you not to be too hasty in your leadership. If you try to drag them too fast, they will drop, exhausted by the wayside and you yourselves will collapse before you reach the place where you want to take them. Gallop steadily, for the land is steep! (1980, 177)

Alternatively, Chief Sulenkama reminds the Prince:

> Now I'm telling you all this because I want to impress the fact upon you that our people still believe implicitly in these things. So whoever is going to lead them must learn to hasten slowly in these matters. (179 – 180)

Jongilanga calls for moderation before his death and disavows the politics of exclusivity that he had preached (241 -243). Like wisdom, personhood is forged through experience and contact with the greater community and its many resources located both in the past and in the present. It is constantly negotiated through understanding and sympathy—through self and community. In framing personhood in communitarian terms, especially in the context of postcolonial politics, it creates the space for subverting extreme forms of individualism. If personhood is linked to independence of the self, it allows for constant questioning of dogma such as the type that leaves the Mapondomise people paralysed at the end of the novel, but sees them reaching out for a pragmatic way forward, which is to register our complex entanglement as human beings. I think this is what Gykye (1995) had in mind when he talked about "moderate communitarianism" as a dialectical view of individualism and communitarianism. I think too that it is this awareness of our entanglement as people across racial, ethnic, gender and class divide that the idea of Ubuntu implies in a range of African communities and specifically in a complex post-colonial/post-apartheid context that South Africa is. It is also about reconsidering values according to their time-bound usefulness and demonstrating that African value systems such as Ubuntu can be reworked as they enter into conversation with other forms of knowledge, whether these are imported or locally generated. The possibility of dialogue between Ubuntu and Chriastian values that we refer to in this volume and that African thinkers like the Arch-Bishop Desmond Tutu (2011) have written about, is a good example. Ubuntu, as some of the papers in this volume also intimate, will have to come to terms as a philosophy and moral value system with an ever changing society challenged by metamorphosing and ever adapting systems of oppression on the African continent and beyond.

BIBLIOGRAPHY

Abrahams, Peter. 1946. *Mine Boy*. Heinemann Educational Books.
Achebe, Chinua. 1958. *Things Fall Apart*. London: Heinemann Educational Publishers.
Biko, Steve. 1978. *I Write What I Like: Selected Writings*. Chicago: The University of Chicago Press.

Fanon, Frantz. 1965. *The Wretched of the Earth*. Harmondsworth: Penguin Books.
Gyeke, Kwame. 1995. *An Essay on African Philosophical Thought: The Akan Conceptual Scheme*. Philadelphia: Temple University Press.
Jordan, J. C. 1980. *The Wrath of the Ancestors*. Alice: Lovedale Press.
Mphahlele, Ezekiel. 1959. *Down Second Avenue*. London: Faber and Faber.
Nwapa, Flora. 1966. *Efuru*. London: Heinemann.
Ogot, Grace. 1966. *The Promised Land*. Nairobi: East African Publishing House.
Oyono, Ferdinand. 1966. *Houseboy*. London: Heinemann
Praeg, Leonhard. 2014. *A Report on Ubuntu*. Scottsville: University of KwaZulu-Natal Press.
Tutu, Desmond. 2011. *God is not a Christian: Speaking Truth in Times of Crisis*. London: Random House.

NOTE ON CONTRIBUTORS

Wonke Buqa received all of his qualifications from the University of Pretoria. In 2005, he graduated BTh honours degree in Theology. In 2007, he received his MTh masters degree in Church History. In 2013, he graduated his second master's degree MA in Practical Theology (Family Therapy) and proceeded with a PhD in Practical Theology in the same institution. Dr. Buqa is an ordained Minister of the Uniting Presbyterian Church in Southern Africa (UPCSA) and serving as a Chaplain in South African Air Force (SAAF). He is constantly consulted for article review based on African writings by various academic institutions in South Africa. Dr. Buqa is currently doing BA Honours in Counselling Psychology with UNISA. In his PhD thesis, 'Exploring *Ubuntu* values in an emerging Multi-racial community: A narrative reflection'. Dr Buqa investigated the meaning of the African philosophy of *Ubuntu* in an emerging multiracial community of Olievenhoutsbosch Township situated along Centurion suburb of Pretoria within the new context of democracy in South Africa from a narrative research perspective. He also argues that *Ubuntu* challenges the status quo. In Olievenhoutsbosch community *Ubuntu* is also perceived as a tool to protect the community against criminality and corruption.

Dominica Dipio is a Professor of literature and film in Makerere University. She obtained a BA with Education and MA in African Literature from Makerere University. She obtained a licentiate in social communications and wrote her PhD on African cinema from the Pontifical Gregorian University in Rome. Professor Dipio has published widely in literature, film, cultural studies and folklore. Among her most recent publications are: "Audience Pleasure and Nollywood Popularity in Uganda: An Assessment"; a monograph, *Gender Terrains in African Cinema*, and four edited books. She has also served as External Examiner and Assessor in universities in eastern, western and southern Africa. Dipio has won several competitive grants and fellowships such as African Humanities Program (AHP), Fulbright and Cambridge Africa Program for Research Excellence (CAPREx). She is a filmmaker with more than ten titles to her credit, most recent of them are: *Word Craft* (2017), *Rainmaking: A Disappearing Practice* (2016), and *Extreme Artists: Ugandan Video Jockeys* (2016). Dipio has also served as a jury member at several international and regional film festivals in Milan, Amiens, Ouagadougou, Zanzibar, as well as in the Uganda Film Festival (UFF) since its inception in 2013.

John L. B. Eliastam, after completing undergraduate studies in theology, served for 17 years as associate pastor and then senior pastor of a church in Cape Town within the Association of Vineyard Churches. For the past ten years John as worked as a consultant and facilitator, with a particular focus on transformation, inclusion, and social cohesion. He works with organisations and communities to help them navigate transitions and develop leaders, with a particular focus on how change, conflict, and diversity impact the world and the way we do business. John has a PhD in Practical Theology from the University of Pretoria. He is a Research Fellow at the University of Pretoria, and for the past three years has been involved in an interdisciplinary research project on the African social value of *ubuntu*. John has been married to Liesl for the past 23 years and has two sons of 19 and 21. John has a deep appreciation for good coffee and a fine red wine, and when he is not working or spending time with his family he is usually to be found on his mountain bike, training for ultra-distance mountain bike races.

Anke Graness is Elise Richter Fellow in the chair of Philosophy in a Global World / Intercultural Philosophy in the Department of Philosophy at the University of Vienna (Austria), and project leader of a FWF-funded research project on the History of Philosophy in Africa at the University of Vienna. She is the author of Das menschliche Minimum. Globale Gerechtigkeit aus afrikanischer Sicht: Henry Odera Oruka (Frankfurt/New York: Campus, 2011). She has also co-edited an anthology on the Kenyan philosopher Henry Odera Oruka, Sagacious Reasoning: H. Odera Oruka in memoriam (Frankfurt/M.: Peter Lang Verlag, 1997; with K. Kresse) and a book on Intercultural Philosophy; Perspektiven interkulturellen Philosophierens. Beiträge zur Geschichte und Methodik von Polylogen (Wien: Facultas/WUV 2012; with F. Gmainer-Pranzl).

Aloo Osotsi Mojola is a professor of philosophy and translation studies at the St Paul's University, Limuru, Kenya and an honorary professor as well as research associate, Faculty of Theology, Pretoria University, South Africa. He is the author of *God Speaks in our own languages.*

Mogomme Alpheus Masoga is an *alumnus* of the University of the Free State (UFS). His doctoral research was entitled: *Dimensions of Oracle-Speech in the Near Eastern, Mediterranean and African Contexts: A Contribution towards African Orality.* Professor Masoga once acted as the Academic Journal Editor at the Development Bank of Southern Africa (DBSA). Professor Masoga is widely published in peer reviewed journals and book chapters. His research focuses on the socio-political and cultural contexts of African Studies including areas such as African Orality, indigenous knowledge systems, education and oral history. Currently, he is a professor of African Studies and

Research Professor in the Faculty of Humanities at the University of Limpopo.

D. A. Masolo is Professor of Philosophy at the University of Louisville, Louisville, Kentucky, USA. Masolo is the author of Self and Community in a Changing World, Bloomington, Indiana University Press, 2010. (Finalist for the Melville Herskovts Award for the Best Scholarly book published on/about Africa in the English language in the year), and African Philosophy in Search of Identity, Indiana University Press, Bloomington, and Edinburgh University Press, Edinburgh, 1994. He is editor (with Ivan Karp) of African Philosophy as Cultural Inquiry, Indiana University Press in association with the International African Institute, University of London, 2000.

Ramadimetja S. Mogale is a Senior Lecturer at the University of Pretoria, Department of Nursing Science. Her program of research is in women's health and women's issues through transdisciplinarity, Afrikan-based methodologies, Afrocentric epistemologies, qualitative research and ethnography.

Fhumulani Mavis Mulaudzi is the Head of Department of nursing Science and Chairperson of the School of Health Care Sciences at University of Pretoria. She is currently the president of Chixi chapter of the Sigma theta tau, member of the CSIR Research ethics committee, and the treasurer of the South African health care Sciences Deans committee. She was a runner up for the Distinguished Women in Science award 2011 for her work in indigenous knowledge system research. She is currently the Editor in Chief of Curationis Journal. Her research interest lies in human rights and ethics, HIV/AIDS, indigenous knowledge system and reproductive health. She is known for promoting the philosophy of Ubuntu in nursing ethics. Her work is recognised and appreciated by her peers both nationally and internationally. This is evident by a number of times that she read papers as a key-note speaker in international and national conferences.

James Ogude is a Senior Research Fellow and the Director at the Centre for the Advancement of Scholarship, University of Pretoria. He has served as a Professor of African Literature and Cultures in the School of Literature and Language Studies at the University of the Witwatersrand, where he worked since 1994, serving as the Head of African Literature and Assistant Dean—Research, in the Faculty of Humanities. He is the author of *Ngugi's Novels and African History: Narrating the Nation*. He has edited five books and one anthology of African stories. His most recent book is *Chinua Achebe's Legacy: Illuminations from Africa* (2015). Ogude has published numerous articles in peer-reviewed journals in the area of African Literature and Popular Culture in Africa. Ogude is currently the Principal Investigator of a University of Pretoria research project on the African philosophy of Ubuntu, which attracted major funding from the Templeton World Charity Foundation. He is the co-Director (with Professor Eileen Julien of Indiana University, Bloomington), of a project on "Arts of Survival: Recasting Lives in African Cities". A member of the South African Academy of Sciences and Ogude also holds a "B" rating for his research from the National Research Foundation of South Africa (NRF)—a rating for researchers who enjoy considerable international recognition by their peers for the high quality and impact of their recent research outputs.

Garnette Oluoch-Olunya is Senior Lecturer in the Department of Language & Communication, and Director of the Centre for Cultural and Creative Industries at the Technical University of Kenya. In her work as a Research Consultant for the GoDown Arts Centre in Nairobi, she is part of the organizing team for the East African Arts Summit, held biennially; *Nai ni Who*, a Nairobi festival that celebrates city diversity, urban geographies and cultures, and identity formations, and coordinator of the Creative Entrepreneurship Course. She is also an Ubuntu project associate fellow with the University of Pretoria, RSA. She holds a PhD in English Literature from the University of Glasgow, and is a member of the Glasgow University Council.

Augustine Shutte is an Honorary Research Associate in the Philosophy Department of the University of Cape Town. Dr

267

Shutte's main areas of interest are philosophy of religion, philosophical anthropology, ethics and contemporary 'Thomist philosophy. He is the author of *Ubuntu: An Ethics for a New South Africa* (2001). Dr. Shutte has since passed on in 2016.

Mpho Tshivhase is a lecturer at the Department of Philosophy at the University of Pretoria. She lectures undergraduate and postgraduate courses in ethics. She holds doctoral degree in Philosophy. She also happens be the first woman of African descent in South Africa to obtain a doctoral degree in Philosophy. Her research interests are personhood, personal uniqueness, and themes of love, autonomy, authenticity, death, and African ethics. She has authored papers in the abovementioned areas, and presented at local and international conferences. She currently works with the student leaders in the Faculty of Humanities. Mpho is the newly elected president of the Philosophical Society of Southern Africa.

Jacomien van Niekerk holds a D.Litt degree from the University of Pretoria, Pretoria, South Africa and teaches literature and literary theory in the Department of Afrikaans at the same institution. She published a monograph on identity and transformation in the nonfiction of Antjie Krog in 2016. Her research interests include African literature, African oral literature, African philosophy, life writing, and postcolonial studies. She is the end-editor of *Tydskrif vir Letterkunde*, a peer-reviewed, Open Access journal for African literature and the treasurer of the International Society for the Oral Literatures of Africa (ISOLA).

INDEX

D

E

F

G

H

I

J

K

L